Communicating in Small Groups
Principles and Practices

Second Edition

Steven A. Beebe
University of Miami

John T. Masterson
University of Miami

Scott, Foresman and Company

Glenview, Illinois
London, England

An Instructor's Manual is available. It may be obtained
through a local Scott, Foresman Representative or by writing
to Speech Editor, College Division, Scott, Foresman and
Company, 1900 E. Lake Avenue, Glenview, IL 60025.

Library of Congress Cataloging-in-Publication Data

Beebe, Steven A.,
   Communicating in small groups.

   Includes bibliographies and index.
   1. Small groups.   2. Interpersonal communication.
3. Group relations training.   I. Masterson, John T.,
II. Title.
HM133.B43   1986   302.3'4   85-18420
ISBN 0-673-18135-9

Acknowledgments

Page 11, From "The Death of the Hired Man" from *The Poetry of Robert Frost* edited by Edward Connery Lathem. Copyright 1930. 1939, © 1969 by Holt, Rinehart and Winston. Copyright © 1958 by Robert Frost. Copyright © 1967 by Lesley Frost Ballantine. Reprinted by permission of Holt, Rinehart and Winston, Publisher.

Page 14, Excerpts from pages 23 and 24 from *Successful Leadership in Groups and Organizations*, Second Edition by Joseph A. Wagner. Copyright © 1973, 1959 by Harper & Row, Publishers, Inc. Reprinted by permission of the publisher.

Page 71, From *Of Human Interaction* by Joseph Luft by permission of Mayfield Publishing Company. Copyright © 1969 by the National Press.

Pages 114, 116, From *Nonverbal Communication in Human Interaction*, Second Edition by Mark L. Knapp. Copyright © 1978, 1972 by Holt, Rinehart and Winston. Reprinted by permission of CBS College Publishing.

Page 151, Sidney B. Simon, Leland W. Howe, and Howard Kirschenbaum, *Values Clarification: A Handbook of Practical Strategies for Teachers and Students*. New York: Hart Publishing Company, Inc., 1972 pp. 292-293.

Pages 152, 153, From "Win As Much As You Can" by William Gellermann in Pfeiffer, J. W. and Jones, J. F. *Handbook of Structured Experiences for Human Relations Training*, Vol. II, University Associates, 1970. Reprinted by permission of William Gellermann.

Page 176, From *Interpersonal Communication: An Introduction*, by Stewart L. Tubbs and Sylvia Moss. Copyright © 1974, 1977, and 1978 by Random House, Inc. Reprinted by permission.

Pages 190, 196, 203, From Brilhart, John K., *Effective Group Discussion*, 3rd Ed., © 1967, 1974, 1978 Wm. C. Brown Company, Publishers, Dubuque, IA. Reprinted by permission.

Page 222, Chart from pp. 26-27 (to be entitled "Leader Behavior and Member Reaction in Three 'Social Climates' ") in *Autocracy and Democracy* by Ralph K. White and Ronald Lippitt. Copyright © 1960 by Ralph K. White and Ronald Lippitt. Reprinted by permission of Harper & Row, Publishers, Inc.

Photo Credits

Preface

The second edition of *Communicating in Small Groups: Principles and Practices* retains the goals of the first edition—to be relevant, practical, and useful. The underlying premise of the textbook is that effective group communication requires a knowledge of the principles and dynamics that characterize small group interaction, together with practice in applying those principles. We have continued to identify useful conclusions of small group communication research. Our approach, then, is a balance of theory and application; our goal is effective communication.

Over the past 15 years the college course in small group communication has evolved from traditional group-discussion formats to more theoretical and research-oriented approach. This evolution has mirrored the rapid development of the speech communication field. The result is a synthesis of theory, research, and practice into the unified discipline of speech communication. In this book, we bring this unified approach to the study of small group communication.

Throughout the book we explore small group theory and research and its relevance to various kinds of small groups. But conceptual understanding must be accompanied by the ability to translate that knowledge into action. In every chapter we suggest ways of converting principles into practices, supplementing our suggestions with case studies and examples drawn from various sectors of society.

In this edition we have expanded our coverage of several small group concepts and have added to our discussion of the different types of groups that exist. In Chapter Two, we provide an overview of four key theories that help us explain and predict small group interaction. We also have added a new section which discusses the power of words in affecting group communication and human relationships. Listening is a key skill that group participants need to possess; we have included a discussion of the barriers that keep us from listening at peak efficiency and identified methods of improving listening competence. We have enriched our discussion of nonverbal communication by including more research conclusions and noting their applicability to small groups. In Chapter Ten, "Leadership," we have suggested ways to manage and organize meetings. We have expanded our treatment of problem solving by noting differences between decision making and problem solving. We also include a discussion of research that helps us describe the moment to moment activity of a group. An important new feature of our problem-solving chapter is a discussion of quality circles and how they are used in government and industry to improve quality and productivity. We have also expanded our discussion of conflict management to include specific suggestions for dealing with different types of conflict. Throughout the book we have updated our treatment of the concepts discussed with contemporary research. We have continued to include a "Practice" section at the end of each chapter; this encourages students to probe, discuss, synthesize, and apply the chapter's content.

We have been greatly aided and encouraged in the preparation of this revision by the critical insights and sound advice of a number of speech communication scholars and fellow educators. Among these are: Isa N. Engleberg, Prince George's Community College; Don Friar, American River College; Theodore Hopf, Washington State University; Richard Kaough, Southern Oregon State College; Elaine Lashley, University of Cincinnati; Patrick A. Sciarra, College of DuPage; and Victor D. Wall, Jr., The Ohio State University.

We are indebted also to the following people who provided feedback on the first edition of the textbook: Randall Alderson, Wagner College; Kimberly Buckingham, San Jose State University; April Christian-Schmidlapp, Edison State Community College; Ray Collins, San Jose City College; Gay Lumsden, Kean College of New Jersey; John L. Vohs, University of California, Davis; Barbara Muller, our acquisitions editor at Scott, Foresman, provided insightful suggestions. This book is better because of her thoughtful and intelligent direction.

It is vital to have the useful advice of reviewers and editors but we particularly want to single out the help and support of our families. We appreciate the patience of our sons, Mark and Matthew Beebe and John and Noah Masterson, who sacrificed time with their dads so this volume could be written. Our spouses deserve special commendation. Nancy Masterson contributed countless hours of her time as a proofreader. Susan Beebe was invaluable as typist, editor, proofreader, and author of the section on research in Chapter Eight.

Steven A. Beebe
John T. Masterson

Contents

1 An Introduction to Small Group Communication

After studying this chapter, you should be able to:

■ Define small group communication.

■ Explain the importance of studying small group communication.

■ List and describe the advantages of working with others in small groups.

■ List and describe the disadvantages of working with others in small groups.

■ Organize and implement the following public small group communication formats: (1) Panel discussion, (2) Symposium presentation, and (3) Forum presentation.

■ Chair a committee meeting.

An Introduction to Small Group Communication

Using a variety of research methods, communication scholars, sociologists, psychologists, and anthropologists have reached a similar conclusion about humankind. Their universal, but perhaps not so startling, conclusion is that *we are social creatures.* We need to establish meaningful human relationships with others. We need to associate with others in groups. We are raised in family groups. We are educated in groups. We worship in groups. We are entertained in groups. We work in groups. When an important problem arises, we seek others' advice. Problem-solving and decision-making groups meet to help find answers to important issues.

This book is about groups. More specifically, it is about communication in **small groups.**

"Why study **small group communication?**" You have probably already asked yourself that question. Or maybe you have asked, "What can a systematic study of small group communication do for me? How will it help me with my career? Will it really help me be a better committee member? Will studying small group communication improve my interpersonal relationships with my family and friends?"

Rather than offer a long list of specific promises about what this book can do for you, let us identify our objective. Our purpose in writing this book is to help you become a better communicator in the context of a small group. We want to give you both a broad understanding of group communication processes and practical advice to help you be a better small group participant. Note that we will be talking primarily about **task-oriented small groups—** groups with a specific objective to achieve, problem to solve, or decision to make.

The communication that occurs in a group will be our focus. In discussing its importance in an organization, Goldhaber describes communication as:

the lifeblood of the organization

the glue that binds the organization
the oil that smooths the organization's functions
the thread that ties the system together
the force that pervades the organization
the binding agent that cements all relationships.[1]

These metaphors apply to a small group as well as to a large corporation. Regardless of the group's size, its members must be able to talk, listen, and respond to others. They must be sensitive to the needs and feelings of other group members. Ideally, group members should have some training in how groups can function efficiently. Without an understanding of the group communication process, members may become frustrated and the meeting may degenerate into an unpleasant, unproductive experience.

WHAT IS SMALL GROUP COMMUNICATION?

As the nation becomes more concerned about the growing nuclear arms race, the President of the United States meets with his chief arms negotiators to discuss arms control.

The city commission has finally decided that it is time to begin formulating plans for a new cultural arts center. The commissioners appoint a subcommittee to help develop the project.

The Board of Directors of American Motors believes that in order to compete with the foreign automobile industry, a new fuel-efficient quality automobile must be produced. They decide to appoint a group of their top-level executives and engineers to begin developing plans for a new automobile.

Each of these three situations involves a group of people meeting for a specific purpose. Although the purposes are quite different, these groups share something in common—something that distinguishes them from, say, a cluster of people waiting for a bus or a bunch of people waiting to get on an elevator. Just what is that "something"? What are the characteristics that make a group a group?

Several scholars have developed definitions of small group communication and group discussion. Here are a few of their definitions:

>... a small group of people talking with each other face to face in order to achieve some interdependent goal.[2]
>... a number of persons who perceive each other as participants in a common activity, who interact dynamically with one another, and who communicate their responses chiefly through words.[3]
>... the process whereby two or more people exchange information or ideas in a face-to-face situation to achieve a goal.[4]

... two or more persons who are interacting with one another in such a manner that each person influences and is influenced by each other person.[5]

... the purposeful, systematic, primarily oral exchange of ideas, facts, and opinions by a group of persons who share in the group's leadership.[6]

Despite the differences in these definitions, there are several common characteristics that may help sharpen your perception of small group communication. Let's examine the similarities.

Meeting with a Common Purpose

The President's disarmament advisors, the city commission, and the Board of Directors of American Motors have one thing in common—their members have a specific purpose for meeting. There is mutual concern for the objectives of the group. While a group of people waiting for a bus or an elevator may share the goal of transportation, they do not have the same *collective* goal. Their individual destinations are different. Their primary concerns are for themselves, not for others. As soon as their individual goals are realized, they leave the bus or elevator. On the other hand, a goal keeps a committee or discussion group together until that goal is realized. Many groups fail to remain together because they never identify their common purpose. While it is true that participants in small groups may have somewhat different motives for their membership, a common purpose cements the group together.

Feeling a Sense of Belonging to the Group

Not only do group members need a mutual concern to unite them, but they should also feel that they belong to the group. It is doubtful that commuters waiting for a bus feel part of a collective effort. However, small group members need to feel a sense of *identity* with a group—that it is *their* group.

Exerting Influence upon One Another

While some groups have an elected or appointed leader, most group members have the opportunity to share leadership responsibilities. Whether they keep the group on schedule, provide information, ask questions to keep the group moving forward, or take notes of the group's meetings, members who perform such tasks assist in leading the group toward its goal. Thus, if we define the role of leader rather broadly, each group member has an opportunity to help lead the group through contributions and suggestions. Even in a small group in which a leader is appointed, all of the members should share the leadership responsibilities. Regardless of its size, a group achieves optimal success when each person accepts some leadership responsibilities.

Communicating Face-to-Face

Group members need to be able to respond immediately, both verbally and nonverbally, to the discussion at hand. To feel a sense of "groupness," they need to interact with one another on a personal, face-to-face basis. In this age of conference telephone calls and swift written correspondence, we can easily communicate with others who are not in our immediate presence. Such communication may, nonetheless, be hindered by sluggish feedback or delayed replies.

In summary, we've defined small group communication as face-to-face communication among a small group of people who share a common purpose or goal, feel a sense of belonging to the group, and exert influence upon one another.

WHY LEARN ABOUT SMALL GROUPS?

Besides defining small group communication, one of our first objectives is to help you understand the value of studying the principles of effective communication in a small group. Consider the following reasons.

1. *You will spend a significant portion of time working in small groups.* Stop reading for just a moment and count how many different groups you are involved with this week. What is your total? Perhaps you thought of only one or two groups you're currently associated with, such as a committee or a work group. But did you consider your friends? How about fraternities, sororities, or religious groups? Your family? If you're employed, did you consider the groups you participate in while on the job? Human beings need to socialize. We have a need to congregate—to associate with others. Unless you're a hermit living in an isolated cave, you communicate with others in groups. And chances are, you will continue to do so. Work groups, social groups, educational groups, family groups, and therapy groups occupy a significant portion of our communication time. While this book will emphasize small groups that exist for the purpose of making decisions, we will still discuss many principles that are applicable to most of the groups with which you associate.

2. *You will understand how groups make decisions and solve problems.* You may not consider many of the groups to which you belong as decision-making or problem-solving groups. You join some groups just for the fun of socializing and being with others. You may think that problem solving or decision making occurs in groups which have only a very specific task. But even in your social groups, problems arise and decisions need to be made. We will discuss various approaches to group problem solving and decision making. An increased understanding of what happens when people make decisions in groups should improve your ability to arrive at higher quality decisions and, consequently, should enhance your enjoyment of working in a group.

3. *You can reduce the uncertainty and anxiety you may have about work-*

ing with others in small groups. We often fear what we do not understand. Your first day on a new job provokes fear and anxiety. You're not sure what to expect. You probably experience some uncertainty on your first day in a new class or a new school. Often, our anxiety and uncertainty can inhibit us and we will not make the most of our situation—whether it is a new job, a new class, or a new group. Most colleges and universities have orientation programs to help reduce students' uncertainty about their new environment. On a new job, we are usually given time to "get broken in" or to "learn the ropes." Employees may go through extensive training programs to help them do a better job. Learning the principles of small group communication and applying specific suggestions for improving its quality can reduce (though not necessarily eliminate) some of the uncertainty and discomfort you may feel working with others in small groups. It helps to know what to expect. Armed with communication theory, you should be in a better position to explain and predict what happens when people communicate in small groups.

4. *You will better understand your own communication behavior.* After participating in a small group discussion, have you ever said to yourself, "Now why did I say that?" or "I don't know why I feel so tense and uncomfortable in this group"? Or, have you ever wondered why you always seem to disagree with someone or why you are not an effective leader of a committee? A study of small group communication should help you answer these questions. We will talk about relationships and leadership, as well as nonverbal communication, conflict management, and reasons for joining groups. As you work with others, a knowledge of small group communication principles and theory should expand your understanding of yourself.

ADVANTAGES AND DISADVANTAGES OF WORKING IN SMALL GROUPS

"What's so great about working in groups?" mutters an exasperated member of the student entertainment committee, just after spending two hours in a meeting with the other committee members. "I could have solved the problem in fifteen minutes. Why do we have to spend two hours rehashing old information?"

"I'm really looking forward to our committee meeting this evening," says an enthusiastic member of an ecology group. "There is always such a great spirit of unity and cohesiveness during each meeting. Even though we sometimes disagree, each group member really seems to respect the ideas and opinions of the others. I think it's because we really enjoy working together as a group."

What's your feeling about working in groups? Maybe you dread attending group meetings. Perhaps you agree with the observation that a committee is a group that keeps minutes but wastes hours. You may have the perception that groups bumble and stumble along until some sort of compromise is reached—a compromise with which no one is pleased. "To be effective," said one committee member, "a committee should be made up of three people. But to get anything done, one member should be sick, and another absent."

Conversely, you could be one of those individuals who enjoys group work. You may relish the challenge of trying to solve problems, make decisions, and accomplish tasks while working with others. We hope you've had more pleasant than unpleasant encounters with group work, but most likely you've had both.

It is easy to become disgruntled with a group if it does not meet our expectations of how a "good" group should behave. One important purpose of this book is to help you appreciate the advantages of working with other people. But we must admit that you will also encounter problems that may lead to frustration and anxiety. Our philosophy is that by understanding both the advantages and the potential pitfalls of working in groups, you will form more realistic expectations about small group work.[7]

Some view groups as a cure-all remedy for complex problems. If a solution to a problem is needed, a group or committee is formed. The work of small groups can result in good solutions, sound decisions, and well-executed projects. And, too, there are some situations and problems that are best not handled by a group at all.

Advantages

Groups have greater resources of knowledge and information. Because of the variety of backgrounds and experiences that individuals bring to a group, there is more information and ideas from which to seek solutions to a problem. And when there is a greater availability of information, the group is more likely to arrive at a better quality solution. For example, when a manufacturing company ponders the decision of whether to develop and market a new product, it seeks input from individuals with expertise in finance, marketing, advertising, personnel, engineering, and management. Only after considering the various points of view will the manufacturer reach a well-informed decision.

Groups can employ a greater number of creative problem-solving methods. Research generally supports the maxim that "two heads are better than one" when it comes to solving problems. Usually groups make better decisions than does an individual working alone because groups have more approaches to or methods of solving a specific problem. It stands to reason that a group of people with various backgrounds, experiences, and resources can more creatively consider ways to solve a problem than can one person. Whether the problem is an issue that concerns the local ecology group, or a major decision that confronts the Board of Directors of General Motors, people who work on problems with other people can capitalize on each other's experiences.

Working in groups fosters improved learning and comprehension of ideas discussed. Imagine that your history professor announces that the final exam next week is going to be comprehensive. History is not your best subject. You realize you need some help. What do you do? Maybe you form a study group with other classmates. Your decision to study with a group of people is a wise move; education theorists tell us that when you can take an active role in the learning process, your comprehension of information will be improved. If you studied for the exam by yourself, you would not have the benefit of asking and answering questions posed by other study group members. Another advantage of working in groups, then, is that it helps increase learning and improves comprehension of the subject under discussion.

Members' satisfaction with the group decision increases because they participate in the problem-solving process. Group problem solving provides an opportunity for group members to participate in the decision-making process. Several research studies suggest that individuals who help solve problems in a group will be more committed to the solution and more satisfied with their participation.

Imagine that while working with a group of other construction workers building a new apartment complex, you've been asked to increase your productivity. You are probably going to be much more responsive to the suggestion if it has evolved from group discussions than if your foreman simply tells you that you need to increase your rate of productivity. If you are consulted, you will be more committed to implementing the recommendation. That way, you have some responsibility in governing your own behavior. Thus, when individuals work together in small groups, they are more satisfied with the group decision that they helped shape.

Group members gain a better understanding of themselves as they interact with others. Working in groups can help you gain a more accurate picture of how others see you. Because of the feedback you receive, you can become aware of personal characteristics that are not known to you, but which are known to others. Of course, whether the interaction is advantageous or disadvantageous depends largely on how you respond to the feedback that others provide. If someone tells you that you are obnoxious and difficult to work with, you may respond by ignoring the comment, disagreeing with the observation, or examining your behavior to see if the criticism is justified. By becoming sensitive to feedback, you can better understand yourself (or at least better understand how others perceive you) than if you worked alone. Group interaction and feedback can be useful in helping you examine your interpersonal behavior and determine whether you want to change your communication style.

Disadvantages

Our discussion thus far suggests that working in small groups can be beneficial for several reasons. Groups make well-informed and better quality decisions more often than do individuals because of the varied experiences individual members bring to a group. With these extra resources, groups can consider more creative methods of solving problems. Group interaction can enhance both comprehension and satisfaction in working on a project. We also learn about ourselves when we work with others because we receive feedback. For these reasons, groups and committees are formed to help solve problems. But, as we noted earlier, problems occur when people congregate. Let's consider some of the disadvantages of working in groups. Identifying these potential problems can help you avoid them.

Group members may pressure others to conform to the majority opinion. Most people don't like conflict and generally try to avoid it. But this tendency to avoid controversy in our interpersonal relationships can affect the quality of a group decision. What's wrong with group members reaching agreement? Nothing, unless group members are agreeing to conform to the majority opinion of the group or even to the leader's opinion. Group members may agree on a bad solution just to avoid conflict. Social psychologist Irving Janis calls this phenomenon "groupthink"—when group members agree primarily to avoid conflict.[8] When we discuss conflict in small groups (Chapter Seven), we'll talk about groupthink in more detail and suggest how to avoid it.

Have you ever had a professor ask your class a question, only to have no one respond? Perhaps you thought you knew the answer yet you did not raise your hand either because you could have been wrong or because no one else was raising a hand and you didn't want to be a "know it all." You didn't contribute because of what others may have thought about you. Thus, you conformed to the standards set by the rest of the group. This happens not only in classrooms, but in other group settings such as board meetings and committee discussions. One disadvantage of working with others in a group situation is that we tend to conform to group pressure or to what other group members are doing (or not doing).

An individual group member may dominate the discussion. In some groups it seems like one person must run the show. That member wants to make the decisions and, when all is said and done, insists that his or her position on the issue is the best one. "Well," you might say, "if this person wants to do all the work, that's fine with me. I won't complain. It will sure be a lot easier for me." Yes, if you permit a member or two to dominate the group, you may do less work yourself, but you then forfeit the advantages of a greater availability of knowledge and of more creative approaches to the group's task. You also lose the advantage of member satisfaction with the group discussion, because other members may feel alienated from the decision making. They don't enjoy working on the project, and the group suffers from the disenchanted members' lessened input.

Try to use the domineering member's enthusiasm to the advantage of the group. If an individual tries to monopolize the discussion, other group members should channel that interest more constructively. The talkative member, for example, could be given a special research assignment. Of course, if the domineering member continues to monopolize the discussion, other group members may have to confront the talkative member and suggest that others be given an opportunity to present their views.

Some group members may rely too much upon others to get the job done.

"Charlie is a hard worker. He'll see that the job is done right."

"Lilian seems to really like taking charge. She is doing such a good job. The group really doesn't need me."

"No one will miss me if I don't show up for the meeting this afternoon. There will be enough people to do the work."

These kinds of statements occur when group members are not aware of the importance of each individual in the group. A danger of working in groups is that we may be tempted to rely on others rather than to pitch in and help. Working together distributes the responsibility of accomplishing a task. But if the responsibility is spread among all group members, shouldn't this shared responsibility be an advantage of group work? It should be. However, when some group members develop an attitude that others can carry the work load, then problems can develop. Just because you are part of a group, don't think you can get lost in the crowd. Your input *is* needed. Don't abdicate your responsibility to another group member. To avoid this problem, try to encourage less talkative group members to contribute to the discussion. Also, make sure each person knows the goals and objectives of the group. Encouraging each member to attend every meeting helps, too. Lack of attendance at group meetings is a sure sign that group members are falling into the "Let Charlie do it" syndrome. Finally, see that each person knows and fulfills his or her specific responsibilities to the group.

Solving a problem takes longer as a group than as an individual. For many people, one of the major frustrations about group work is the time it takes to accomplish tasks. Not only does a group have to hassle with the logistics of finding a time and a place where everyone can meet (sometimes a serious problem in itself), but a group simply requires more time to define, analyze, research, and solve problems than do individuals working by themselves. It takes time for people to talk and listen to others. Still, such input usually results in a better quality solution. You have to remind yourself and the group, "If we want a better quality solution, it is going to take time, patience, and understanding."

But if you realize that it takes too much time to solve problems in groups, you may decide that problems requiring an immediate decision may be better handled by an individual. In the heat of battle, the commander usually does not call for a committee meeting of all his troops. True, the troops may be more satisfied with the decision if they feel they can participate in making it, but the obvious need for a quick decision overrides any advantages that may occur from meeting as a group. Thus, while this book is about small group communication, you should also know when it may be more efficient to solve problems individually. Remember that solving problems in groups requires more time.

TYPES OF SMALL GROUPS

We have discussed the key characteristics of a small group, the importance of studying small group communication, and several advantages and disadvantages of working in groups. Besides understanding what a small group is and why you should study it, you need to keep in mind that small group communication can range from a relatively unstructured, spontaneous discussion of an issue to a more formal, preplanned presentation.

Groups are formed for several reasons. As we will discuss in Chapter Three, some groups originate to fulfill our basic needs for association and fellowship. Others are formed to solve a specific problem, to make a decision, or to gather information. To give you an idea of the variety of purposes and formats for group meetings, we will identify several types of groups and three types of public group communication formats.

Primary Groups

In "The Death of the Hired Man," poet Robert Frost mused, "Home is the place where, when you have to go there,/They have to take you in." Your family provides one of the best illustrations of a **primary group.** Communication in families does not usually follow a prescribed agenda; family conversation is informal. Conversation is also informal within other primary groups, such as informal cliques of friends or workers who interact over an extended period of time. Primary group members associate with one another for the joy of fellowship—to fulfill their basic need to associate with others.

The main task of the primary group is to perpetuate the group so that members can continue to enjoy each other's companionship. Because we want to maintain these ties, we may be eager to conform to the behavior of the group. Teenagers who embrace the latest clothing style or current music group often do so, not only because they may genuinely enjoy what's currently in vogue, but also because they need to fit in with the rest of their peers. Primary groups do not meet regularly to make decisions unless a meeting is needed to perpetuate the social patterns of the group. As with any group, there are some who may assert more influence than others. But the key reward of belonging to a primary group is simply the satisfaction of being a member.

Study Groups

As a student, you are no doubt familiar with **study groups.** These are groups whose primary purpose is to gather information and learn new ideas. As we have already noted, one advantage of participating in a group is that you learn by being involved in a discussion. With several individuals, a study group also has the advantage of sharing a greater amount of information and ideas.

Study groups are not formed just for learning the facts taught in a formal classroom setting. Often a study group may try to gather information about a particular issue or problem. Their prime purpose is not to solve the problem, but to research an idea so that others may make an informed choice. Staff meetings and briefing sessions are examples of non-classroom group situations in which the primary purpose of the meeting is to learn and study.

While, strictly speaking, a study group is formed only to learn about a topic, often such groups are formed because of a desire to promote a particular belief or point of view. Churches, political parties, and organizations which focus on drug or alcohol abuse are examples of organizations which may sponsor a study group to promote a change in attitudes or behavior.

Therapy Groups

A **therapy group,** also called an encounter group or T-group, strives to provide treatment for the personal problems of the individuals who belong to the group. Such groups are led by a professional who is trained to help members overcome, or at least manage, individual problems in a group setting. We have noted that an important advantage of group work is that members gain a better understanding of themselves as they communicate with others. This is an important reason why there is group therapy. Members learn how they are perceived by others. By participating in a therapy group, people with similar problems can benefit from how others learned to cope. Groups such as Weight Watchers and Alcoholics Anonymous also provide positive reinforcement when members have achieved their goals. By experiencing therapy with others, a T-group takes advantage of the greater amount of resources of knowledge and information available to the group.

Committee Meetings

A **committee** is a small group that can be formal or informal. Brilhart defines a committee as a "small group of people given an assigned task or responsibility by a larger group (parent organization) or person with authority."[9] Most of you have probably sat through several of these meetings. You may have a negative reaction to serving on a committee—many people do. They regard committee work as time-consuming, tedious, and ineffective, except in increasing the sale of aspirin! Organizations such as schools, churches, businesses, and hospitals include committees within their organizational hierarchies.

By interacting with others in therapy groups, members can utilize feedback to learn more about themselves and how they are perceived by others.

These groups make decisions, solve problems, and implement policies. Some committee members are appointed to a *standing committee* (one that remains active for several years); other members serve on an *ad hoc committee* (one that disbands once its special task has been completed).

While committees vary tremendously in their scope and purpose, they have enough consistent characteristics that permit us to suggest a few guidelines to help you organize, lead, and participate in committee meetings. Joseph Wagner identifies several characteristics of committee meetings:

1. The meeting should begin and end on time.
2. Neither the chairman nor the members are required to stand when they speak.
3. The chairman may discuss business as freely as any of the other members.
4. It is not necessary to secure recognition from the chair before speaking.
5. Usually, debate is neither limited nor suppressed by a motion to vote immediately.
6. A matter may be discussed even though there is no formal motion to vote immediately.

7. Although the atmosphere is informal, the chairman must guide and control the group. Majority rule must be insured, and yet the minority's rights must be protected.[10]

If you are appointed or elected to serve as chairperson of a committee, you should be familiar with the special responsibilities expected of you. You need a clear understanding of the purpose of your committee. As a chairperson you must locate a suitable meeting room and make sure that the committee members know when and where the meetings will take place. While parliamentary procedure helps organize large groups, small group discussions generally need not implement the formality of parliamentary procedure. Wagner suggests that the chairperson of a committee meeting assume the following responsibilities:

1. Call the meeting to order.
2. Start discussion with a few comments on the nature of the committee's problem.
3. Avoid digressions and small talk. Follow the agenda.
4. Do not talk too much; draw out the quiet members of the group.
5. When a point is saturated, move on to the next.
6. Summarize frequently in order that the members may keep a mental picture of their progress before them.
7. Prepare a committee report when, after one meeting or many, your group has completed its work.[11]

Public Communication Formats

The group formats we have discussed thus far usually do not have an audience listening to the group deliberations. There are a variety of formats, however, that are designed so that others can listen to the discussion. **Public communication formats** help audience members understand all sides of an issue, particularly if individuals with diverse points of view are involved in the discussion. The three public communication formats we will consider are **panel discussions, symposium presentations,** and **forum presentations.**

Panel Discussions

You have undoubtedly seen numerous posters advertising panel discussions and inviting you to attend. A panel discussion is the most frequently used group-discussion format, usually selected for the benefit of *informing* an audience about an issue or specific problem. A panel discussion is defined as a group discussion which takes place before an audience with the purpose of (1) informing the audience about issues of interest, (2) solving a problem, or (3) encouraging the audience to evaluate the issues of a controversial question.

A panel discussion usually has an appointed chairperson or moderator to organize the presentation. It is the moderator's job to help keep the discussion on track. The moderator usually opens by announcing the discussion question. Most panel discussions include at least three panelists; if more than eight or nine are on the panel, it is difficult for all of them to participate equally. Since the panel is presented for the benefit of the audience, care should be taken so that the audience can see and hear the discussion clearly. Panelists usually sit in a semicircle or behind a table. While panel members should be informed about the subject they will discuss, they should not rehearse their discussion; the conversation should be extemporaneous. Panelists may use some notes to help them remember facts and statistics, but they should not use a prepared text. After announcing the discussion topic, the moderator briefly introduces the panel members to the audience, perhaps noting each one's qualifications for being on the panel. The moderator may then direct a specific question to one or more panelists to begin the discussion. An effective moderator encourages all panelists to participate. If one panelist seems reluctant, the moderator may direct a specific question to him. Or, if a panelist tends to dominate the discussion, the moderator may politely suggest that other panel members be given an opportunity to participate. Rather than let the discussion continue until the group has nothing more to say on the issue, it is best to set a specific time limit on the discussion. Most panel discussions last about one hour, but the time limit can be tailored to the needs of the audience and the topic. At the conclusion of the discussion, the moderator may either summarize com-

Choose the public group communication format which will best serve your group's objective. In this case, a panel format was chosen to help inform the audience about a specific issue.

ments made by the group members or ask another group member to do so. Often, the summary statement is followed by an invitation to the audience to ask the panel questions.

Symposium Presentations

A symposium is another public discussion format in which a series of short speeches is presented. Usually a central theme or issue pervades all of the speeches. Unlike panelists in a panel discussion, the participants in a symposium either come with prepared speeches or speak extemporaneously from an outline. The speakers are usually experts who represent contrasting points of view. For example, imagine that your physics instructor has invited four experts in the field of nuclear energy to speak to your class. Each expert has selected a specific aspect of nuclear energy to present. Your instructor will probably give a brief introduction of the speakers and announce the central topic of discussion. The speakers may be asked to address themselves to a discussion question. Then each will speak from eight to ten minutes. The speakers will probably not engage in informal conversation between speeches; it is likely that they know in advance what general areas the other speakers will discuss. After the speeches, your instructor may provide a concluding statement to summarize the major ideas presented. The audience is frequently given an opportunity to participate in an open forum following the symposium.

Technically, a symposium is not really a form of group discussion because there is little or no interaction among the participants. But a symposium often concludes with a more informal panel discussion or a forum. A major advantage of the symposium discussion lies in the ease of organizing it: just line up three or four speakers to discuss a designated topic. In addition, when speakers with contrasting viewpoints are asked to present their ideas, a lively discussion often follows. But make sure that the speakers know their time limits and address their assigned topics. An able moderator can prevent a symposium presentation from digressing into irrelevant issues. It is also wise to announce a time limit for the audience forum following a symposium.

Forum Presentations

Group discussion encourages more interaction and participation than other forms of communication (such as public speaking). A forum presentation takes maximum advantage of the principle that participation from many people can result in improved decisions. The word *forum* originated with the Romans. The forum was the public marketplace where Roman citizens could assemble and voice their opinions about the issues of the day. A forum discussion generally follows a panel discussion or symposium presentation. Forum discussions can also come after a single speaker's presentation. A forum permits an audience to get involved in the discussion. Rather than play a passive role such as in a panel discussion, the audience directs questions and responses to a chairperson or to a group of individuals. When holding a news conference, the President of the United States presents a prepared statement, followed by questions and responses from reporters—a forum. Some talk radio stations have forum discussions on topical issues of the day. Many communities still conduct town meetings in which its citizens can voice their opinions about issues affecting the community. The audience in a forum has an opportunity to provide feedback. Comments from audience members can sometimes be used to determine how successfully a speaker or panel enlightened the audience. The questions and responses also give the featured speakers an opportunity to clarify and elaborate their points of view.

AN INTRODUCTION TO SMALL GROUP COMMUNICATION: PUTTING PRINCIPLE INTO PRACTICE

Groups are an integral part of our society. In this chapter we have noted why it is important to study small group communication. To help summarize how you can apply some of the principles presented about the nature of groups, consider these suggestions:

- Work in small groups to benefit from the knowledge and information that others have, but which you are lacking.
- Work in small groups to take advantage of the other members' creative approaches to problem solving and decision making.
- When you want to improve your understanding and comprehension of a subject or issue, form a discussion group and talk about the topic with others.
- If it is important that people are satisfied with decisions that affect them, work in small groups so that they can participate in the discussion process. They will be more likely to support the decision if they have a genuine opportunity to contribute to the discussion.
- You can usually learn something about yourself when you work with others in small groups.
- Try not to let others pressure you to conform to the majority opinion of the group just for the sake of agreement.
- When working in a small group, don't let one or two members dominate the discussion. If you do, you lose many of the advantages of working in groups.
- Don't fall into the trap of relying too much on other group members. Assume your fair share of the responsibility for getting things done.
- You will probably be less frustrated if you realize that groups take more time to work together to accomplish a task than you do when you work alone.

- If you are given the task of organizing a public group discussion, consider one of the following formats: (1) panel discussion, (2) symposium presentation, or (3) forum presentation.
- If you are asked to serve as the chairperson of a committee, be sure to (1) draw out quiet members of the group, (2) limit your own talking, (3) move on to the next point when the discussion at hand is no longer productive, and (4) frequently summarize the comments of others.

PRACTICE

Get-Acquainted Activities

The following activities are designed to help you get to know your classmates better. These "discussion starters" can be used in most small group situations.

Activity 1: If you were in a gift shop, what kind of gift would you buy for the various members of your group to make them feel good about themselves as well as about you? Share with the group. React to the gifts others give you. Try to be honest. Would the gifts really make you feel good about yourself? About them?

Activity 2: Describe the kind of house you think each member now lives in or may live in later. If group members are not married, what kind of husband or wife would each member choose? How would they raise their family? What kind of work? Hobbies? Entertainment? Share with the group. React to others' perceptions of you.

Activity 3: Each member can give you a five-minute soliloquy about himself or herself.

Activity 4: Describe to the group what your name means to you.

Activity 5: If members of the group could change their names and be someone else, who do you think they would choose to be? The figure can be from the past or the present, or a character from a play or novel. Share with the group. React to others' insights of you. Would you really like to be such a person?

Activity 6: Describe what you do least well. Members take turns. Then describe what you do best.

Activity 7: Try to picture each member of the group at age eight or nine. What kind of a person was he or she? Aggressive? Shy? A leader? A follower? It may help to close your eyes and develop a mental image of the person. Share with the group.

Activity 8: Each member of the group should draw or symbolize their family tree. Explain how you see yourself in comparison to your mother, father, brother, sister, son, daughter, etc.

Activity 9: Each member of the group should draw or symbolize their life line. Use symbols and pictures to illustrate your life; symbolize where you have been and where you think you are going.

Agree-Disagree Statements[12]

Read each statement once. Mark whether you agree (A) or disagree (D) with each statement. Take five or six minutes to do this.

———————   **1.** A primary concern of all group members should be to establish an atmosphere in which all feel free to express their opinions.

———————   **2.** In a group with a strong leader, an individual is able to achieve greater personal security than in a leaderless group.

———————   **3.** There are often occasions when an individual who is a part of a working group should do what he thinks is right regardless of what the group has decided to do.

———————   **4.** It is sometimes necessary to use autocratic methods to obtain democratic objectives.

———————   **5.** Sometimes it is necessary to change people in the direction you think is right, even if they object.

———————   **6.** It is sometimes necessary to ignore the feelings of others in order to reach a group decision.

———————   **7.** When the leader is doing his best, one should not openly criticize or find fault with his conduct.

———————   **8.** Democracy has no place in a military organization, an air task force, or an infantry squad when actually in battle.

———————   **9.** Much time is wasted in talk when everybody in the group has to be considered before making a decision.

———————   **10.** Almost any job that can be done by a committee can be done better by having one individual responsible for the job.

———————   **11.** By the time the average person has reached maturity, it is almost impossible for him to increase his skill in group participation.

After you have marked the above statements, break up into small groups and try to agree or disagree *unanimously* with each statement. Try especially to find reasons for differences of opinion. If your group cannot reach agreement or disagreement, you may change the wording in any statement to promote unanimity.

Notes

1. Gerald M. Goldhaber, *Organizational Communication,* 2nd ed. (Dubuque, Iowa: Wm. C. Brown Company, Publishers, 1979), p. 2.

2. John K. Brilhart, *Effective Group Discussion,* 3rd ed. (Dubuque, Iowa: Wm. C. Brown Company, Publishers, 1978), p. 5.

3. Dean C. Barnlund and Franklyn S. Haiman, *The Dynamics of Discussion* (Boston: Riverside Press, 1960), p. 20.

4. R. Victor Hamack, Thorrel B. Fest, and Barbara Schindler Jones, *Group Discussion: Theory and Technique,* 2nd ed. (Englewood Cliffs, New Jersey: Prentice-Hall, Inc., 1977), p. 12.

5. Marvin E. Shaw, *Group Dynamics: The Psychology of Small Group Behavior,* 2nd ed. (New York: McGraw-Hill Book Company, 1976), p. 11.

6. David Potter and Martin P. Andersen, *Discussion in Small Groups: A Guide to Effective Practice,* 3rd ed. (Belmont, California: Wadsworth Publishing Company, Inc., 1976), p. 1.

7. Our discussion of the advantages and disadvantages of working in small groups is based, in part, upon: Norman R. F. Maier, "Assets and Liabilities in Group Problem Solving: The Need for an Integrative Function," *Psychological Review* 74 (1967): 239–49.

8. Irving L. Janis, "Groupthink," *Psychology Today* 5 (November 1971): 43–46, 74–76.

9. Ibid., p. 15.

10. Joseph A. Wagner, *Successful Leadership in Groups and Organizations,* 2nd ed. (New York: Chandler Publishing Company, 1973), p. 23.

11. Ibid., p. 24.

12. Developed by Alvin Goldberg, University of Denver.

2 Small Group Communication Theory

After studying this chapter, you should be able to:

■ Discuss the nature and functions of both theory and theory construction.

■ Explain the relevance of theory to the study of small group communication.

■ Explain the model of small group communication presented in this chapter.

■ Identify some of the components of small group communication.

■ Explain the power of words to create.

■ Describe some verbal barriers to communication.

■ Discuss four general theories that apply to small group communication.

Small Group Communication Theory

"Well it sounds good in theory, but in reality . . ."
"Theoretically speaking . . ."
"Yes, but that's only a theory."

Theory. It is a word we encounter almost daily in our casual conversations, in the classroom, and on news broadcasts. We hear of theories of evolution, the theory of relativity, quantum theory, social exchange theory, the continental drift theory. On less formal levels we watch fictitious criminal investigators on television as they examine evidence and develop theories about what took place at the scene of a crime. There are theories of personality development and theories of child-rearing (in fact, there are practically as many theories of child-rearing as there are parents). In short, we are surrounded by theories— some simple, some complex; some formal, some informal; some scientific, some unscientific. Yet few of us have taken the time to find out what theory *is*. What are theories? What good are they? Where do they come from? How do we build them? What do we do with them after we've got them?

In our experiences as students and teachers we have found that many people are intimidated by the word **theory**. To many, studying theory is an esoteric activity which has no real relevance except for the scientist or the professional academician. Today's students seem to be interested in relevant, practical kinds of knowledge, the assumption here being that theory is neither relevant nor practical. But as Dance and Larson so aptly put it, "Theorizing is a very basic form of human activity."[1] Theory is *very* practical. It is an activity in which we all engage whenever we attempt to explain or predict the events in our lives. On a rudimentary level we theorize when we reflect on our past experiences and make decisions based on these experiences. Theory, then, has two basic functions: *to explain* and *to predict*. We will discuss these functions more fully later in the chapter.

In this chapter we will examine some of the central issues of group communication theory. First, we will continue our discussion of the nature of theory and the theory-building process. Second, we will turn our attention to the relevance and practicality of theory in the study of small group communication. Third, we will discuss four theoretical perspectives for the study of small groups. Finally, we will present a theoretical model of small group communication.

THE NATURE OF THEORY AND THE THEORY-BUILDING PROCESS

We have said that theories are very practical. Let's examine this statement more closely. Suppose you are in the habit of doing your weekly grocery shopping every Thursday after your late afternoon class. On each visit to the store you are pleased to see, upon entering, that there are several checkout lanes open with no lines of people behind any of them. "Ah," you say, "I'll be out of here in short order." With your cart before you, you proceed up one aisle and down the next. To your dismay you notice that each time you pass the checkout lanes, the lines have grown until, by the time you have filled your cart, there are at least six people waiting in each lane. You now have a twenty-minute wait at the checkout.

If the situation described above were to occur once, you would probably curse your luck and chalk it up to a twist of fate. But if you find that the same events occur each time you visit the market, you begin to see a consistency in your observations which goes beyond luck or fate. When you notice this consistency, you have taken the first step in building a theory. You have observed a *phenomenon*. You have witnessed a *repeated pattern* of events for which you feel there must be some *explanation*. And so you ponder the situation. In your mind you organize all of the facts available to you: the time of your arrival, the condition of the checkout lanes when you enter the store each time, and the length of the lines when you have completed your shopping. Lo and behold, you discover that you have been arriving at the store at approximately 4:45 each afternoon and reaching the checkout lanes about twenty-five minutes later. Between the time of your arrival and the time of your departure, thousands of workers have "called it a day" and headed for home, with a small but significant percentage of them stopping off at the store on the way. *Voilà*—you have a theory. You have organized your information to explain the phenomenon.

Assuming that your theory is accurate, it is now very useful for you. Having *explained* the phenomenon, you may now reasonably *predict* that under the same set of circumstances, events within the phenomenon will recur. In other words, if you continue to do your weekly shopping after your late class on Thursdays, you repeatedly will be faced with long checkout lines. Given this knowledge, you can adapt your behavior accordingly, perhaps by doing your shopping earlier or later in the day.

Our lives are very theory-directed. When we call the weather service to get the latest forecast before our outings, the information we receive is a prediction based on a theoretical explanation of the relationships among various geographic, atmospheric, and astronomic conditions. On a more immediate level it is a theory we have about ourselves (*self-concept*) which influences the choices we make throughout the day. We tend to do things which we see as being consistent (*predictable*) with our self-concepts. In essence, this self-concept or "self-theory" serves to explain ourselves to ourselves, thereby allowing us to predict our own behavior so that we can successfully select realistic goals. This is theory at its most personal and pervasive.

Theory building is a common, natural process of human communication. We notice consistencies in our experience, examine the consistent features of that experience and their relationships to one another, and build an explanation of the phenomenon which allows us to predict future events and, in some cases, to exercise some control over the situation. There are, of course, very elaborate and formal theories, but even in these we can see the fundamental features of explanation and prediction. In George Kelly's definition of theory we find reference to these features:

> A theory may be considered as a way of binding together a multitude of facts so that one may comprehend them all at once. When the theory enables us to make reasonably precise predictions, one may call it scientific.[2]

Theory is crucial to the study of small group communication. The explanatory power of good theory helps us understand the processes involved when we interact with others in a group setting. The predictive precision of theory allows us to anticipate probable outcomes of various types of communicative behavior in the group. Armed with this type of knowledge, we can adjust our own communicative behavior to help make group work more effective and more rewarding.

THEORY: A PRACTICAL APPROACH TO GROUP COMMUNICATION

As we have seen in our excursion through the market, the development of theory is a very practical pursuit. It is theory, both formal and informal, which helps us make intelligent decisions about how to conduct ourselves. Working in small groups is no exception. Each of us brings a set of theories to small group meetings—theories about ourselves, about other group members, and about groups in general. Once in the group, we regulate our behavior according to these theories. We behave in ways which are consistent with our self-concepts. We deal with others in the group according to our previous impressions (theories) of them. If we believe (theorize) that groups are essentially ineffectual, that "a camel is a horse designed by a committee," or that "if you really want to get something done, do it yourself," then we will probably act accordingly and our prophecy will be fulfilled. If, on the other hand, we come to the group convinced that groups are capable of working effectively, and if we are equipped with knowledge about how to achieve this, then we will behave very differently and contribute much more to the group's effectiveness.

Explanatory Function

To be practical, theories of small group communication must suggest ways in which we can make the process of group discussion more efficient and more rewarding. The **explanatory function** of theory is important in this regard. If we understand why some groups are effective while others are not, or why certain styles of **leadership** are appropriate in some situations but not in others, then we are much better prepared to diagnose the needs of our own groups. By studying theories of group interaction we try to gain an understanding of the overall process and the ways in which different facets of it are related.

Predictive Function

While understanding a process gives us a measure of satisfaction, it is the **predictive function** of theory which has even greater practicality. Consider the following hypothetical situation:

> The dean of student affairs at your college has become sensitive about reports from students that the activities scheduled for orientation week each year are silly. Specifically, students have been reacting to two of the dean's favorite activities at the first orientation mixer—a pass-the-orange-under-your-chin race and a find-your-own-shoes-in-the-middle-of-the-room relay race. Consensus among students seems to be that they feel undignified during these activities, that they are being treated more as children than as adults. Bewildered, the dean remembers how much the Class of '53 enjoyed these activities and is at a loss about what to do. Therefore, the dean has appointed a group of students to investigate the matter. You are one of those students.
>
> The committee is composed mostly of juniors and seniors. The dean feels they have been around long enough to "know the ropes." As president-elect of next year's sophomore class you are the youngest committee member. There are six members altogether. The chairperson is a graduating senior.
>
> At the first meeting you arrive ready to work. The committee has been charged with the task of planning a schedule of activities which are "more closely aligned with the needs of today's college men and women" and you are excited about being a part of a decision-making process which will have a real effect. To your dismay, the other members of the group seem to disregard the task at hand and spend the meeting discussing the prospects for the basketball team, hardly mentioning orientation week activities for next fall. You leave the meeting confused, but hopeful that the next meeting will be more fruitful. You resolve to take a more active role and to try to steer the meeting more toward the committee's task.
>
> At the second meeting you suggest that the committee really should discuss

orientation week. The group concurs and proceeds to make jokes about past experiences with orientation week activities. When the chairperson makes no effort to keep the group on the track, you feel overwhelmed and bewildered.

There are many theories which, if you were familiar with them, might help you understand what is going on in this group—leadership theories, theories of group growth and development, problem-solving theories, various theories of interpersonal interaction, and so on. Basing your observations on theory you might say, for example, that your inferior status as the youngest committee member reduces your ability to exert influence over the group process. Or you might say that the chairperson's leadership style is inappropriate to the task and situation. You might say that every group seems to go through a period of orientation and that the time spent on "trivia" is a necessary part of the group process.

All of these theories might be correct to a *degree*. At least you have a way of describing your group experience systematically. But the test of practicality has not yet been met. While understanding a process carries with it a degree of satisfaction, the more important question is what do you *do* with your understanding? Once you know something about group communication, how do you *use* what you know to help the group function more effectively?

As in the medical field, a diagnosis of the problem is useless unless it suggests some course of treatment. Nevertheless, diagnosis—*explanation*—is the necessary first step. Our *understanding* of the process leads us toward ways to *improve* the process, and herein lies the usefulness of the predictive quality of theory. Let's go one step farther. By understanding our own group and group communication in general, and by being aware of the alternative behaviors which are open to us, we can use theory to select those behaviors which will help us achieve the goal of our group. In other words, if we can reasonably predict that certain outcomes will follow certain types of communication, then we can regulate our behavior to achieve the most desirable results. If, in our example of the dean's advisory committee, we know that a necessary orientation period is coming to a close and that some task-oriented statements will help the group along toward its goal, we can choose to make such statements. In this way, theory *informs* our communicative behavior in small groups. We no longer behave randomly; we behave with understanding and purpose.

Some of the theories presented in this book provide explanations which can help you understand small group phenomena. These descriptive theories are referred to as *process theories*. Other theories, called *method theories,* reflect a prescriptive approach to small group communication. These "how-to-do-it" theories are particularly useful in helping establish formats for solving problems and resolving conflicts in the group. Both types of theories contribute to the knowledge and skill which can help you become a more effective communicator. Central to your effectiveness as a communicator is the ability to use spoken words, which is the subject of our next section.

VERBAL DYNAMICS IN THE SMALL GROUP

The most obvious yet elusive component of small group communication is the spoken word. Words lie at the very heart of who and what we are. Our ability to represent the world symbolically gives us the capacity to foresee events, to reflect on past experiences, to plan, to make decisions, and to consciously control our own behavior. Words are the tools with which we make sense of the world and share that sense with others.

The Power of the Spoken Word

Groups cannot function without spoken words; **speech communication** is the vehicle through which the group moves toward its goals. Spoken words "call into being" the realities, or potential realities, that they represent. Thus a verbal description of an idea for a new product at the board meeting of a manufacturing company creates a vision of that new product for the board members. Presented effectively, the description may result in new or changed attitudes and behaviors; the idea may be adopted. Words, then, have the power to create new realities and change attitudes; they are immensely powerful tools. While this fact may seem obvious, it often goes unnoticed. We spend so much of each day speaking, listening, reading, and writing, that our language seems commonplace. It is not. Through language we reduce our uncertainty and unravel the immense complexity that is our world.

Uncertainty. Dean Barnlund and others have proposed that the aim of speech communication is to reduce uncertainty.[3] According to this principle, the process of speech communication serves to organize and "make sense" out of all the sights, sounds, odors, tastes, and sensations present in our environment. As Barnlund states, "Communication occurs any time meaning is assigned to an internal or external stimulus."[4] Thus, when we arrive at our meeting room and begin to shiver, this sensation brings to mind the word "cold." Within ourselves, or on an *intrapersonal level,* we have reduced uncertainty about the nature of an experience. The room is *too cold.* Giving verbal expression to our experience organizes and clarifies that experience.

At the *interpersonal level* of speech communication we can see the reduction of uncertainty principle even more clearly. As we interact with another group member over a period of time, we say that we are "getting to know her." This is a good assessment of the situation. And as we "get to know" someone, we progressively discover what it is that makes that person unique. We reduce uncertainty about her. By developing an explanation of her behavior, we can predict how she is likely to respond to future communication and events. We base our predictions on what we know about her—her beliefs, attitudes, values, and personality characteristics. In essence, we build a theory which allows us to explain her behavior, to predict her future responses, and to control our own communicative behavior accordingly. In other words, the theory helps reduce our uncertainty about her.

Complexity. "Getting to know" someone is a process of progressively reducing uncertainty—and a lot of uncertainty exists, especially at the outset of a relationship. Think back to your first day at college or to your first day in group communication class. You were probably surrounded by many unfamiliar faces. At times such as these, most of us feel a sense of tentativeness—a feeling of "What am I doing here?" and "Who are all of these other people?" Feelings of uncertainty soar. You encounter an attractive member of the opposite sex in the cafeteria line. You summon up some courage and speak: "Hi! Are you a freshman? What do you think of school so far?" This takes a bit of courage because you don't know what kind of response your advances will elicit. And so you are tentative. You make "small talk" and look for signs in the other's behavior which might indicate whether further communication is desired. You communicate, observe the response, and base further communication on your interpretation of that response. This is a very complex process, particularly when we consider that all of this communicating, observing, responding, and interpreting goes on in both individuals simultaneously!

The complexity of the process creates the uncertainty. Many communication theorists have noted that whenever we communicate with another person there are at least six "people" involved: (1) who you think you are, (2) who you think the other person is, (3) who you think the other person thinks you are, (4) who the other person thinks he or she is, (5) who the other person thinks you are, and (6) who the other person thinks you think he or she is. All six of these "people" influence and are influenced by the communication—a very complex matter indeed, and one that contributes to our uncertainty about interpersonal relationships. Nevertheless, we persist in communicating and we find that on the interpersonal level, communication reduces our uncertainty about other people.

Small groups: more complexity and more uncertainty. Let us look at the even more complex dynamics of the small group. If we have six "people" involved when two people interact, how many such entities are present among eight interactants? Readers who are mathematically inclined have probably already surmised that the numbers grow exponentially rather than arithmetically with the addition of each new member to the group. When eight people interact we have literally thousands of factors which both influence communication and are influenced by it—factors such as "who I think Ted thinks Sally thinks George is" or "who I think Bonnie thinks Tom thinks I am."

Fortunately, we don't consciously think about all of these factors all of the time. It would be horribly debilitating to do so. Nevertheless, these dynamics subtly influence us whenever we interact. When we interact in groups, the number of influencing factors is staggering.

Words As Barriers to Communication

While words can empower us to create new realities and to influence attitudes and behaviors, they can also impede the process that they facilitate. While speech communication gives us access to the ideas and inner worlds of other group members, it can also—intentionally or unintentionally—set up barriers to effective communication.

If you grew up in the United States you can probably remember chanting, defensively, "Sticks and stones can break my bones but names can never hurt me." Even as you uttered these lines you knew it was a lie you were using to protect yourself. We often unwittingly communicate in ways that threaten and make others feel defensive. When a group member feels a need to protect himself, he will shift his attention from the group's goal to his own personal goal of self-protection, thus creating a barrier to effective group process. We will expand on the subject of defensive and supportive communication in Chapter Five. For now, let's look at a more subtle but pervasive word barrier that general semanticists call **bypassing.**

Bypassing. The meanings of the words we use seem so obvious to us that we assume they elicit the same meaning in others, but nothing could be further from the truth. Bypassing takes place when two people assign different meanings to the same word. Many words are open to an almost limitless number of interpretations. Consider, for example, the words "love," "respect," and "communication." You may know precisely what you mean when you say that the department's account is "seriously overdrawn," but how is that to be interpreted by others? How serious is "seriously"?

It has been estimated that the 500 most frequently used words in the English language have over 14,000 dictionary definitions. And dictionary definitions reflect only a tiny percentage of all possible meanings. Add to that the influence of our different cultures and experiences and it's amazing that we can understand each other at all.

In groups, the problem of bypassing is compounded by the number of people involved; the possibility for multiple misunderstandings is always present. This points to the importance of good *feedback* among group members. Feedback is any response by a listener that lets the speaker know whether or not he has been understood accurately. To overcome word barriers, we must understand that words are subjective. We need to check that what we understand from others is really what they intend.

THEORETICAL PERSPECTIVES FOR THE STUDY OF SMALL GROUP COMMUNICATION

Thus far in the chapter we have discussed the nature of theory and its relationship to effective small group communicaton. We have also shown that uncertainty and complexity are pervasive characteristics of small groups while speech communication is the driving force that moves the group toward its goals.

The purpose of small group communication theory is to explain and predict small group phenomena. Given the complexity of the process and the number of variables that affect small group communication, no single theory can account for all of the variables involved; nor can one theory systematically relate the variables to each other. Therefore, a number of different approaches to group communication theory have emerged in recent years. Each seeks to explain and predict group behavior while focusing on different facets of the group process. Individually and in concert, all of these theories give us insight into the subject. Four of these theoretical perspectives are described briefly here: *field theory, social exchange theory, rules theory, and systems theory.*

Field Theory and Small Group Communication

Social psychologist Kurt Lewin was one of the first theorists and researchers in the area known as *group dynamics.* His theory of human behavior suggests that individuals move about within a subjective world that he called a *psychological field* or *life space.* This subjective field, said Lewin, can best be conceptualized in its distance from other objects within the field. As the individual moves in this perceptual space she is motivated by needs and goals and her behavior is explainable in terms of her pursuit of these goals. But as she approaches her goals, she will encounter barriers which she must overcome.

Groups are an inseparable part of the psychological fields of individuals. They have a life space of their own with characteristic forces and tensions that impel them toward goals and exert influence on individuals in the group. Thus, said Lewin, the group is influenced by individual needs, while the individual is affected by group standards.[5]

Social Exchange Theory and Small Group Communication

Exchange theory is a simple but powerful theory that explains human behavior in terms that sound like a blend of behavioral psychology and economic theory. According to this theory, relationships can be described in terms of their rewards and costs, profits and losses. Rewards are pleasurable outcomes associated with particular behaviors; costs include such things as mental effort, anxiety, or even embarrassment.[6] Moving from specific behaviors to the overall quality of relationships, we see *profit* as equal to rewards minus costs. Thus, as long as rewards exceed costs, the relationship remains attractive.

As we shall see in later chapters, small group variables such as cohesiveness and productivity are directly related to how rewarding the group experience is to its members. The basics of exchange theory are useful in their descriptiveness. Keep them in mind as you read the remaining chapters and as you observe working groups.

We study small group communication theory so that we can understand the various behaviors in our groups and can accordingly adapt our own behaviors to help further the goals of our groups.

Rules Theory and Small Group Communication

Rules theory begins with the assumption that in order for successful communication to take place, the interactants must share a set of rules that structure communicative behavior. The rules of grammar that order our words in a logical, followable sequence are one example. But we also share rules about such things as how to greet another person, how to take turns at speaking, and how to insult or be sarcastic.

Susan Shimanoff defines a rule as "a followable prescription that indicates what behavior is obligated, preferred, or prohibited in certain contexts."[7] Let's examine this definition more closely. A rule, to be a rule, must be *followable.* This implies that we have a choice about whether to follow a rule or not. If we had no choice, we would be conforming to a law of nature, not a rule. Rules are *prescriptive;* that is, failure to conform may result in some form of penalty such as criticism or social ridicule. Furthermore, rules dictate *behavior.* They tell us what to do or not to do, but they do not dictate how we should think, feel, or interpret.[8] Finally, rules are *contextual.* While some rules are relatively stable (such as the rule that says we should apologize for stepping on someone's toe), others vary from situation to situation. Many of the **norms** that small groups develop would fall into this category. For example, a group may develop a norm that says it's all right to start each meeting fifteen minutes late, a pattern that might not be tolerated in other groups.

Systems Theory and Small Group Communication

Perhaps the most prevalent approach to small group communication is that of systems theory. In many respects, systems theory represents the most promising perspective on small group communication in that it is flexible enough to encompass the vast array of variables that influence small group interaction.

One way to approach the concept of **system** is to think of your own body. The various organs of your body make up systems (digestive, nervous, circulatory, etc.) which, in turn, make up the larger system which is you. Each organ is dependent on the other organs properly functioning; a change in one part of the system effects changes in the rest of the system. Furthermore, the physiological system cannot be seen in isolation from the environment that surrounds it; to maintain the proper functioning of your physiological systems, you must adjust to changes outside of the body. A decrease in oxygen at a higher elevation will cause more rapid breathing; a rise in temperature will induce perspiration, and so forth. In other words, your body is an *open* system composed of *interdependent* elements. It is a system that receives *input* from the environment (food, air, water), *processes* that input (digestion, oxygenation, etc.), and yields an *output* (elimination of waste materials, carbon dioxide, etc.). *Like the human body, a small group can be described as an open system composed of interdependent variables that receives input, processes the input, and yields an output.*

An Open System. Groups do not operate in isolation; they are continually affected by interactions with the outside environment. New members may join while former members leave, demands from other groups or organizations may alter the group's goals, and even the climate may affect the group's ability to work.

Interdependence. This concept is important to the study of small group communication. The various components of the group process are interrelated in such a way that a change in one component may alter the relationships among all of the other components. A shift in **cohesiveness** can change the level of productivity. The loss of a group member or the addition of a new member effects a change that is felt throughout the system. **Interdependence** in the small group system is what makes the study of small group communication so fascinating and so difficult. None of the variables involved may be understood properly in isolation.

Input Variables. We may categorize the variables of small group communication by viewing them as parts of subsystems categorized according to the systems theory concept of input, process, and output. Input variables in the small group system include such things as group members, group resources (funds, tools, knowledge, purposes, relationships to other groups or organizations, and the physical environment).[9]

Process Variables. These variables relate to the procedures the group follows to reach its goals. Many of these variables are represented in the model in the next section.

Output Variables. Output variables represent the outcomes of group process. These may range from problem solutions and decisions to personal growth and satisfaction.

While systems theory does not provide any specific explanation for small group phenomena, it serves as a useful organizational strategy. Indeed, all of the theories identified in this section are incomplete pictures of human behavior. But each provides some general insight into the maze of forces that affect small group communication.

A THEORETICAL MODEL OF SMALL GROUP COMMUNICATION

At this point we can see that a theoretical model which takes into account all of the elaborate networks of sender, receiver, and message variables in a small group would be hopelessly complicated even before we included other variables central to the study of small group communication. We must, then, settle for a model that is less than comprehensive but which suggests the features and relationships critical to an understanding of small group communication.

Figure 2–1 represents such a descriptive model. This framework depicts small group communication as a constellation of variables, each of which is related to every other. Speech communication—what we say and how we say it—is the process by which these relationships are established and maintained. Our model includes only those variables which we feel are absolutely essential. We'll provide an in-depth discussion of these variables later in the book; for now, note the brief discussion that follows.

- *Speech Communication.* What we say, how we say it, to whom we say it, all comprise speech communication. This is the primary object of study in small group communication research.
- *Leadership.* In Chapter One, part of our definition of small group communication concerned *mutual influence.* Leadership refers to behavior which exerts influence upon the group.
- *Goals.* All groups have goals. The goal may be to provide therapy for its members, to complete some designated task, or simply to have a good time. Individual group members also have goals. Often individual goals complement the group goal. Sometimes they do not.

Figure 2-1   Constellation of Variables in Small Group Communication

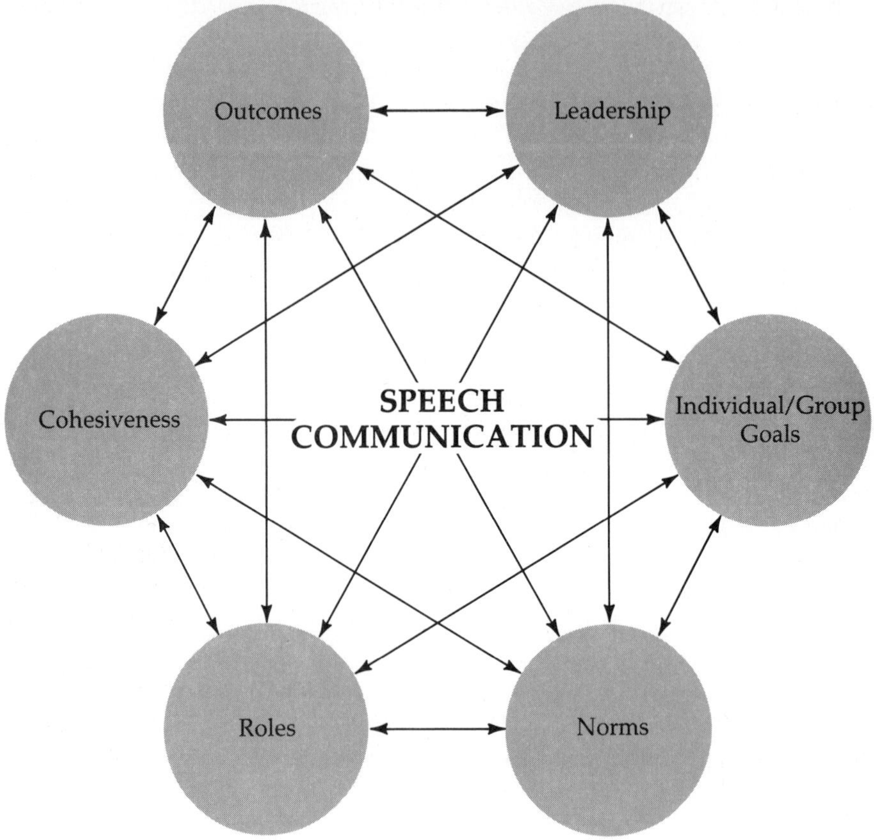

- *Norms.* Norms establish which behaviors are permitted or encouraged within the group and which behaviors are forbidden or discouraged. Every group, from your family to the president's cabinet, develops and maintains norms or rules. Some norms are observed formally, as when a group operates according to parliamentary procedure. Other norms are established informally, as when a group always begins its meetings fifteen minutes late.

- *Roles.* Roles are sets of expectations we hold for ourselves and for others in a given context. Different people play different roles in different groups. Researchers have identified several functional roles which need to be filled in order for a small group to reach maximum satisfaction and productivity.

- *Cohesiveness.* Cohesiveness is the degree of attraction group members feel toward one another and toward the group. Feelings of loyalty help unite the group.

- *Outcomes.* Frequently used as measures of the effectiveness of small group interaction, outcomes are generally rated by researchers along two dimensions: (1) the quality or effectiveness of the group's product, decision, or problem solution, and (2) the satisfaction felt by individual group members.

Small group communication theory seeks to *explain* the relationships among these and other variables and to *make predictions* based on such explanations. Thus, the theories presented in this book help us eliminate most of the complexity and uncertainty which surface at every level of group interaction.

SMALL GROUP COMMUNICATION THEORY: PUTTING PRINCIPLE INTO PRACTICE

Theorizing is a basic form of human activity, not an esoteric endeavor reserved for scientists and academicians. The theories discussed throughout this book explain consistencies in communicative behavior observed within small groups. If we can attain a theoretical grasp of small group communication, we can more successfully make predictions and control our behavior accordingly.

At the present, no single theory of small group communication systematically relates all of the major variables. We have offered a model of small group communication which identifies several areas of theory and research which we consider essential to understand small group communication.

PRACTICE

1. Make a list of informal "theories" you have about an ordinary day (e.g., Professor X is boring, I'm afraid of speaking in class, etc.). On what basis did you formulate these theories? How do they affect your behavior? What might cause you to alter these theories?
2. Make a list of your beliefs about working in small groups. How do these beliefs affect your behavior in small groups?
3. Based on your experience in groups and the model presented in Chapter Two, make predictions about how changes in one facet of small group communication affect the other facets.
4. What areas of uncertainty can you identify within the small group context? How does communication function to reduce uncertainty in these areas?

Notes

1. Frank E. X. Dance and Carl E. Larson, *The Functions of Human Communication: A Theoretical Approach* (New York: Holt, Rinehart & Winston, 1976), p. 4.

2. George A. Kelly, *A Theory of Personality: The Psychology of Personal Constructs* (New York: W. W. Norton & Company, Inc., 1963), p. 18.

3. Dean Barnlund, *Interpersonal Communication: Survey and Studies* (Boston: Houghton Mifflin Company, 1968).

4. Dean Barnlund, "Toward a Meaning Centered Philosophy of Communication," in *Nothing Never Happens,* Johnson et al., eds. (Beverly Hills: Glencoe Press, 1974) p. 213.

5. For a broader discussion of Field Theory see: Stephen W. Littlejohn, *Theories of Human Communication* (Belmont, CA: Wadsworth Publishing Company, 1983), pp. 219–20.

6. Ibid., p. 205.

7. Susan B. Shimanoff, *Communication Rules: Theory and Research* (Beverly Hills: Sage Publications, 1980), p. 57.

8. Littlejohn, *Theories of Human Communication,* p. 63.

9. John K. Brilhart, *Effective Group Discussion,* 4th edition, (Dubuque, IA: William C. Brown, Publishers, 1982), p. 25.

3 Group Formation

After studying this chapter you should be able to:

▪ Discuss two classification systems of interpersonal needs and describe their relationship with group formation.

▪ Explain the potential conflict between individual goals and group goals.

▪ Suggest ways in which mutuality of concern can be established in a work group.

▪ Identify and explain four factors in interpersonal attraction.

▪ Identify and describe three factors in group attraction.

▪ Facilitate a group's movement through the first phase of formation.

▪ Apply your knowledge of group formation toward greater effectiveness as a communicator.

Group Formation

Are you considering or being considered for membership in any particular group right now? A fraternal organization? A sports club? A political action group? Are you thinking about getting married? Granted, a marriage starts with only two people, but it has a way of becoming a group of three or more.

To which groups do you already belong? Can you identify a circle of friends you might refer to as "your group"? Do you belong to clubs? Teams? If you think about it, you can probably generate a rather long list of groups, from the past and in the present, to which you belong. From the moment we are born into our first group, the family, we move through a succession of group memberships. Some are formally organized, some are loosely structured; some we choose; others are assigned. But *our membership in groups does not happen randomly*. Groups meet specific needs and perform special functions. To understand group formation, then, requires that we examine the needs and functions around which groups form.

Upon learning of our work on this book, a friend of ours said, "I don't know how you can even stand to think about it. I hate committee work. I'll do anything I can to avoid working in groups. I'd rather do things my own way." This fairly prevalent attitude toward groups ignores the pervasive influence which groups have on our lives (discussed in Chapter One). So, we prodded our friend a bit and asked him if there wasn't at least one group in his life which provided him with some pleasure. "Well," he faltered, "there is my bowling team . . . and, come to think of it, I enjoyed working with a group of political strategists in the last election. My religion and human rights discussion group at the church is pretty interesting, . . . and of course there is my family." He added, "But there's a difference between *those* groups and the committees I have to serve on as part of my job." Although he might be in the wrong job, we admit there is a difference, at least in our initial perception, between groups to which we choose to belong and those to which we are assigned. But the fact remains that even the groups and committees to which we are assigned at work or in school are the result of *choices we have made*.

As professors, we do not enjoy every university committee on which we serve, but these committees are a part of the larger group which we *did* choose—the academic community. You may not have selected the group with whom you work in class, but you *did* select that class. We may still say that all of the groups to which we belong reflect *personal decisions.* Some groups we chose directly; others are the result of prior choices we have made.

WHY DO PEOPLE JOIN GROUPS?

An understanding of the diversity of reasons that draws people to groups can help us unravel the complexity of small group interaction. Groups are many things to many people. To one member of a committee the group's problem is an exciting vehicle toward greater self-understanding. To another group member it is merely an uninteresting but necessary obstacle on the way to reaching a personal goal. These two individuals differ dramatically in their motivation for joining the group and in their commitment and contribution to it. In this chapter we will first examine the needs and goals which lead individuals into joining small groups and then we will explore the impact of these needs and goals on small group communication.

We have already suggested that the answer to the question "Why do people join groups?" has many dimensions. These dimensions can be placed into several broad categories: (1) **interpersonal needs,** (2) individual goals, (3) group goals, (4) interpersonal attraction, and (5) group attraction.

INTERPERSONAL NEEDS

Maslow's Hierarchy

Abraham Maslow asserts that all humans have basic needs and that these needs can be arranged in a hierarchy; that is, we do not concern ourselves with higher-level needs until lower-level needs are satisfied.[1] At the bottom of the hierarchy are two levels of needs that Maslow termed *physiological needs* and *safety needs.* Our physiological needs are for air, water, and an adequate supply of food. Our safety needs are for security and protection. Maslow called these two levels *survival needs;* their satisfaction is necessary to our basic existence. During our childhood years the family satisfies these needs for us.

Once our survival needs are fulfilled, we can turn our attention to the higher-level needs that Maslow called *psychological needs.* They are the need to belong, the need for esteem, and the need for self-actualization. These needs may affect our group memberships throughout our lives.

Belongingness need. Maslow posits that once we have satisfied our basic survival, physiological, and safety needs, we turn our attention to a social or *belongingness need.* We need to feel that we are a part of some group. Here again, the family provides for us, but as we get older we begin to look outside of the family to satisfy this need. Peer groups gain importance. Do you remember the "in" group and the "out" group in high school? At that time, our affiliation needs were at their strongest. To be a social pariah seemed a fate worse than death. Consequently, teams, clubs, and cliques took care of this need for us.

Esteem need. Once we have developed a sense of belonging, Maslow says that we have a need for respect or *esteem.* We need to feel not only that we are accepted, but also that we are worthwhile and valued by others. We cannot, of course, receive this positive feedback from others if we are in isolation. We need a group of people whose opinions we value to tell us that we're OK.

Self-actualization need. Finally, Maslow says, we have a need for self-actualization. This need is of a character different from the first four needs. The former needs Maslow calls "deficiency needs" because they represent a perceived void which we fill by drawing on the resources of other people. Maslow calls self-actualization a "being" need. Basically, *self-actualization* involves being all that we are capable of being, and living life to its fullest potential. Having taken care of our "deficiencies" by drawing on others, we are ready to give of ourselves. We are ready to function as autonomous beings, operating independently in quest of our own full potential. We no longer need groups to take care of our deficiencies; instead, we need groups in which we can find and express our wholeness. While this need level is, perhaps, the most difficult to grasp conceptually, we can still see consistency throughout Maslow's hierarchy: *People need groups to satisfy interpersonal needs.* It is also clear that people differ from one another in their motivation for joining groups. This difference may be reflected in the communicative behavior of group members. The person who simply wants to *belong* may interact in a manner different from the person who needs the esteem and respect of the group.

Schutz's Theory

In an elaborate theory of interpersonal behavior, William Schutz suggests that three basic human needs influence individuals as they form and interact in groups. These needs are **inclusion, control,** and **affection.**[2]

Inclusion need. Like Maslow's belongingness need, we join groups to fulfill our need for *inclusion.* We need to be recognized as unique individuals. We need to feel that we are understood. When people try to understand us it implies that we are worthy of their time and effort. In this respect, we see that Schutz's *inclusion need* is also related to Maslow's *esteem need.*

Control need. The need for *control* is a need for status and power. We need to have some control over ourselves and over others and, sometimes, to give others some control over us, as when we seek their guidance and direction.

Affection need. The need for *affection* drives us to give and receive emotional warmth and closeness. The degree of our need for inclusion, control, and affection varies, but groups provide us with a setting in which such needs can be satisfied.

In a broad sense, groups are more than collections of people with a common goal; they are arenas in which individual needs are satisfied or frustrated. Schutz asserts that we join groups to satisfy our inclusion, control, and affection needs, and that these needs influence group process throughout the life of the group. He has observed that in the initial stages of group formation, communication aims primarily toward inclusion needs. Group members are friendly but cautious as they "feel each other out" and try to gain the acceptance of other group members. As the group progresses, control needs become more evident when the members contest issues and vie for leadership. Schutz observes that as conflicts are resolved we turn toward our affection needs. The expression of positive feelings characterizes this phase. The progression, Schutz says, is cyclical.

Continuing cycle of group process. Group formation from Schutz's perspective is a process not limited to the initial coming together of the group. Rather,

It is often the commonality of individual goals that is responsible for the formation of a group. However, groups can be frustrated by the various degrees of commitment brought to the group by its members.

the pattern repeats as the group develops over time. The process of group decision making is characterized by a series of smaller decisions on the way toward achieving the group's primary goal. For example, a group of engineers planning a bridge must make decisions regarding concerns that range from the location and frequency of their meetings to the design and materials for the bridge. While we can observe a linear progression through developmental phases over the life of the group (as we shall in Chapter Eight), we can also witness this cyclical pattern of formation and reformation whenever the group approaches each new meeting and each new decision. If we could visualize this process we might see something akin to a large jellyfish moving through the water. The jellyfish floats in the water in a relatively disorganized state until it decides (that is, if jellyfish can decide at all) to move forward, at which time it organizes itself, contracts, and propels itself through the water until it returns to a restful, less organized state. Group process moves through a similar series of contractions until it reaches its ultimate goal.

A group is defined, in part, by a common purpose. Within that purpose are several smaller goals. As a group reaches each of these goals, it momentarily loses a bit of its definition until a new goal replaces the old. As we accomplish each new goal, we begin a new cycle of inclusion, control, and affection behaviors. Let's look at an example:

Harv: Well. It's been hard but we've finally found a date for the banquet that we can all agree on.

Juanita: For sure. For a while I thought we'd never agree but y'know, I think we've made the best decision now.

Betsy: Yeah. We're over the major hurdle. Feels good, doesn't it?

Phil: Amen. We're organized now and ready to go for it! This is getting to be fun.
           (Laughter, followed by a pause)

Juanita: Well, here we are. What do we do next?

Phil: I guess we ought to talk about the theme and the speakers.

Harv: Hold on there! The speakers are irrelevant if no one is there to hear them. We've got to talk first about how we're going to publicize.

Phil: C'mon, Harv. How can we publicize if we don't have a theme?

Betsy: Here we go again.

In this example we can see the end of one cycle and the beginning of the next. The members expressed their positive feelings about the group and its accomplishment and experienced a lull in the conversation before regrouping for another attack on a new facet of their problem. The sense of "groupness" or cohesiveness peaks during the affection phase and then falls off, only to rebuild around the next task. But like the jellyfish which coordinates its processes around its task of propulsion, the small group does not end up back where it started. The whole process moves forward. To say that the phases are cyclical, then, is somewhat misleading. Certain types of communicative behaviors recur, but the whole process moves forward. Frank E. X. Dance captured the essence of this process when he described human communication as having the properties of a helix.[3] The helix, like a bedspring, is both linear and circular. It turns in on itself and yet always moves forward. Seen in this light, the process of group formation does not cease, but pulses throughout the life of the group.

INDIVIDUAL GOALS

Theories of interpersonal needs provide us with some of the psychological bases for group formation. Another important factor is *individual goals.* Goals have a more tangible and obvious effect on our selection of group memberships. What is it that you want out of life? Prestige? Status? Power? Anonymity? Recreation? Education? Personal growth? In other words, what goals do you have which exist apart from any particular group membership?

Individual goals are instrumental in determining which groups we join. Obviously, if we enjoy flower arranging and wish to improve our skills, we may join the garden club. If personal growth is our aim we will join a T-group or encounter group. If we desire status and power we will seek a group which we perceive will bring us such status and power. Sometimes the prestige associated with a particular group is enough to make membership attractive to us. This is often a motivation for joining a particular sorority or fraternity. *Whatever our individual goals may be, we bring them with us when we join a group.*

GROUP GOALS

Group goals are identifiable goals which transcend the group members' individual goals. Certain professionals and fraternal organizations devote their activities to serving community needs. For example, the Lions Club is well known for its significant contribution toward cures for eye disease and the prevention of blindness. Individual members have many different goals which lead them to join the club: the chance to "rub elbows" with other professionals from the community, the pleasure of camaraderie and fellowship, the prestige of membership, the sense of belonging, or the genuine interest in serving the community. While individual goals may vary, the group goal takes precedence.

Of course, somewhere along the way it was an individual or small group of individuals who proposed the group goals, which suggests at least some initial commonality among individual goals. But once the individuals adopt group goals, their individual goals are superceded. The multiplicity of needs and goals which individuals bring into small groups may be incompatible with the group's goal. This is a potential source of problems in small group communication. Consider the following situation:

The First Church in the town of Roseville has a Building and Grounds Committee. This committee, charged with the responsibility of overseeing the regular maintenance and upkeep of the church building and surrounding property, makes sure that the lawns are mowed, the hedges trimmed, the furnace maintained, the roof patched, and so forth. The committee consists of the following members:

Robert Bomblast. Robert has been an accountant for a local firm for twenty-three years. He has always felt that his firm has never given him a chance to show his true leadership ability. He sees this committee, of which he is chairperson, as his big chance to prove himself and show the world what a truly fine administrator he is. He has another ulterior motive: he wants very much to be the new part-time business manager for the church when "Old George," the present manager, dies or becomes too senile to do the job. This committee, then, is Robert's stepping-stone to greatness.

"Marmalade." No one is sure of "Marmalade's" real name. Found ten years ago wandering around the sanctuary saying, "Wow . . . wow . . . wowwwww . . . wowwwwwwwww," he is your basic burn-out. The church members took him under their wing. He has been sweeping floors and doing other odd jobs around the church since that time. The pastor thought it would "do Marmalade some good" to get involved with a responsible committee, so he assigned him to this one.

Polly Prim. Polly is the president of Roseville's Garden Club. She has been complaining that the landscaping around the church "lacks imagination." She has struggled for the last three years, trying to get on the committee. Finally, she is on it.

Merry Midwest. In all of her forty-seven years, Merry has not been outside of her home state. She loves her country, her state, her community, her home, and her family. She especially loves her church because of the sense of warmth and community she feels there. She has served on every committee in the Church and when she is not serving on a committee she misses a sense of "fellowship." Merry has high needs for inclusion. She is pleased to be on this committee.

Thurman Jester. Ever since his vacation trip to Dallas, Thurman wears a white belt and off-white shoes to work every day (and strongly urges his employees at the insurance office to do the same). He is committed to keeping up with the trend setters, and Dallas, he feels, is where trends are set. Thurman was also impressed by a forty-foot neon cross he spotted outside a church in Dallas. Thurman is highly motivated by control needs.

Now imagine that this group has come together for their first monthly meeting, that the church custodian has just resigned, and that the roof of the church leaks. The group goal is to provide adequate maintenance for the building and grounds. All of the members are, to some degree, committed to the group goal. However, this commitment means different things to the different members. For each, an individual need or goal shapes his or her perception of what the group should be doing. They are conscious of their personal goals but most of the members are not consciously aware that their behavior is motivated by a desire to satisfy interpersonal needs. Merry Midwest may interpret her own behavior as a desire to serve, while the underlying unconscious motive may be a need for inclusion. Thurman Jester has the personal goal of putting a neon cross outside the church. But Thurman may not be aware of his need to control others.

Whether our individual needs and goals are conscious or not, they influence our perception of the group members and the group's task. If a group goal is the desired end result of a group, and an individual goal is the desired end result of an individual, then we can predict that there will be some overlap between individual and group goals in any given group. Differences between these goals may help or hinder the group. The conflict between individual and group goals is often the reason why some groups can't get off the ground.

Returning to our church committee example, try to imagine what the first meeting or two could be like. Even better, ask some friends or classmates to play the roles of the various characters. Each has a personal agenda—an individual goal—which will have a profound effect on his or her behavior in the group. Robert is seeking personal gain; "Marmalade" is unpredictable; Polly will attempt to get the committee busy on landscaping projects; Merry just wants to feel a part of something; and Thurman wants to make his mark on the world with a forty-foot neon cross. Each of these characters will direct his or her communication in the group toward a particular goal; but we have here at least five goals, none of which is compatible with the more immediate need for fixing the leaky roof and hiring a new custodian. While all the characters have come together ostensibly for the same purpose, each has a different idea of what the group should be doing. If each member pulls in a different direction, the results can be disastrous. The group may go nowhere, and, to compound matters, each member will probably perceive the others as uncooperative! For this reason, it is essential that groups question the **mutuality of concern** of group members during the initial stages of group formation.

Establishing Mutuality of Concern

When we join a group we often assume that other group members share our commitment to the group's task. If there is a problem to be solved we take it for granted that others view the problem in much the same way that we do. But as we have seen in the earlier example of the building and grounds committee, each person may view the problem differently. Many small groups function poorly because they begin to propose solutions before they have defined the problem to everyone's mutual satisfaction. We will explore this further in Chapter Eight.

Groups can also be frustrated because people bring different levels of commitment or *concern* to the group. Suppose that you have been appointed to a student government group whose task is to recommend whether your college should institute a plus/minus system of grading or continue with a straight A,B,C, and D grading policy. If you are a freshman or sophomore, this policy change could have a direct effect on your grade point average over your four years in college. But if you are a graduating senior, a policy change would have little or no effect on you. Hence the level of concern over the problem can vary from member to member. Once again, we can see individual goals interacting with the group goal. Those whom the problem affects directly will probably become more active within the group than will those who are not as concerned with the problem. This can lead to needless conflict, as when some members resent having to carry the bulk of the work load.

The degree to which members are concerned with the group's task needs to be clarified at the outset. Each group member should state clearly her or his personal needs and goals regarding the topic area. Patton and Giffin make some suggestions about how to begin this process in your group:

> To clarify a mutual concern with others you start with tentative, trusting behavior, clearly stating your personal view of the situation and how you feel about it. Your comment may be something like this; "I see a need to reconsider course requirements for the English major, and I feel this need is very important." The keynote elements are "I see . . ." and "I feel. . . ." These elements indicate a personal viewpoint (not the only possible viewpoint) and signify that another group member may see or feel differently.
>
> At this stage your interpersonal manner, way of stating your viewpoint and attitude toward other members can indicate a good, or poor, understanding of this phase of the decision-making process. You must state clearly and honestly your viewpoint and your feelings; by all means be genuine and sincere. But show your expectation that others in the group will do the same, comfortably disagreeing as necessary. Your manner of stating your viewpoint and feelings should be genuine and honest, but it should deliberately and overtly tell other members you can tolerate expressed differences of viewpoints or feelings when they state their position.
>
> As each group member in effect says "This is the way I see it . . ." and "This is how I feel about it. . . ," the nature and degree of common concern can be diagnosed. If honesty prevails, it will become apparent whether a group can work well together on the problem previously thought to be of mutual concern. All members must be prepared to discover that others do not share their view and concern. In fact, it may be discovered that there is no common concern at all. In such case it is better to discover this early than late; it can save time, energy and, possibly, interpersonal emotional wear and tear.[4]

While individual needs and goals may bring a group together in the first place, they can also break the group apart. The success or failure of a group depends, in part, upon the degree to which the group's goal is assumed by the individuals as their own goals. Unsatisfied or unclarified individual needs and goals can become *hidden agendas*—goals toward which individuals are working while seemingly working toward the group goal. Such hidden agendas can be extremely disruptive to the group. Establishing mutuality of concern can help to reduce this disruptive influence.

Having explored some of the relationships among interpersonal needs, personal goals, and group goals, we turn now to two other factors which have an influence on our selection of groups: *interpersonal attraction* and *group attraction.*

INTERPERSONAL ATTRACTION

Often, we are attracted to groups because we are attracted to the people who compose them. While there are many factors which influence interpersonal attraction, four of these are especially significant: similarity, complementarity, proximity/contact/interaction, and physical attractiveness.

Similarity

One of the strongest influences in interpersonal attraction is **similarity.** Remember your first day on campus? That feeling of newness, strangeness and aloneness? You needed a friend, and you probably found one. Who did you look for to be your friend? Did you seek out someone whom you perceived to be very different from yourself? Probably not. If the principle of similarity in interpersonal attraction applies here, you probably looked for someone to talk to who appeared to be in the same situation—another lonely newcomer, or perhaps someone dressed similarly to the way you dress.

Who are your closest friends? Do you share many of the same attitudes, beliefs, and values? Do you enjoy the same activities? More than likely, you do. We are often attracted to people whom we consider to be like ourselves. A probable explanation for this phenomenon is that similar backgrounds, beliefs, attitudes, and values make it easier to understand one another—and we all like to feel that we are understood.

Complementarity

As you read the previous section on similarity, some of you probably were shaking your heads and saying to yourselves, "No, that's not the way it is at all. My best friend and I are about as similar as an orchid and a fire hydrant!" As the saying goes, "no generalization is true ... including the present one," and so it is with the principle of similarity. While there is some truth to the statement that "birds of a feather flock together," it is also true that "opposites attract." Thibaut and Kelley suggest that some interpersonal relationships are based primarily on similarity while others are based on **complementarity.**[5] At times we may be attracted to others who exhibit qualities which we do not possess but which we admire. While the principle of similarity seems to be the more pervasive phenomenon, we can all cite instances of complementarity. For at least a partial explanation of attraction through complementarity we can look to Schutz's theory of interpersonal needs which we discussed earlier in this chapter. According to Schutz's theory, a person with a high need to control would be most compatible with a person who has a high need to be controlled. The same would be true in terms of needs to express and receive inclusion and affection. These needs are complementary rather than similar.

Proximity/Contact/Interaction

We tend to be attracted to people who are physically close to us, people who live and work with us, and people whom we see and talk with often. If we know that we have to live or work close to another person, we may ignore that person's less desirable traits in order to minimize potential conflict. Furthermore, proximity, contact, and interaction breed familiarity, and familiarity has a positive influence on interpersonal attraction.[6] Interaction with another person helps us "get to know" that other person, and through this process we may uncover similarities and discover ways in which we can satisfy each other's interpersonal needs. It is not, then, the actual physical distance between people which influences attraction, but the interpersonal possibilities which are illuminated by proximity, contact, and interaction.

Physical Attractiveness

At least in the initial stages of interpersonal attraction, physical attractiveness influences us. In a given culture, if person is physically beautiful, others tend to want to affiliate with him or her.[7] However, there is evidence that this factor diminishes in importance over time and that physical beauty is more important to males than to females.[8]

In sum, we seem to be attracted to others who are likely to understand us, who can fulfill our needs, who may complement our personalities, and who are physically appealing. We perceive these people as potentially rewarding to us. As such, they constitute a powerful influence on our selection of groups.

GROUP ATTRACTION

While we may be attracted to a group because of our attraction toward the members who compose it, we may also be attracted to the group itself. Such attraction usually focuses on the group's activities, goals, or simply on the desirability of group membership.

Group Activities

While research support is not extensive in this area, it seems fairly clear that people who are interested in the same activities tend to form groups.[9] A person who enjoys intellectual pursuits may join a literary discussion group. Bridge players may join a bridge club. Beyond these obvious examples, people may

Like the students of the police academy above, we join groups because we are attracted to their goals.

be attracted to the activities of a group in a more general sense. Some of us may join groups simply because we enjoy going to regular meetings and joining in group discussions, regardless of the group's specific aims or goals. The structure and human contact provided by groups are potentially rewarding in and of themselves.

Group Goals

Another factor that may attract us to a group is the goal for which the group meets. If, for example, we believe that the spread of nuclear power must be curtailed, we may join a group which is dedicated to such curtailment. If we are personally committed to preserving and protecting our natural environment, we may join Friends of the Earth, the Sierra Club, the Audubon Society, or any organization which professes a goal similar to our own.

Within this factor of group attraction we can also see elements of attraction mentioned earlier: similarity in interpersonal attraction and the relationship between individual and group goals.

Group Membership

Sometimes it is not the people, the activities, or the goals of a group which attract us but *membership itself.* Sometimes we perceive that membership, such as one in an exclusive club or honor society, brings us prestige, acceptance, or professional benefits outside of the group. Membership in some civic organization, for example, may be "expected" of a young executive because it provides good public relations for the firm.

Our needs for affiliation—Maslow's belongingness need and Schutz's inclusion need—can make group membership attractive to us. You probably know of "professional" committee members who move from group to group because their lives seem "incomplete" without some type of group membership. The need for affiliation is basic to human nature. Group membership can help satisfy that need.

GROUP FORMATION: PUTTING PRINCIPLE INTO PRACTICE

While we have treated separately the topics of interpersonal needs, individual goals, group goals, interpersonal attraction, and group attraction, we have really been examining an arena where all of these factors come together—the small group. You may have noticed some continuity and intrinsic relationships between the variables described. For example, there is a clear relationship between an individual's need for affiliation and the attractiveness of group membership. Similarity in interpersonal attraction and the attractiveness of a shared group goal is another point at which we can see the interface between variables.

The dynamic interrelatedness of *all* of the variables which affect small group processes makes the study of small group communication challenging and exciting. As you move through the rest of this book, it is important that you retain what you have previously learned. Only when we've fit all of the puzzle pieces together can we see a clear picture of small group communication.

In this chapter we have zoomed in on one part of the puzzle: those needs and goals which motivate us to join groups and which influence our behavior within those groups. In the formative, initial stages of group development, uncertainty is at its peak—uncertainty about the group, about its goals, and about our place within it. How you communicate at this sensitive stage of group development provides the basis for future interaction. As you join new groups, keep in mind the following:

- At the first meeting of any new group, individual anxiety levels are relatively high. Members are often uncertain who the others are, what their roles are to be, and what to say to whom. At this stage it can be helpful if you share a little information about yourself and encourage others to do the same. Many group leaders will ask the members to say a few words about themselves. This strategy "breaks the ice" and provides some familiarity on which to base further discussion. In short, it reduces our uncertainty and helps us relax.

- As we join new groups the question of what brings these particular people to this particular place is one which we often ignore, frequently to the detriment of the group. Individual agendas, hidden or otherwise, can confound the group's progress unless the agendas are examined openly. The section in this chapter on establishing mutuality of concern is important. Never assume that everyone in your group shares your level of commitment to the group and its task. This area of potential uncertainty needs to be clarified. Failure to do so can lead to the complaint which we often hear (and sometimes voice) that "a couple of us are doing all the work while others just sit back." One way to overcome this problem, as Patton and Giffin suggested, is openly and honesty to tell the group how you feel about the group and its task, with the clear expectation that others will do the same.

  There are, of course, some prior questions which you need to ask yourself: "Why am *I* a part of this group? What do *I* want to accomplish here? What are *my* goals? What do I want from these people . . . and what can I give to them?"

- If you ask and answer the questions listed above, you may find that you are attracted to a group because you are attracted to its members. If that is your *only* attraction, think twice before you join. When a group is dedicated to a common purpose, they will probably resent a member who is there for purely social reasons.

In sum, people are attracted to groups for different reasons and join groups to satisfy a variety of needs. An understanding of these factors in group formation should guide your communicative behavior in groups.

PRACTICE

1. This chapter suggests one strategy for establishing mutuality of concern. What are some other strategies that groups could use to establish mutuality of concern?

2. Use the First Church case study and play the roles of the committee members. Observe the relationships between individual and group goals.

3. Observe a videotaped group discussion. Periodically stop the tape and identify the phase of the group's cycle in which the group is operating (inclusion, control, affection). What are the verbal and nonverbal cues that lead you to this conclusion? Continue the tape and note the group's strategies for passing from one phase into the next. As the group repeats the cycle can you observe any differences in their communicative behavior?

4. Make a list of the groups with which you are affiliated. For each one, identify its members, its activities, and its goals. Then note your individual goals in regard to each group. Examine the results. What is your primary attraction to each group? Are your individual goals compatible with the group's goals? Do you have any hidden agendas? Do your answers to these questions explain any of your attitudes about or behaviors within these groups?

Notes

1. Abraham Maslow, *Toward a Psychology of Being* (Princeton, N.J.: D. Van Nostrand Company, 1968).

2. William Schutz, *The Interpersonal Underworld* (Palo Alto, Calif.: Science & Behavior Books, 1958).

3. Frank E. X. Dance, "A Helical Model of Communication," in *Human Communication Theory* (New York: Holt, Rinehart & Winston, 1967), pp. 294–98.

4. Bobby Patton and Kim Giffin, *Decision-Making Group Interaction* (New York: Harper & Row, Publishers, Inc., 1978), pp. 118–19.

5. John Thibaut and Harold Kelley, *The Social Psychology of Groups* (New York: John Wiley & Sons, Inc., 1959).

6. Robert Zajonc, "Attitudinal Effects of Mere Exposure," *Journal of Personality and Social Psychology* 9 (1968): 1–29.

7. Marvin Shaw, *Group Dynamics: The Psychology of Small Group Behavior* (New York: McGraw-Hill Book Company, 1981), p. 93.

8. D. Krebs and A. A. Adinolf, "Physical Attractiveness, Social Relations, and Personality Style." *Journal of Personality and Social Psychology* 31 (1975): 245–53.

9. Marvin Shaw, *Group Dynamics: The Psychology of Small Group Behavior* (New York: McGraw-Hill Book Company, 1981), p. 85.

4 Relating to Others in Small Groups

After studying this chapter, you should be able to:

■ Describe how an individual develops and defines self-concept.

■ Identify the *task, maintenance,* and *individual* roles that group members assume.

■ Identify several group norms that often develop in small group discussions.

■ Describe several effects of status differences upon communication in small groups.

■ Describe how power affects relationships in small groups.

■ Identify factors that foster trusting relationships with others.

■ Apply guidelines for appropriate self-disclosure in small groups.

■ Describe the Johari Window and its applications to group communication.

■ Describe how individual group member relationships develop over time.

Relating to Others in Small Groups

$\mathbf{D}$o you consider yourself a leader or a follower in small group meetings? Do you usually talk a lot or a little when you serve on a committee? Do you think you are a good or mediocre group member? Perhaps your answers depend upon the quality of the relationships that you have with others in the group.

Relationships refer to the feelings, roles, norms, status, and trust that both affect and reflect the quality of communication between ourselves and others. If the members of your group are old friends, your relationship with them will obviously be different than if you have just met for the first time. Have you served on a committee with three or four other people, all of whom you felt were much better qualified than yourself to contribute to the discussion? Your feeling of inferiority undoubtedly affected your relationship with the other group members.

In small group communication, and in other communication contexts as well, the quality of the interpersonal relationships between people often determines what they say to one another.

According to relational communication theorists, every message we communicate to one another has both a content dimension and a relationship dimension. The content dimension of a message refers to the specific information, thoughts, and ideas that are conveyed to someone. The relationship dimension refers to message cues that provide hints about whether we like or dislike the person we are communicating with. For example, language formality and nonverbal cues provide important information about the relationship between two individuals having a conversation. Whether you are giving a public speech, talking with your spouse, or communicating with others in a small group, you are providing information about the substance of ideas and thoughts as well as about the feelings you have toward your listener.

In this chapter we are going to emphasize those elements of your communication that affect the quality of the interpersonal relationships you establish with other group members. Specifically, we are going to concentrate on five variables that have an important effect upon the relationships we establish with others in small groups. First, we will discuss how **roles** are formed and how the roles we assume during the course of a group discussion affect our relationships with others. Second, we will discuss the development of group **norms,** or standards, and how they influence our relationships with others in small groups. Third, we will describe how differences in **status** within a group can affect interpersonal relationships and have an impact on the quality and productivity of the group's discussion. Fourth, we will consider the power others have to influence group members. And finally, we'll talk about *trust* —how trusting relationships are developed and how varying degrees of trust affect group members.

ROLES

Stop reading this chapter for just a moment and reflect upon this question: Who are you? A simple question, you probably think. Perhaps it took you little time to answer. Maybe you responded by repeating your name. Or, maybe you said you are a student—a label that summarizes your current status as you read this book. Ask yourself the "Who are you?" question again. Get a pencil and write ten different responses.

Who Are You?

1. I am _____ .

2. I am _____ .

3. I am _____ .

4. I am _____ .

5. I am _____ .

6. I am _____ .

7. I am _____ .

8. I am _____ .

9. I am _____ .

10. I am _____ .

It may not have taken much effort for some of you to come up with a profile of who you think you are. But for others, labeling multiple aspects of **self-concept** may be more difficult. As you relate to others in small groups, your concept of self—who you think you are—affects your communication and relationships with other group members. In addition, your self-perception will have an impact upon how others relate to you.

In an attempt to reduce some of the uncertainty that occurs when people communicate in groups, we quickly label the behavior of others. We assign them roles, or sets of expectations. For example, Gloria seems like a leader; she usually takes charge and delegates responsibility. But Hank doesn't talk much. He will probably just follow the recommendations of others rather than initiate many ideas of his own—or at least this is the way we may label him. In a small group, a role is the result of (1) our expectations about our own behavior—our *self-concept,* (2) the perceptions others have about our position in the group, and (3) our actual behavior as we interact with others. Since our self-concept largely determines the roles we assume in small groups, let's talk about how self-concept develops. Put another way, we'll discuss how we come to learn who we think we are.

Self-Concept Development: Role Formation

How do you know who you are? Why did you respond as you did when you were asked to consider the question, "Who are you?" Your self-concept is influenced by a number of factors. First, other people influence who you think you are. Your parents gave you your name. Perhaps a teacher once told you that you were good in art, and consequently you think of yourself as artistic. Maybe your music teacher or your brother or sister told you that you cannot sing very well. And because you believed them, you may now view yourself as not very musically inclined. Thus, we listen to others, especially those whose opinions we respect, to help shape our concept of self.

A second factor that helps you define your self-concept is the various reference groups with whom you affiliate. If you are attending college now, you may describe yourself as a student. If you are a member of a fraternity or sorority, you may consider that group association a distinguishing characteristic which sets you apart from others. Your religious affiliation, your political party, and your membership in civic and social organizations all contribute to the way you perceive yourself.

You also learn who you are by simply observing and interpreting your own behavior. Just before you are ready to leave your dorm, house, or apartment, you may look in the mirror to see if your hair is OK and if your clothes are wrinkle free. You try to see yourself as others will see you. You stand back and look at yourself, almost as if you were looking at someone else, evaluating what you see and forming an impression of who you are. Of course, as both the observer and the observed, your impressions are subject to bias. You may be too critical in evaluating who you are and in assessing your self-worth or self-esteem. Your high expectations for your own behavior, when compared with your perceptions of your actions, may result in a distorted view. For example, you may aspire to become a great opera singer; yet, your only singing opportunity comes when you sing in the shower. Even though you may have an excellent voice, your self-expectations have not been fulfilled so you tell others that you are not a very good singer. The contradiction between your expectations and your actual experiences affects your self-concept and self-worth.

Diversity of Roles in Small Groups

As you become part of a small group, you bring with you your perceptions, expectations, and experiences you have had with other groups of people. Your self-expectations thus provide a foundation for the roles that you will assume in the group. Yet your role is also worked out jointly between you and the other group members. As noted by Brown and Keller, "At the heart of every relationship lie the self-images of the persons involved, each created by interaction with the other."[1] As you interact with others, they form impressions of you and your abilities. As they reward you for your actions in the group, you learn what abilities and behaviors will be reinforced. These may, in turn, become part of your self-concept. Consider the following example:

> Ken has long had an interest in physics and nuclear energy. When his small group in the group communication class considers a discussion of peaceful uses of nuclear energy, Ken is enthusiastically supportive. Other group members soon recognize Ken's knowledge and interest in the subject. Ken enjoys providing resources and information for the group. He soon emerges as the group member who provides most of the information and coordinates the group's research efforts. It is a role he enjoys, and the rest of the group appreciates his contributions.

Ken's role as idea initiator, information contributor, and coordinator was the result of his interest and ability (which was reflected in his self-concept). The group's need and desire to have him serve as a leader also helped determine his role.

Thus far, we have noted that people assume roles because of their interests and abilities and because of the needs and expectations of the rest of the group. There are times, however, when some roles are formally assigned to group members. When police officers arrive on the scene of an accident, their leadership roles are generally unquestioned. In task-oriented small groups, a group member may be assigned the role of secretary, which includes specific duties and responsibilities. Or a chairperson may be elected to help coordinate the meeting and delegate responsibilities. Assigning responsibilities and specific roles helps reduce uncertainty. The group can sometimes get on with the task at hand more efficiently if some of the roles are assigned. Of course, even if a person has been elected or assigned the role of chairperson, the group may reject his or her leadership in favor of the leadership of another group member who may better meet the needs of the group.

The kinds of roles we have discussed so far are **task roles**—they help accomplish the task of the group. There are also two other kinds of roles. **Maintenance roles** assist in maintaining the social dimension of the group. A group member who tries to maintain a peaceful, harmonious group climate by mediating disagreements and resolving conflicts performs a maintenance function. **Individual roles,** the third general role type, call attention to individual contributions to the group. These individual roles are often counterproductive to the group. Someone who is more interested in seeking self-recognition than in promoting the general benefit of the group is adopting an individual role.

A comprehensive list of possible roles that individual group members can assume has been compiled by Benne and Sheats.[2] Perhaps you can identify the various roles you have assumed while participating in small group discussions.

Group Task Roles

Initiator-contributor:	proposes new ideas or approaches to group problem solving. A person who occupies this role may suggest a different approach to procedure or organizing the problem-solving task.
Information seeker:	asks for clarification of suggestions. An information seeker also asks for facts or other information that may help the group deal with the issues at hand.
Opinion seeker:	asks for a clarification of the values and opinions expressed by other group members.
Information giver:	provides facts, examples, statistics, and other evidence that pertains to the problem the group is attempting to solve.
Opinion giver:	offers beliefs or opinions about the ideas under discussion.
Elaborator:	provides examples based upon his experience or the experience of others that help to show how an idea or suggestion would work if the group accepted a particular course of action.
Coordinator:	tries to clarify and note relationships among the ideas and suggestions that have been provided by others.
Orienter:	attempts to summarize what has occurred and tries to keep the group focused on the task at hand.
Evaluator-critic:	makes an effort to judge the evidence and conclusions that the group suggests.
Energizer:	tries to spur the group to action and attempts to motivate and stimulate the group to greater production.
Procedural technician:	helps the group achieve its task by performing tasks such as distributing papers, rearranging the seating, or running errands for the group.
Recorder:	writes down suggestions and ideas of others. Makes a record of the group's progress.

Group Building and Maintenance Roles

Encourager:	offers praise, understanding, and acceptance of others' ideas and suggestions.
Har-monizer:	mediates disagreements that occur between other group members.
Compro-miser:	attempts to resolve conflicts by trying to find an acceptable solution to disagreeing group members.
Gate-keeper and expediter:	encourages the participation of less talkative group members and tries to limit lengthy contributions of other group members.
Standard setter:	helps to set standards and goals for the group.
Group observer:	keeps records of the group's process and uses the information that is gathered to evaluate the group's procedures.
Follower:	basically goes along with the suggestions and ideas of other group members. Serves as an audience in group discussions and decision making.

Individual Roles

Aggressor:	destroys or deflates the status of other group members. May try to take credit for someone else's contribution.
Blocker:	is generally negative, stubborn, and disagreeable without apparent reason.
Recogni-tion-seeker:	tries to seek the spotlight through boasting, reporting on personal achievements.
Self-confessor:	uses the group as an audience to which he reports personal, non-group oriented feelings, insights, and observations.
Playboy:	has a general lack of involvement in the group's process. Lack of interest may result in cynicism, nonchalance, or other behaviors that indicate lack of enthusiasm for the group.
Dominator:	makes an effort to assert his authority through manipulating group members or attempting to take over the entire group. May use flattery or assertive behavior to dominate the discussion.
Help-seeker:	tries to evoke a sympathetic response from others. Often expresses insecurity or feelings of low self-worth.
Special interest pleader:	speaks for a special group or organization that best fits his own biases, to serve his individual need.

In looking at the list of roles that people often assume in a task-oriented group, you might be tempted to label group members according to these role classifications. You may have easily recognized yourself as a harmonizer or a follower and said, "Yes, that's me. That's the role I usually take." Or you may have tried to classify other group members into the categories outlined above. While identifying role characteristics may help you understand the nature and function of roles in small group communication, stereotyping and labeling others can lock them into roles. Bormann and his colleagues have extensively studied role behavior in groups and note that most group participants, when asked to analyze group role behavior, will often categorize group members into roles corresponding to the category labels.[3] As you identify the roles exhibited by other group members, be flexible in your role classifications. Realize that you and other group members can assume several roles during the course of a group discussion. In fact, it would indeed be rare if a group member served only as an "encourager," "opinion seeker," or "follower." A role is a dynamic concept; it changes as perceptions, experiences, and expectations change. It is possible for an individual to assume certain leadership responsibilities during one meeting and play more of a supporting role at other meetings.

Since a role is worked out jointly between you and the group, you will no doubt find yourself assuming different roles in different groups. Perhaps a

Your role in a group develops as you interact with other group members; depending on your situation, your role can change from group to group.

committee of which you are a member needs someone who can serve as a procedural leader to keep the meeting in order and on the agenda. Because you recognize this need, and no one else seems to be keeping the group organized, you may find yourself steering the group back on to the topic, making sure all members have a chance to participate. But in another committee, where others serve as procedural leaders, you may become known as the person who can come up with good ideas. Whether consciously or not, you develop a role unique to your talents and the needs of the group. Your group role, then, changes from group to group.

If you understand the formation of group roles and the functions various roles serve, you should be in a better position to help the group achieve its purpose. For example, groups need members to perform both maintenance and task functions. Task functions help the group get the job done, and maintenance functions help the group run smoothly. If no one is performing maintenance functions, you could point out this problem to the group. *You* could assume some responsibility for maintenance functions. If you notice one or more individuals hindering the progress of the group because they have adopted an individual role (blocker, aggressor, recognition seeker, etc.), you could bring this matter to the attention of the group or the offending group member. Explain that individual group roles can reduce the efficiency of the group and can often lead to social conflict among group members. While you cannot assume complete responsibility for role distribution within your group, your insights can help solve some potential problems.

NORMS

You have undoubtedly seen a movie or television show about the Old West in which villains ransacked homes, stores, and banks, and the young and old alike feared marauders because of their total lack of respect for the law. According to the way movies depict western history, people like Wyatt Earp were among the first able to enforce the law and restore peace and order. In small groups as well as in the Old West, rules and regulations are necessary to keep peace and order. While a small group of people communicating with one another does not need Wyatt Earp to enforce order, the group probably does need certain norms to help its members feel comfortable with their roles and relationships.

Identifying Group Norms

Norms are rules or standards that determine what is appropriate and inappropriate behavior. They establish expectations of how group members should behave. The norms that develop within a group reduce some of the uncertainty that occurs when people congregate. Our speech, the clothes we wear, the clothes we don't wear, and how and where we sit are all determined by group norms. Group norms also affect group member relationships.

If you recently joined a group, how do you know what the group's norms are? Do most groups draft a formal list of them? Should you just ask someone in the group, "Excuse me, but could you tell me what the norms are for this group? I don't want to say or do anything stupid." No, most groups do not formally state their norms, but, when given an opportunity, many group members can identify certain standards of behavior that their group considers acceptable. One way to identify norms is to observe any repeated behavioral patterns. Note, for example, any consistencies in the way people talk or dress. In trying to identify normative behavior in a group, consider the following questions:

1. How do group members dress?
2. What are the group members' attitudes toward time? (e.g., Do group meetings begin and end on time? Are members often late to the meetings?)
3. What type of language is used by most group members? (e.g., Is swearing acceptable? Is the language formal?)
4. Do group members use humor to relieve tension?
5. Do group members formally address the leader of the group?
6. Is it proper to address other group members by their first names?

Answers to these questions will help pinpoint some of the group's norms. Some groups even develop norms for developing norms. For example, group members may discuss what type of clothing will be worn to the meetings. The group may talk about what should be done with group members who are absent or tardy.

Besides observing consistent patterns of behavior in groups, noting when someone breaks the rules can also reveal group norms. If a group member arrives late to the meeting and other group members look at that member with a frown or grimace, they are probably signaling that they don't approve of the norm violation. If, after certain obscene words are used, another group member says, "I wish you wouldn't use words like that," you can be certain that for at least one person a norm has been broken. Thus, punishable offenses indicate violated norms. Often the severity of the punishment corresponds to the significance of the norm.[4] Punishment can range from subtle nonverbal expressions of disapproval (which may not even be noticed by the person expressing them) to death. The hangman's noose was often the ultimate punishment for those who violated the norms or laws of the Old West.

Conforming to Group Norms

What influences how quickly and rigidly we conform to the rules and standards of the group? According to Reitan and Shaw, there are at least five factors that affect individual conformity to group norms.[5]

The personality characteristics of the group members. In summarizing the research, Shaw notes:

> ... more intelligent persons are less likely to conform than less intelligent persons; women usually conform more than men, at least on traditional tasks; there is a curvilinear relationship between age and conformity; persons who generally blame themselves for what happens to them conform more than those low on self-blame; and authoritarians conform more than nonauthoritarians.[6]

Thus, the group members' past experiences and unique personality characteristics influence how they conform to the established norms.

The clarity of the norm and the certainty of punishment for breaking it. The more ambiguous a group norm, the less likely it is that the group member will conform. The military spells out behavior rules clearly so that little if any ambiguity remains. A new recruit is drilled on how to talk, march, salute, and eat. Failure to abide by the rules results in swift and sure corrective sanctions. Thus, the recruit quickly learns to conform. In some small group discussions, particularly when the group first meets, there is much uncertainty about how to act. Yet as soon as the rules become clear and norms (particularly those which suggest how the group should proceed) become established, group members will usually conform. The clearer the norms, the more likely it is that the members of the group will conform.

The number of people who have already conformed to the norm. Imagine walking into a room with five or six other people. Three lines have been drawn on a blackboard, one of which is clearly shorter than the other two. But one by one, each person is asked which line is shortest, and each says that all the lines are the same length. Finally, it is your turn to judge which of the lines is the shortest. You are indeed perplexed because your eyes tell you that one line is definitely shorter. Yet can the other members of your group be wrong? You tell your questioner that all of the lines are the same length. You conform. You do not want to appear odd to the other group members. Such factors as the size of the group, the number of people who agree with a certain policy, and the status of those who conform contribute to the pressure for conformity.

The quality of the interpersonal relationships that have developed in the group. A group whose members like one another and respect one another's opinions is more likely to support conformity than is a less cohesive group. Employees who like their jobs, bosses, and co-workers, and take pride in their work are more likely to support the group norms than if they have negative or frustrating interpersonal relationships with their employers or colleagues.

The greater the sense of group identification, the greater the likelihood of group conformity. If group members can readily identify with the goals of the group, they are more likely to conform. Church members who support the doctrine of a particular church and like the other church members are probably going to conform to the wishes of those in leadership positions. In addition, group members who feel they will be a part of the group for some time to come are more likely to conform to the group norms.

Although violating a group norm usually results in group disapproval and, perhaps, chastisement, such a violation can occasionally be beneficial to the group. Some norms may be detrimental to the group. Just because there is unanimous conformity to a rule does not necessarily mean that the rule is beneficial. For example, if a norm of low productivity were to develop, group work output would be adversely affected. In Chapter Seven we will discuss how over-conformity can hurt a group striving for a high-quality decision.

STATUS

> "My dad can run faster than your dad."
> "Oh, yeah? Well, my dad is smarter than your dad."
> "No, he's not!"
> "Oh, yes he is!"
> "Says who?"
> "Says me. Wanna make something of it?"

Even as children we were concerned about status—who is better, brighter, and more beautiful. *Status* refers to an individual's position of importance. A person with higher social status generally has more prestige and commands more respect than do persons of lower status. Those with high status we want to talk to and talk about, see and be seen with. We are interested in the lives of high-status individuals. Fan magazines and weekly newspapers available at the supermarket checkout counter are filled with features about the famous and near famous—status achievers and status seekers. The President of the United States, television personalities, authors, and athletes often provide the names that make "name dropping" a status seeker's pastime.

Privileges Accorded to High-Status Group Members

In television's long-running situation comedy "All in the Family," Archie Bunker's territorial claim to his chair suggests that within his family group he enjoys certain high-status privileges. He removes lower-status individuals from his seat. Similarly, most of us would probably like to be perceived as enjoying some status within a group. Because occupying a position of status fulfills our need for attention, it also builds our self-respect and self-esteem. Bormann suggests that high-status positions are pleasant because:

> The group makes a high-status person feel important and influential. They show
> him deference, listen to him, ask his advice, and often reward him with a greater

share of the group's goods. He gets a bigger office, more secretaries, better furniture, more salary, a bigger car, and so forth. Even in communication-class discussion groups, the high-status members receive considerable gratification of their social and esteem needs. One of the most powerful forces drawing people into groups is the attraction of high status.[7]

Perhaps you have participated in small groups in which the status of an individual afforded him or her certain special privileges that were not available to the rest of the group. The chairperson of the board may have a private dining room or a private executive washroom while other members must eat in the company cafeteria and use public washroom facilities. Faculty members may have certain privileges, such as discounts at the university bookstore, that are not available to students. Status differences in the military are strictly observed. The number of stripes and stars on a uniform serve as not-so-subtle status markers.

Effects of Status Differences

In small groups, the status or social rank of group members exerts a significant effect upon interpersonal relationships. Status differences and similarities affect with whom and how much we talk. An individual's status, or the reputation the individual has before joining a group, certainly affects the role that the individual assumes. In addition, norms that help groups determine how they will deal with status differences and what privileges they should allow those with greater prestige readily develop. Several researchers have observed how status differences affect the relationships among members of a small group. Consider the following research conclusions:

1. High-status group members talk more than low-status members.[8]
2. High-status group members communicate more with other high-status members than they do with those of lower status.[9]
3. Low-status group members tend to direct their conversation to high-status group members rather than to those of lower or equal status.[10]
4. Low-status group members communicate more positive messages to high-status members than they do to those of equal or lower status.[11]
5. High-status group members are likely to have more influence upon the group's decision making than low-status members.[12]
6. High-status group members usually abide by the norms of the group more than do low-status group members. (The exception to this research finding occurs when high-status members realize that they can violate group norms and receive less punishment than low-status group members would receive; thus, depending upon the situation, they may violate certain group norms.)[13]
7. Group members are more likely to ignore the comments and suggestions made by low-status members than those made by high-status members.[14]

8. Low-status group members communicate more irrelevant information than do high-status members.[15]

9. High-status members are less likely to complain about their jobs or responsibilities.[16]

10. Communication with high-status group members can replace the need for the upward movement of low-status members in the group's status hierarchy.[17]

11. High-status group members tend to talk to the entire group more than members of lower status do.[18]

12. In small group communication and discussion courses, the leader of the small group is usually the member with the highest status. (The exception to this conclusion occurs when the leader emerges because of his or her capability and competence, and not necessarily because of popularity. That kind of leader holds a lower status than does a more popular, well-liked group member.)[19]

Observing Status Differences to Predict Group Dynamics

Knowing how status affects the relationships between group members helps you predict who will talk with whom. If you can perceive status differences, you can also predict the content of the messages communicated in a small group discussion. These research conclusions suggest that the social hierarchy of a group affects group cohesiveness, group satisfaction, and even the quality of a group's solution.

POWER

Sociologist Robert Bierstedt once observed that "In the entire lexicon of sociological concepts, none is more troublesome than the concept of **power.** We may say about it in general only what St. Augustine said about time, that we all know perfectly well what it is—until someone asks us."[20] While there is much debate in scholarly literature over definitions of power as well as its relationship with other variables such as status and authority, there is general agreement that power, at its core, involves the ability of one person to control or influence some other person.[21] Our power in a small group, then, is reflected in our ability to get other group members to conform to our wishes.

We are all aware that certain group members have more power within the group than do others. Sometimes the source of their power is clear to us, as when there are large status differences in the group, but in other cases the sources of power are not so clear. In order to map out the territory of social power in small groups, let's look at three broad concepts: *power bases, power processes,* and *power outcomes.*

Power Bases

Your power base in any group is the sum of resources you possess that you can use to exert control over others. Because no two group members have exactly the same resources, each operates from a different power base. But what are some of these power bases? French and Raven[22] identified six specific power bases in their study of small groups: *legitimate power, referent power, expert power, informational power, reward power,* and *coercive power.*

Legitimate power, also called authority, is derived from the group members' view that certain positions carry with them privileges. Many of the benefits reported in the previous section for high-status group members reflect this kind of power base.

Referent power is the power of interpersonal attraction. Recall from Chapter Three that we are attracted to people who we admire and want to "be like." Put simply, those we like have more power over us than those we do not like.

Expert power stems from the belief that a group member possesses knowledge that other group members need but do not have. As the saying goes, knowledge is power.

Informational power is the power of effective communication. It derives from an ability to clearly and articulately express your views in ways that are reasonable and compelling to other group members. Much of this textbook is aimed at helping you develop this kind of power.

Reward power is based on your ability to provide rewards for desired behaviors. If you are in a position to help another group member gain additional money, status, power, acceptance, and so forth, this gives you a degree of power over that person. Of course we need to qualify this idea by reminding you that group members are motivated by different needs and goals. What is rewarding to one may not be rewarding to others.

Coercive power is the negative side of reward power. It is based on the perception that another can punish you for acting or not acting in a certain way. The possibilities for demotion, reduced salary or benefits, forced overtime hours, and firing are examples of resources that can make up this power base.

Power Processes

Power processes are the ongoing interactions between group members. Through interaction we put our resources to work for us. But interaction itself can be an important source of power in the group. Communication researcher Charles Berger observed that "persons who talk most frequently and for the longest periods of time are assumed to be the most dominant group members. In addition, persons receiving the most communication are assumed to be most powerful."[23] However, it is also true that the person who talks the longest or loudest is not always the most powerful in every situation. Therefore we need to consider two additional power concepts: assertiveness and control.

Whether potential or actual, power in a small group is the ability to get members to agree with our wishes.

Assertiveness refers to the number of attempts an individual makes to influence the behavior of others. *Control* is a measure of the effectiveness of these attempts, or the number of times these attempts are successful. In other words, the power held by a group member can be represented by a ratio of attempts to successful attempts. Given the interdependence of small group variables, this ratio will be influenced by many factors, including the power bases discussed previously.

Power Outcomes

As we have seen, power may be potential or actual. Whereas power bases and power processes represent potential sources of power, power outcomes are the measure of the actual power of a group member. Who wins the argument, who makes the final decisions, and who achieves higher status within the group are all results of the development and use of power.

TRUST

What do used-car salespeople, politicians, and insurance agents have in common? They are often stereotyped as those whose credibility is suspect. The untrustworthy images evoked by these professionals are not always justified, but when people want something from us, whether it is our money or our vote, we are often suspicious of the promises they make. When we trust people, we have faith that they will not try to take advantage of us and that they will be mindful of our best interests. In developing interpersonal relationships in small groups, the degree of trust we have in others affects our relationships with them.

"Sure, I can be at next Tuesday's group meeting," says Carl, a member of the social committee. But since you know about Carl's poor attendance record at previous group meetings, you aren't too confident that he'll be there. On the other hand, Diane says she will try to get the entertainment for the annual picnic. Diane follows through with her promises; if she says she will do something for the group, it will be done. What specific qualities foster more trust in some people than in others? Why do we take greater risks with some group members than with others? First, we will consider how trust in relationships affects group members. Then we will suggest how to elicit more trust as you interact with others.

Have you ever participated in a group in which you felt you couldn't trust the other group members? If you have, you probably did not enjoy working in the group and would avoid working in that group again. A study by Leathers gives some idea of what may happen if group members don't trust one another.[24] Leathers arranged for a person to work in a group and instructed this group member to earn the other members' trust. Once a trusting relationship was established, this group member started to disagree with and criticize the "trusting friends" (the subject of Leathers' study). The subjects' nonverbal behaviors suggested they were uncomfortable and tense. The subjects became more defensive and began to respond to the criticism with insulting remarks. In short, the new lack of trust produced increased anxiety within the entire group. Thus, if group members do not trust one another, the potential exists for less satisfactory discussions.

Developing Trusting Relationships

Why do we trust some people more than others? What is it about your closest friend that enables you to comfortably confide your most private feelings? How can group members develop trusting relationships? First, realize that developing trusting relationships takes time. Just as a role you assume during the course of a group discussion requires time to develop, so does the confidence you place in others need time to evolve. Second, remember that we base trust upon the previous experiences we have had with others. You probably would not walk up to a stranger and give your bank account number. But you would more than likely trust this number to your spouse or to a friend you have known for several years. As we communicate with others, we gradually learn whether we can or cannot trust them. Trust builds on past experiences. First we observe how an individual completes various tasks and responsibilities. Then we decide whether we can rely upon that individual to get things done.

Perhaps you have a friend you can always count on to help you. Your friend has helped you in the past so you trust that that help will be extended to you in the future. Trust, then, develops when we are able to predict how another person will behave under certain circumstances. Put another way, trust helps us reduce uncertainty as we form expectations of others. We trust people who offer us support and who we believe will continue to do so in the future. As you participate in a group, you trust those who, because of their actions and support in the past, have given you every reason to believe that they will support you in the future. Group members establish trusting relationships as they develop mutual respect for one another and as the group becomes more cohesive.

However, even time and experience cannot guarantee trust. A certain amount of *risk* is always involved whenever we trust another person. As Reichert suggests, "Trust is always a risk, a kind of leap in the dark. It is not based on any solid proof that the other person will not hurt you ... trust is always a gamble."[25] Sometimes the gamble does not prove profitable. For example, if you have recently worked in a small group with several people in whom you placed little confidence, you may be reluctant to trust others in future groups. If you have developed a close relationship with a friend only to have that friend betray your trust, you may be reluctant to develop a close relationship with someone else. Thus, your experiences in past groups, be they good or bad, affect the way in which you relate to people in future groups.

Self-Disclosure

One of the most important ways to establish and maintain trusting relationships with others is through self-disclosure. **Self-disclosure** is the deliberate communication of information about yourself to others. We have noted that establishing trust in our interpersonal relationships requires both time and a certain degree of risk. The two variables of time and risk are also involved during self-disclosure. When we reveal personal, private information, we open ourselves to the possibility that others might reject us. John Powell, author of the book *why am i afraid to tell you who i am?*, says we hesitate to self-disclose because, "...if I tell you who I am, you may not like who I am, and it's all that I have."[26]

Appropriate self-disclosure should be well-timed to suit the occasion and the expectations of the individuals involved. "Telling all" too soon may violate what the other person expects. It would not be appropriate to talk about the intimate escapades of your life (for example, your financial net worth or your romantic endeavors) when you first introduce yourself to someone else. The other person may feel uncomfortable and want to terminate the relationship. Thus, when we first meet someone, we usually reveal information that is not too threatening or personal. As we establish a trusting relationship with an individual, we may feel more comfortable about discussing private feelings and concerns. Powell notes that the information we reveal about ourselves often progresses through several predictable levels:

Level five: *Cliché communication.* We first establish verbal contact with others by saying something that lets the other people know that we acknowledge their presence. Standard phrases like *Hi, how are you?, Nice to see you, Beautiful weather, isn't it?,* and *How's it going?* signal the desire to initiate a relationship. Recall a recent group meeting during which members met for the first time. Chances are that the first words you spoke or heard could be labeled cliché communication.

Level four: *Facts and biographical information.* After using cliché phrases and responses to establish contact, we reveal nonthreatening information about ourselves, such as our names, hometowns, or occupations. Many groups have each member deliver a brief introduction to the rest of the group as the first item on the agenda.

Level three: *Personal attitudes and ideas.* After introducing ourselves and getting down to business, we then respond to various ideas and issues, noting where we agree and where we disagree. When we share our personal ideas, attitudes, and values, we open ourselves to greater possibilities for rejection by other group members. Sharing personal attitudes and ideas, then, involves more risk.

Level two: *Personal feeling.* Talking about our personal feelings makes us even more vulnerable than discussing our attitudes and ideas, particularly when we talk about our feelings regarding ourselves or others.

Level one: *Peak communication.* According to Powell, this is the ultimate level of self-disclosure. People seldom reach this level. Only with our closest friends or people who we have known for some time will we share personal insights that may result in our being rejected by others. Task-oriented small group discussions rarely achieve peak communication. The highest level of self-disclosure may take much time and trust to develop.[27]

We have discussed these five levels of self-disclosure as a means of describing the self-disclosure process, so do not preoccupy yourself with trying to classify all of your personal communication with others into one of these categories. Analyses like "I'm now talking to someone in level four and maybe next week I'll reach level two," should not be your concern. Such thinking may detract from an otherwise spontaneous conversation. While we do not advocate using self-disclosure as a tool to manipulate others into trusting relationships, we do encourage developing greater awareness of the self-disclosure process to help evaluate your relationships with others in small groups.

One researcher has described five characteristics of appropriate self-disclosure.[28] Consider his summary statements about self-disclosure. First, *self-disclosure is a function of the ongoing relationship.* This statement means that self-disclosure is not something you do just once. Rather, it means continually sharing information about yourself with others.

Second, *self-disclosure occurs reciprocally* (i.e., when you self-disclose to me, I will probably self-disclose to you). We refer to this reciprocal nature of self-disclosure as the "dyadic effect." When you reveal information about yourself to others, they will probably share information about themselves with you—at least, they probably will if you give them an opportunity. If you are talking constantly about yourself and rarely give other group members a chance to talk, they probably will not respond. If you want to create a climate of trust in your group, you must be willing to share with others.

Third, *appropriate self-disclosure is timed to fit what is happening in your group.* For example, if your group is discussing where the new highway coming through town should be located, it would not be appropriate to talk about how much you enjoy taking automobile trips with your family through the country. In other words, don't self-disclose just for the sake of self-disclosing. Your comments should be relevant to the discussion at hand.

Fourth, *self-disclosure should deal with what is happening among the people who are present.* Not only should your self-disclosure be timed to fit the occasion, but it should also be appropriate for the people in your group. You need not talk about your troubled relationship with your spouse if it clearly is of no concern to the others present. You may find someone who will listen to you, but if the others present have no interest in your self-insights, keep your confessions to yourself.

Finally, you should realize that *self-disclosure usually moves by small increments* (i.e., it takes time). Earlier, we made the point that establishing trusting relationships with others generally is not something that can be rushed. If you work with a group of people and will be meeting for only two or three sessions, don't feel compelled to enter into a self-disclosure "truth session" and expect others to follow suit during the opening moments of your first session. While you may feel that "really getting to know one another" would be healthy for group members, don't try to rush genuine self-disclosure. If you do, you may inflict more harm than good. Group members may interpret your efforts to establish trust as prying into their personal lives. While we caution you from disclosing too much too soon, you should nonetheless persevere in trying to get to know other group members. Self-disclosure is a useful way to improve relationships.

The Johari Window

The **Johari Window** model nicely summarizes our discussion of how willingness to self-disclose affects and reflects our relationships with others. The model can apply to dyadic relationships (relationships between two people) as well as to relationships among several group members. The Johari Window describes four types of information about you. The model, as shown in Figure 4–1, identifies four quadrants.

Imagine that the model represents you as you communicate with others in a small group. At first glance, all four quadrants in the diagram seem to be the same size. But that may not be the case (in fact, it probably isn't). Quadrant one is called the *open area*. It refers to information that others know about you and that you are also aware of. The more information that you reveal about yourself, the larger quadrant one will be. Put another way, the more risks you take by self-disclosing, the larger the open area will be. The open area might include such information as your age, your occupation, and other things you mention about yourself.

The *blind area* occupies the second quadrant. This area consists of information that other people know about you, but that you do not know. Do you remember when, in grade school, someone may have put a sign on your back that said, "Hit me"? Everyone was aware of it but you. The blind area of the Johari Window works in much the same way. For example, you may see yourself as generous, but others may see you as a tightwad. Perhaps you've been in a group with a group member who thought she was the group leader, but wasn't aware that she did not command respect and approval. As you learn how others see you, the blind area of the Johari Window gets smaller. In order for it to shrink, others must tell you how they perceive you. Generally, the more we accurately know about ourselves and about how others see us, the better are our chances to establish open and honest relationships. Still, you must remember that the process of learning about how others see us should

Figure 4-1   The Johari Window[29]

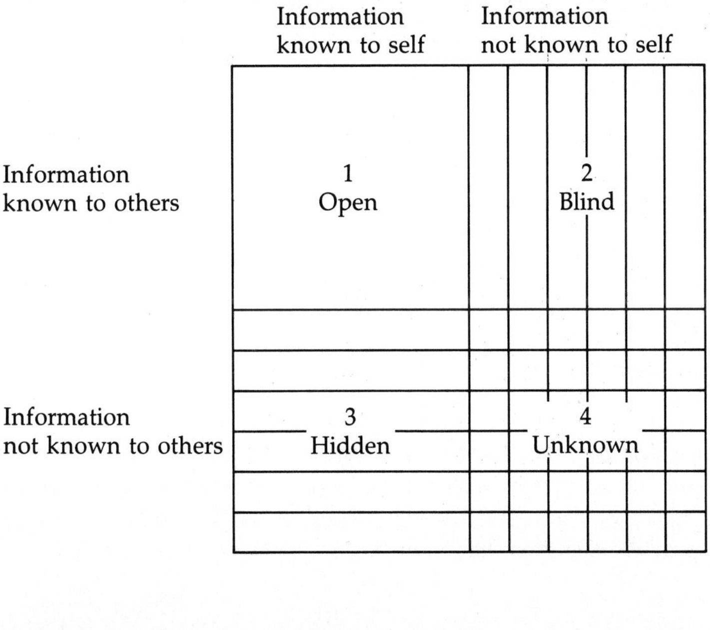

	Information known to self	Information not known to self
Information known to others	1 Open	2 Blind
Information not known to others	3 Hidden	4 Unknown

follow the same guidelines that we suggested for self-disclosure. Don't, for example, expect lots of verbal feedback about your performance in a group until you get to know the group members well and they get to know you. In other words, don't expect too much feedback too soon. Certainly, there are times when feedback would be useful to you, but many people may want to know more about you first. As we suggested earlier, appropriate self-disclosure should be timed to fit what is happening in the group and should be appropriate for the people present.

The *hidden area* labels the third quadrant of the Johari Window. This area consists of information that you know about yourself, but that others do not know about you. You can probably think of many facts, thoughts, and feelings that you would not want anyone else to know. They may be feelings you have about yourself or feelings about other group members. Most advocates of self-disclosure do not claim that *everything* about us should be shared with others. Once again, we stress that appropriate self-disclosure is timed according to the situations and the people involved. It is selective. Yet, on the other hand, hidden agendas occasionally can hinder small group discussions. We are not suggesting that you reveal *all* of your secrets to another person to foster trust. And, we cannot tell you specifically what you should reveal and what you should not reveal to other group members. The important principle to remember, however, is that *self-disclosure can foster trusting relationships.* The other person, though, must be able to accept what you have selected to reveal. Otherwise, the revelation may result in a decrease, rather than an increase, of communication.

The fourth quadrant in the Johari Window depicts the *unknown area.* This area consists of information that is unknown to both you and others. Perhaps you do not know how you will react under certain stressful situations. Maybe you are not sure what stand you will take on an issue next year. Other people may also not be aware of how you would respond under certain conditions. Your potential, your untapped resources, are unknown. We assume that this area exists because eventually some of these things become known to yourself, to others, or to both you and others.

The Johari Window illustrates how self-disclosure can affect small group work. This model provides a deeper understanding of the relationships between what others know about you and what you know about yourself. People trust us only when they perceive us as trustworthy. Both our self-concept and the perceptions others have toward us determine our role in a group. Norms in small groups sometimes develop in response to the perceived expectations we have about others in our group. And certainly the status that group members enjoy is a direct result of the perceptions others have about them.

THE DEVELOPMENT OF GROUP
RELATIONSHIPS OVER TIME

As we have talked in this chapter about developing relationships with other group members, one theme has consistently predominated our discussion: *It takes time for relationships to develop.* There is some tension and anxiety the first time you participate in a small group. You are uncertain what your role in the group will be. The group has not met long enough for norms to develop. True, certain standards of behavior already exist because of the common culture that the group may share. But these expectations provide only skeletal guidance for behavior. Status differences among group members can also create tension. Bormann has defined this initial uneasiness as **primary tension.** According to Bormann, primary tension is:

> the social unease and stiffness that accompanies getting acquainted. Students placed in a discussion group with strangers will experience these tensions most strongly during the opening minutes of their first meetings. The earmarks of primary tensions are extreme politeness, apparent boredom or tiredness, and considerable sighing or yawning. When members show primary tension, they speak softly and tentatively. Frequently they can think of nothing to say, and many long pauses result.[30]

Thus, you should expect to find some primary tension during initial meetings. It is a normal part of group development. A group leader can minimize this tension, however, by helping group members get to know one another. Get-acquainted exercises and brief statements of self-introduction can ease primary tension. While groups that will be meeting only once might deem getting to know one another as impractical, using a few minutes to break the ice and manage some of the primary tension can help create more satisfying interpersonal relationships among group members.

After the group resolves the primary tension, develops group norms, and becomes more comfortable with roles (i.e., group members have fairly realistic expectations about how other group members will react to them), another type of tension develops. **Secondary tension,** as labeled by Bormann, occurs as conflicts arise and as differences of opinion emerge. Whether recognized as a personality conflict or simply as a disagreement, secondary tension surfaces when group members try to solve the problem, accomplish the task, or resolve specific issues facing the group. The presence of secondary tension usually establishes group norms. Joking or laughing often helps manage secondary tension. Regardless of how cohesive a group may be, some conflict over procedure will normally develop as group member relationships form. In Chapter Six we will discuss the phases of a group's growth and development in more detail, and in Chapter Nine we will consider some suggestions for managing the conflict and controversy that result from secondary tension.

RELATING TO OTHERS IN SMALL GROUPS: PUTTING PRINCIPLE INTO PRACTICE

We have focused on four variables that affect and reflect our relationships with others in small groups: roles, norms, status, and trust. An understanding of how these concepts affect your performance and the performance of other group members will help you explain and predict the types and quality of relationships that are formed in small groups. As you attempt to apply the information that we have presented in this chapter, consider these suggestions:

Roles

- Having a clearer understanding of your own self-concept and self-worth will help you understand your role as you work with others in small groups.

Power

- A group member who is powerful is one who can influence the behavior of other group members.
- People develop power in a group because they can provide information, expertise, rewards and punishment, or because they are well liked or have status in the group.
- People who talk often and for long periods of time in group discussions are assumed to be powerful, influential group members.

Trust

- In most groups, don't expect trusting relationships to form too soon—it takes time for trust to develop.
- Self-disclosure is an important factor in developing trusting relationships with others.
- An effective group includes some members who perform task role functions and others who perform maintenance role functions. Most group members perform both task and maintenance role functions.
- If no one performs group maintenance functions, point out this fact to the group or assume the responsibility for performing them yourself.
- If you observe one or more group members hindering the progress of your group because they are adopting an individual group role (blocker, aggressor, recognition-seeker, etc.), bring this to the attention of the group or the offending group member.

- Don't try to fit yourself or other group members into just one or two group roles. You and other group members can assume several roles during the course of a discussion.

Norms

- You can identify group norms by noting repeated patterns of behavior.
- Another way to identify group norms is by noting what kind of offenses group members punish.
- The personalities of the group members, the clarity of the norm and the certainty of punishment for breaking it, the number of people who have broken the norm, the quality of relationships among group members, and the sense of group identification all help determine whether members will conform to the group norms.

Status

- You can identify the status of group members by the privileges high-status group members receive.
- If you can spot status differences in small groups, you will be able to predict who talks to whom.
- By becoming aware of the status differences among group members, you can predict the content of the messages communicated.
- If you are aware of the status differences, you can predict the quality of interpersonal relationships in a small group.
- Don't think that self-disclosure just happens once when the group first gets together; it is a function of ongoing group relationships.
- Don't talk solely about yourself without giving others a chance to self-disclose.
- Don't self-disclose merely for the sake of self-disclosing. Your self-revelations should be relevant to the discussion at hand.
- Appropriate self-disclosure should deal with what is happening among the persons who are present.
- Don't rush the self-disclosure process; appropriate self-disclosure moves by small increments.
- Familiarizing yourself with the Johari Window should give you a deeper understanding of the relationship between what others know about you and what you know about yourself as you interact with others.
- Get-acquainted exercises and brief statements of self-introduction during the first group meeting can help manage primary tension.

PRACTICE

Johari Window Exercise

The purpose of this exercise is to help you understand the Johari Window as presented in this chapter. In essence, we are asking you to construct a Johari Window for a group in which you participate. Of course, you should realize that the impression you have of the others and the impression they have of you may be based only upon a very brief opportunity to meet with one another. Your instructor will give you additional suggestions for completing this activity.

1. Form groups of three to five people.

2. Check five or six adjectives from the list below that best describe your personality *as you see it*.

3. Select three or four adjectives that describe the personality of *each person in your group* and write them on separate sheets of paper. Distribute these lists to the appropriate group members.

4. Fill in square number one ("known to self and known to others") with adjectives from the list that both you and at least one other member of your group have selected to describe your personality.

5. Fill in square number two ("not known to self but known to others") with those adjectives others in your group used to describe you, but you did not use to describe yourself.

6. Fill in square number three ("known to self but not to others") with adjectives you have used to describe yourself, but no one else used to describe you.

able	dependable	intelligent	patient	sensible
accepting	dignified	introverted	powerful	sentimental
adaptable	energetic	kind	proud	shy
bold	extroverted	knowledgeable	quiet	silly
brave	friendly	logical	reflective	spontaneous
calm	giving	loving	relaxed	sympathetic
caring	happy	mature	religious	tense
cheerful	helpful	modest	responsive	trustworthy
clever	idealistic	nervous	searching	warm
complex	independent	observant	self-assertive	wise
confident	ingenious	organized	self-conscious	witty

	known to self	not known to self
known to others	1	2
not known to others	3	unknown

Notes

1. Charles T. Brown and Paul W. Keller, *Monologue to Dialogue* (Englewood Cliffs, New Jersey: Prentice-Hall, Inc., 1973), p. 2.

2. Kenneth D. Benne and Paul Sheats, "Functional Roles of Group Members," *Journal of Social Issues* 4 (Spring 1948): 41–49.

3. Ernest G. Bormann, *Discussion and Group Methods: Theory and Practice,* 2nd ed. (New York: Harper & Row, Publishers, Inc., 1975), p. 209.

4. S. Schacter, "Deviation, Rejection, and Communication," *Journal of Abnormal and Social Psychology* 46 (1951): 190–207.

5. H. T. Reitan and Marvin E. Shaw, "Group Membership, Sex-Composition of the Group, and Conformity Behavior," *Journal of Social Psychology* 64 (1964): 45–51.

6. Marvin E. Shaw, *Group Dynamics: The Psychology of Small Group Behavior* (New York: McGraw-Hill Book Company, 1976), p. 253.

7. Bormann, p. 215.

8. J. I. Hurwitz, A. F. Zander, and B. Hymovitch, "Some Effects of Power on the Relations Among Group Members," in *Group Dynamics: Research and Theory,* D. Cartwright and A. Zander, eds. (New York: Harper & Row, Publishers, 1953), pp. 483–92.

9. Ibid.

10. Ibid.

11. D. C. Barnlund and C. Harland, "Propinquity and Prestige as Determinants of Communication Networks," *Sociometry* 26 (1963): 467–79.

12. Shaw, p. 246.

13. George C. Homans, *The Human Group* (New York: Harcourt Brace and World, Inc., 1950).

14. John K. Brilhart, *Effective Group Discussion* (Dubuque, Iowa: Wm. C. Brown Company, Publishers, 1978), p. 36.

15. H. H. Kelly, "Communication in Experimentally Created Hierarchies," *Human Relations* 4 (1951): 36–56.

16. Ibid.

17. Ibid.

18. Bormann, p. 215.

19. Ibid.

20. Robert Bierstedt, "An Analysis of Social Power," *American Sociological Review* 6 (1950): 7–30.

21. Marvin E. Shaw, *Group Dynamics: The Psychology of Small Group Behavior* (New York: McGraw-Hill Book Company, 1981), p. 294.

22. J. R. P. French and B. H. Raven, "The Bases of Social Power," in D. Cartwright and A. Zander, eds. *Group Dynamics* (Evanston, IL: Row, Peterson, 1962), pp. 607–23.

23. Charles R. Berger, "Power in the Family," in Michael Roloff and Gerald Miller, eds. *Persuasion: New Direction in Theory and Research* (Beverly Hills, CA: Sage Publications, 1980), p. 217.

24. Dale Leathers, "The Process Effects of Trust-Destroying Behavior," *Speech Monographs* 37 (1970): 180–87.

25. Richard Reichert, *Self-Awareness Through Group Dynamics* (Dayton, Ohio: Pflaum/Standard, 1970), p. 21.

26. John Powell, *why am i afraid to tell you who i am?* (Niles, Illinois: Argus Communications, 1969), p. 12.

27. Ibid., pp. 54–58.

28. Joseph Luft, *Of Human Interaction* (Palo Alto, California: National Press, 1969), pp. 132–33.

29. Joseph Luft, *Group Processes: An Introduction to Group Dynamics* (Mayfield Publishing Company, 1970).

30. Bormann, pp. 181–82.

5 Improving Group Climate

After studying this chapter, you should be able to:

■ Observe a group discussion and identify behaviors which contribute to a defensive or supportive group climate.

■ Identify examples of confirming and disconfirming interpersonal responses.

■ Explain three types of listening in small groups.

■ Describe two major barriers to effective listening.

■ Observe, identify, and describe at least four factors in group cohesiveness.

■ Explain communication networks and their effect on group climate and individual satisfaction.

■ Describe the relationships between group size, composition, and climate.

■ Explain the relationship between group climate and productivity.

■ Communicate in ways which are more likely to improve group climate.

Improving Group Climate

What does the word "climate" call to mind? If you've taken a course in geography or meteorology, or have studied weather patterns, you may think of temperature gradients, barometric pressure, and how bodies of water, latitude, ocean currents, and mountains affect the weather of a particular region. Look out your window. What is the weather like? Does today's weather make you want to curl up with this book? Go to the beach? Go skiing? Would you say that climate affects your desire to engage in certain activities? How do you feel about a cold, snowy night spent in front of a roaring fire in a cozy room? As we write these words, the temperature is in the low seventies, there is a gentle breeze blowing, and the sun is shining brilliantly outside the window. And it's almost February! Be assured that the climate has an effect on your authors' abilities to be productive.

Group climate is roughly analogous to geographical climate. A variety of factors interact to create a group feeling or atmosphere. How group members communicate, to whom they communicate, and how often they communicate influence member satisfaction as well as productivity. We hope that you have participated in groups where there was a genuine sense of warmth, trust, camaraderie, and accomplishment. Our question in this chapter is how can we communicate in ways which help the group establish such a climate? We begin with a case study from one of your author's recent personal experiences.

A CASE STUDY

Not long ago I received a telephone call from a good friend. His message was rather mysterious. He said that he and his wife had a business proposition for me and my wife which they would like to discuss at our earliest convenience. No, he really didn't want to discuss any of the details over the phone. When could we meet? Tuesday evening? At my place? They'd see us then.

Our curiosity piqued, we anxiously awaited the Tuesday evening rendezvous. What could our friends possibly have up their sleeves? The appointed hour arrived. The bottle of wine was being chilled. Right on time, the doorbell rang. ("Unusual," we thought, "they're usually a half hour late.") Our next surprise was that our friend George was dressed in a three-piece suit, his wife Margaret in a tailored dress. My wife and I looked at each other in our jeans, bare feet, and shirts, then returned our gaze to George and Margaret and asked whether they had just returned from a funeral. They laughed nervously(?) at the joke (?!), marched past us, and began to set up a small demonstration board on our dining room table. Turning down our offer of wine, they asked if we could begin the meeting. This was becoming stranger by the moment. My wife Nancy and I were beginning to feel like we had invited insurance agents into our home even though we knew that wasn't the case. These were people with whom we have gone camping, hiking, canoeing, and with whom we've spent many an evening over many a beer. Something didn't fit, but our curiosity was aroused so we decided to play along.

It wasn't long before the experience began to get frustrating. George and Margaret asked us what we wanted out of life. We suggested that they probably ought to have some idea of that by now—that most of our goals were inward, state-of-being kinds of goals, like having a greater awareness of ourselves and others, peace of mind, and so forth. This answer agitated our guests who responded by suggesting that it might be nice if we never again had to worry about money. We agreed that that would, indeed, be pleasant. At this, they seemed to breathe a little more easily and proceeded to haul out charts, graphs, and illustrations which, they claimed, proved that we could double our present income in a little over a year—in our spare time, of course.

After an hour, George and Margaret were still refusing to tell us what it was we would have to sell (we'd figured *that* much out) or to whom we'd have to sell it. ("Please bear with us until the end," they said.) Something was definitely wrong. Here I was sitting in my own dining room with my wife, my friends, and a glass of wine, yet I felt as if I were back in junior high being asked to please hold all my questions until the end. I've had the same experience with life insurance and encyclopedia salespeople. They were treating us not as people, but as faceless members of that great mass of consumers whom sales manuals target and who serve as the inspiration for countless commercials where housewives dance, sing, and extol the virtues of airtight plastic containers, soap powders, and kitchen floors that shine like new.

George and Margaret were still making their pitch. They had finally revealed the name of the company and its line of products and were now setting about the task of showing how rapidly the company had grown due to its unique marketing concepts, fine products which sell themselves (of course), and so forth. It didn't matter. I had already decided not to do it. I felt dehumanized, abused by my friends. Why hadn't they simply told us that they were involved with the company (which we had heard of long before) and that they'd like to explore the possibilities of our becoming involved as well? With friends, it would be a much more effective approach; certainly a more honest one.

The formal part of the presentation was over. They were asking for our comments and questions. I was ready and "loaded for bear." As a teacher of speech communication I am well versed in the art of critiquing oral presentations and visual aids. I proceeded to evaluate their entire presentation, emphasizing their failure to adequately analyze their audience and to adapt their communicative style accordingly. George and Margaret were shocked and hurt. They had not, they said, come into our home to be criticized. They had come in good faith with an honest proposal from which we all stood to benefit. If they had offended us, they were sorry. No, they still did not care for a glass of wine. We'd get together again sometime soon.[1]

DEFENSIVE COMMUNICATION

This case study illustrates many of the principles discussed in this text. Clearly, some group norms were being violated, particularly the interpersonal expectations of openness and honesty. Likewise, group roles to which all of us had adjusted were altered dramatically as new roles of "salesperson" and "critic" were introduced. Messages, both verbal and nonverbal, were being interpreted differently (e.g., their "professional" attire seemed "out of place" to us). We have recounted the scenario because it is a particularly good example of the type of communication which fosters a *defensive climate* in the small group.

Let's take a closer look at the case study above. From the first telephone call, information was withheld—a pattern which repeated itself throughout the entire episode. When George and Margaret arrived they were dressed in a very businesslike fashion, suggesting (once funeral attendance was ruled out) a change in what had become a typical pattern of interaction for the two couples. George and Margaret took *control* of the conversation. They maintained control of information and, to an extent, controlled others' choices (through limiting alternative responses). The response to George and Margaret was defensive, verbal aggression. The author gave an evaluative critique of the presentation which aroused further defensiveness, hurt, and anger in a cyclical process which left old questions unanswered and new ones unasked—a very uncomfortable and unproductive evening. The specific examples of **defensive communication** we find occurring here are *strategy, control,* and *evaluation.*

DEFENSIVE AND SUPPORTIVE CLIMATES

For several years Dr. Jack Gibb observed communicative behavior of people in groups and identified the types of behaviors which contribute to a *defensive climate* and those behaviors which develop *supportive climates.* As Gibb suggests, a defensive climate is clearly counterproductive in any group.

> The person who behaves defensively, even though he also gives some attention to the common task, devotes an appreciable portion of his energy to defending himself. Besides talking about the topic, he thinks about how he appears to

others, how he may be seen more favorably, how he may win, dominate, impress, or escape punishment, and/or how he may avoid or mitigate a perceived or an anticipated attack.[2]

The key to building a supportive climate in the group lies, of course, in communication, and in this case it is not so much *what* we communicate as *how* we communicate it. It is possible to deliver the same "core" message in ways which evoke either support or defense. Consider some examples based on Gibb's categories.

Evaluation *vs* Description

Part of the problem-solving process in small group communication concerns the generation and evaluation of ideas. Unfortunately, not all ideas are perfect and this needs to be discovered if the group is to reach the most effective decision. When someone puts forth a less-than-perfect idea we can respond in essentially one of two ways: We can say "Listen, you cretin, that's the most ridiculous and outlandish idea I've heard in a decade." Or, we can say, "As I think through that idea and apply it to our problem, I run up against some other problems. Am I missing something?" Now imagine yourself on the receiving end of the first comment. Imagine that it is your supervisor (whom you are trying to impress) who says it to you. Think of all the others in the group who are looking at you, waiting for a response. How do you feel? Not very good? You have just been "put down" and are likely to be quite defensive. This is an example of evaluation (albeit an extreme one). We can see that the latter response, an example of description, is much more effective and supportive. Your idea may, in fact, be terrible, but at least the second response is not an attack. Instead, it allows you to "save face." It also keeps the door open for further discussion of your idea. Quite possibly, further investigation into your bad idea may lead to a better idea (*see* Chapter 6).

In a nutshell, *evaluation* is "you" language: It directs itself to the *other person's* worth or the worth of that person's ideas. As a result, it can provoke much defensiveness. *Description,* on the other hand, is "I" language: It describes the *speaker's* thoughts about the person or idea. This type of response leads to more interpersonal trust and greater group cohesiveness.

Control *vs* Problem Orientation

Communicative behavior which aims at controlling the behavior of others can produce much defensiveness in other group members. This pattern characterizes many aggressive salespeople who, quite intentionally, manipulate us into answering a series of trivial questions which lead up to the final question of whether or not we want to buy the product. Various persuasive tactics aim at controlling behavior (as any student of television commercials can observe). Implicit in attempts to control lies the assumption that the controller knows what is good for the controllee. It's the "I know what's good for you" assumption. When we become aware of this attitude we frequently get defensive.

In a group, a more effective approach seems to be *problem orientation.* If others perceive you as a person who genuinely strives for a solution which will benefit all concerned (rather than just for yourself), this perception will contribute to a supportive climate, greater cohesiveness, and increased productivity.

Strategy *vs* Spontaneity

Like controlling behavior, strategy suggests manipulation. In the example with which we began this section we can see the effects of strategy on the group's climate. As George and Margaret were perceived as acting with hidden motivations and withholding information, your author and his wife became defensive. They felt used and manipulated. Again, this sort of behavior places the self before the group and does not lead to the most effective problem solutions.

On the other hand, if others perceive you as a person who acts *spontaneously* (that is, not from hidden motivations or agendas) and as a person who immediately and honestly responds to the present situation, you are likely to contribute to a more supportive climate.

Neutrality *vs* Empathy

If you behave in a detached, uncaring fashion, as if the people in your group and the outcome of the group's process don't concern you in the least, your behavior will probably arouse some defensiveness. Expressions of involvement and concern for the group task and other group members is perceived as supportive.

Superiority *vs* Equality

As the saying goes, "Some folks've got it and some folks ain't." If you feel that you belong to the former set, the small group meeting is not the time to tell the world. You probably know of people who approach others in the class after tests have been returned and always ask: "What'd ya get?" Frequently this question is merely a preface to showing you their superior grade. Sound familiar? Most of us label this behavior as obnoxious. It makes us feel defensive. In groups, some people preface their remarks with words such as "obviously" or point out their greater knowledge of the facts, their greater experience, or some such strategy to make themselves appear to be in a position superior to other group members. Most likely, their behavior will meet with some resistance. A more supportive climate is produced when we indicate a willingness to enter into participative planning with mutual trust and respect.

Certainty *vs* Provisionalism

Do you know people who always have all the answers, whose ideas are "truths" to be defended, who are intolerant of those with the "wrong" (that is, different) attitudes? These highly dogmatic people are well known for the defensiveness they can produce in others. Our usual response is to want to prove them wrong. This behavior is counterproductive in groups. We are likely to be more effective if our attitudes appear to be held *provisionally:* that is, if we appear flexible and genuinely committed to solving problems rather than simply taking sides on issues. If we leave ourselves open to new information and if we can admit that, from time to time, we may be wrong about something, we will be more effective group members and will help build a more supportive group climate.

As a communicator, you control your own actions. Your knowledge of defensive and supportive behaviors will help you make your group work more effectively. Another area of research and application in group climate is the area of interpersonal confirmation and disconfirmation. This body of research deals not with those communicative behaviors which you initiate, but with the ways in which you respond to other group members.

DISCONFIRMING AND CONFIRMING RESPONSES

Group process often seems to go nowhere. Questions are left unanswered and ideas remain ignored. One of the most frequent complaints among group members is that communication in the group seems disconnected and disjointed, fostering vague feelings of uneasiness as if the members are being disregarded.[3] Unfortunately, this is a common phenomenon and one which does not lead to the satisfaction of task, process, or individual needs. While attending a series of committee meetings, one of your authors noted that hardly anyone directly acknowledged what anyone else said. Rather, the meetings proceeded as a series of soliloquies. It was not surprising that most of the group members expressed dissatisfaction with the group's process and frustration with the group's inability to reach decisions.

In an investigation of communication in effective and ineffective groups, Evelyn Sieburg examined the ways in which group members responded to the communicative acts of others. In this seminal study and in later work with Carl Larson, Sieburg identified several types of responses which she classified as *confirming* or *disconfirming.* Simply stated, **confirming responses** are those which cause people to value themselves more, while **disconfirming responses** are those which cause people to value themselves less.[4] Sieburg's identification of confirming and disconfirming responses has been one of the most salient contributions to our understanding of group climate.

Some forms of interpersonal responses are obvious examples of confirmation and disconfirmation, like when a person responds to another with overt praise or sharp criticism. But there are more subtle ways in which group members confirm and disconfirm one another. Sieburg and Larson identify some of those behaviors as follows:

Disconfirming Responses

1. *Impervious response.* When one speaker fails to acknowledge, even minimally, the other speaker's communicative attempt, or when one ignores or disregards the other by not giving any ostensible acknowledgment of the other's communication, this response may be called impervious.
2. *Interrupting response.* When one speaker cuts the other speaker short or begins while the other is still speaking, his response may be called interrupting.
3. *Irrelevant response.* When one speaker responds in a way that seems unrelated to what the other has been saying, or when one speaker introduces a new topic without warning or returns to his earlier topic, apparently disregarding the intervening conversation, his response may be called irrelevant.
4. *Tangential response.* When one speaker acknowledges the other person's communication but immediately takes the conversation in another direction, his response may be called tangential. Occasionally, individuals exhibit what may appear to be direct responses to the other, such as "Yes, but ..." or "Well, you may be right, but ...," and then respond with communicative content very different from that which preceded. Such responses may still be called tangential.
5. *Impersonal response.* When a speaker conducts a monologue, when his speech communication behavior appears intellectualized and impersonal, contains few first-person statements and many generalized "you" or "one" statements, and is heavily loaded with euphemisms or clichés, the response may be called impersonal.
6. *Incoherent response.* When the speaker responds with sentences that are incomplete, or with rambling statements difficult to follow, or with sentences containing much retracing or rephrasing, or interjections such as "you know" or "I mean," his response may be called incoherent.
7. *Incongruous response.* When the speaker engages in nonvocal behavior that seems inconsistent with the vocal content, his response may be called incongruous. For example, "Who's angry? I'm not angry!" (said in a tone and volume that strongly suggest anger). Or, "I'm really concerned about you" (said in a tone that suggests lack of interest or disdain).

Confirming Responses

1. *Direct acknowledgment.* One speaker acknowledges the other's communication and reacts to it directly and verbally.

By directly acknowledging another's communication, either verbally or through eye contact, you are contributing to a supportive group climate which ultimately will enable your group to reach its goal.

2. *Agreement about content.* One speaker reinforces information expressed by the other.
3. *Supportive response.* One speaker expresses understanding of the other, reassures him, or tries to make him feel better.
4. *Clarifying response.* One speaker tries to clarify the content of the other's message or attempts to clarify the other's feelings. The usual form of a clarifying response is to elicit more information, to encourage the other to say more, or to repeat in an inquiring way what was understood.
5. *Expression of positive feeling.* One speaker describes his own positive feelings related to prior utterances of the other; for example, "Okay, now I understand what you are saying."[5]

The implication of this research for improving our communicative effectiveness and thus the effectiveness of our groups is this: By using confirming responses rather than disconfirming responses when we communicate with other group members, we contribute toward a supportive, trustful climate in the group and therefore promote greater group effectiveness and individual satisfaction.

DEFENSIVENESS AND UNCERTAINTY

Take a moment and imagine yourself alone at night in a strange city. You have just stepped off a bus and, as it roars off into the night, you realize that you have gotten off at the wrong stop. The street is unfamiliar to you. A couple of sinister looking characters eye you from a doorway. Your senses sharpen. There is nothing in this environment that you can trust. You don't want to let down your guard. Anything could happen to you.

This is probably not a time when you'll ponder what to buy your mother for her birthday or how to approach your boss for that raise you think you deserve. You're too busy trying to figure out how to preserve yourself in this alien environment. What will you do if one of those sinister characters follows you? You are expecting the unexpected.

Now imagine yourself in your hometown on the street where you live. Again, it is nighttime and you're walking alone. But now the sensation is different. You are familiar with your surroundings. You know what to expect. If you live in a rough neighborhood, even the danger is familiar and you know what you will do if you feel threatened. Here you may find your mind wandering from your immediate surroundings.

The point is this: When our surroundings are unfamiliar—that is, unfamiliar and potentially dangerous—we become preoccupied with those immediate surroundings. When we can't trust this environment, we become more self-centered. We relate to our interpersonal environments in much the same way. When we attend a party where we know virtually no one, we are likely to be a bit self-conscious for a while. At home with our families, we are more relaxed. When our surroundings are familiar, when there is little uncertainty, and when there is *trust,* there is no need for us to be defensive. We tend to trust that which is familiar and predictable.

When we perceive others' behavior as threatening to our emotional security or our position in the group, our uncertainty about our role in the group increases. Individual needs are elevated to a place equal to or even greater than the group's task and process needs. If we respond defensively we are likely to evoke further defensiveness from the rest of the group. In a defensive, disconfirming climate there is an absence of trust in one another. To say that we cannot trust another suggests that the other's behavior is unpredictable—we don't know for sure how he or she will respond to us. It's like being in that unfamiliar neighborhood. We're simply not sure what's going to happen so we guard ourselves against all contingencies. This type of uncertainty is counterproductive in a problem-solving group. On the other hand, in a supportive, confirming climate where mutual respect and trust prevail, individuals are more certain about their own well-being. This security, in turn, allows the individuals to increase their concentration on the task and the process needs of the group.

LISTENING

One of the most common sources of defensiveness and disconfirmation is the tendency most of us have to exercise poor listening habits. If we have not been actively attending to what another has been saying, our responses will be perfunctory at best, and apathetic, impervious, or tangential at worst. In groups, it is even easier to be a poor listener than it is in interpersonal situations because the probability that we will have to respond to the speaker is reduced; there are all of those others who can pick up the conversation. *But groups cannot reach their maximum effectiveness unless their members listen actively to one another.*

Listening is a skill that can be improved with practice. It is *an active process through which we select, attend, understand, and remember.* Listening takes effort. To listen effectively, we must actively select and attend to the messages we are receiving. This involves filtering out the other stimuli that compete for our attention: the hunger pangs we're starting to feel, the groceries we need to pick up on the way home, the attractive person to our left. To improve any skill takes knowledge and practice. In this section we'll provide some knowledge. The practice is up to you. Are you listening?

Types of Listening

Glatthorn and Adams have proposed a new explanation for listening. They suggest that the three types of listening are hearing, analyzing, and empathizing.[6]

Hearing is the fundamental type of listening on which the other two types are built. *"Hearing is receiving the message as sent."*[7] Glatthorn and Adams point out that in order to achieve this seemingly simple objective, you must perform several complex operations. You must:

> *receive the sounds as transmitted;*
>
> *translate these sounds into the words and meanings that were intended;*
>
> *understand the relationship of those words in the sentences spoken;*
>
> *note the relevant nonverbal cues that reinforce the message;*
>
> *comprehend the entire message as intended.*[8]

Viewed in this way, hearing becomes a great deal more than a physiological response to stimuli. To say "I hear you" takes on a whole new level of meaning.

Analyzing is *"discerning the purpose of the speaker and using critical or creative judgment."* Analyzing involves hearing but goes far beyond; it includes making judgments about unspoken messages, as well as the broader context in which messages were received. For example, many messages in small groups are aimed at persuading other group members. Often these messages contain emotional appeals such as "Our group's failure to stand up in support of anti-abortion laws is tantamount to murder!" Hearing this message is not difficult, particularly if the nonverbal behavior of the speaker reinforces it. But analyzing is a bit trickier. An appropriate response requires that we analyze the content of the message, the intent of the speaker, and the context within which the transaction is taking place. We need to consider the persuasive strategy the speaker is employing, his or her degree of commitment to the issue, the nature and objectives of the group, and the probable positions other group members hold on the issue. In short, to respond with maximum effectiveness, we need to consider multiple factors instantaneously. Glatthorn and Adams claim that analyzing involves the following steps:

> *Hearing the message accurately;*
> *Identifying the stated purpose;*
> *Inferring the unstated purpose;*
> *Determining if a critical or creative judgment is required;*
> *Responding accordingly.*[9]

Empathizing is the most complex and difficult type of listening. It requires concentration, a sensitivity to the emotional content of messages, an ability to see the world from the point of view of the speaker, and a willingness to suspend judgment. Empathizing involves elements of hearing and analyzing but again moves beyond them. It involves these steps:

> *Hearing the message accurately;*
> *Listening to the unstated purpose;*
> *Withholding judgment;*
> *Seeing the world from the perspective of the speaker;*
> *Sensing the unspoken words;*
> *Responding with acceptance.*[10]

Often problems that affect the group are expressed obliquely; not in the words themselves, but in the feelings behind the words.

Cindy: You all can do whatever you want. I'll go along with anything.

Toni: You sound as if you're not "all here" tonight. Is it something you can talk about?

Cindy: Oh, I'm having some problems at home. It'll all work out but I can't get it out of my mind. I'm sorry if I'm a little distant tonight.

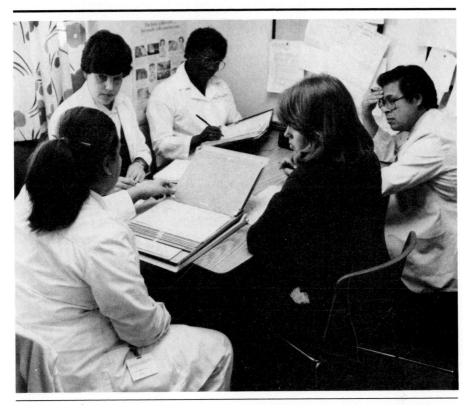

By listening effectively, we select, understand, and remember what is said by others. Listening is hard work, but it is essential for an effective group meeting.

      Floyd: That's OK. We understand.

In this dialogue we can see that Cindy has a problem that she brought with her to the group. While her problem does not affect the group directly, it can be a potential source of misunderstanding and conflict. Her seeming disinterest in the group may be a cause for unwarranted anger:

      Cindy: You all can do whatever you want. I'll go along with any-
                thing.
        Lou: Dammit Cindy, I'm not going to let you get away with that.
                This group needs your ideas as much as anyone's and you
                just can't sit back and let us do all the work.

This insensitive response reflects Lou's failure to empathize, which results in a disconfirming response to Cindy. The empathizing response we saw previously, however, was accepting and supporting. It promoted the group's understanding of the situation which led to a more positive group climate.

Barriers to Effective Listening

We said earlier that listening is the process of selecting, attending, understanding, and remembering. The previous discussion suggests that there are a number of levels at which this process can take place. To fully attend to, understand, and remember what another is saying at any of these levels requires that we overcome the common obstacles to effective listening. There are many such barriers—outside distractions, an uncomfortable chair, a headache—but we will focus briefly on two prevalent and serious barriers: prejudging and rehearsing.

Prejudging the Communicator or the Communication. Sometimes there are people we simply don't like, or with whom we always disagree. Because we are creatures of consistency, we anticipate that what these people will say will be offensive and we begin to "tune them out." An example of this is the tendency many of us have not to listen carefully to the speeches of politicians who hold political beliefs different from our own. In a group it is important to overcome the temptation of ignoring those we think are boring, pedantic, or offensive. Good ideas can come from anyone, even those people we don't like. Likewise, it is important that we do not prejudge certain topics as being too complex, boring, or controversial. This can be difficult, especially when a cherished belief is criticized or when others say things about us that we might not want to hear. But these are precisely the times when communication needs to be clear, open, honest, and confirming. And to do that, we need to listen.

Rehearsing a Response. This barrier, in our experience, is perhaps the most difficult to overcome. It is the tendency we have to rehearse in our minds what we are going to say when the other person is finished. One of the reasons for this barrier is the difference between speech rate and thought rate. Most people speak at a rate of about 100 to 125 words-per-minute. But we have the capacity to think or listen at a rate of 400 or more words-per-minute! This gives us the mental time and space to wander off while keeping "one ear" on the speaker. The thought/speech differential is better used, though, to attend fully to what the speaker is saying—and not saying. When we learn to do this, our responses can be more spontaneous, more accurate, more appropriate, more confirming, and more supportive.

Effective listening skills can contribute a great deal to building a supportive, more cohesive group. Cohesiveness is an important factor in the life of a group and is the subject of the next section.

GROUP COHESIVENESS

If this were a textbook in Introductory Physics we would define "cohesion" as the mutual attraction which holds together the elements of a body. This, of course, is a small group communication textbook, but we offer a very similar definition of **group cohesiveness.** *Cohesiveness is the degree of attraction which members feel toward one another and the group.* It is a feeling of loyalty, of "groupness," of *esprit de corps.* Cohesiveness results from the interaction of a number of variables including group composition, individual benefits derived from the group, task effectiveness, and, first and foremost, communication.

Composition and Cohesiveness

As we noted in Chapter Three, people often join groups because they feel an attraction toward the people in that group. Factors we've discussed earlier, such as the similarity of group members or the degree to which group members' needs complement each other, are influential in the development of group cohesiveness. If we can choose our own groups rather than being randomly assigned to them, there is a greater likelihood that a strong sense of cohesiveness will develop. According to Hare:

> Since individuals who desire to be close to people will choose others who prefer closeness, it is generally true that "birds of a feather flock together." However, individuals who like to initiate tend to choose those who like to receive, so that it is also true that "opposites attract."
>
> Groups containing a larger number of mutual choices on either a "work" or "play" criterion are often said to be highly "cohesive" in that they will "stick together" longer than groups in which there are few mutual choices.[11]

Individual Benefits and Cohesiveness

By viewing cohesiveness as a combination of forces holding us in a group, we can clearly see that the membership which brings us personal satisfaction must be important. Depending on the nature of the group, its members can derive benefits of affiliation, power, affection, and prestige. We like to be with groups of people in which these needs are mutually satisfied. Such groups can become important reference groups in that they allow us to validate our judgments about ourselves and others.[12] *An important determinant of group cohesiveness, then, is the degree to which a particular group is capable of meeting our needs in comparison to the ability of any other group to meet those same needs.* If we perceive that we are deriving benefits from our group that no other group could provide, our attraction toward that group will strengthen considerably. This factor partially accounts for the intense attraction most of us feel toward our families or our closest friends.

Task Effectiveness and Cohesiveness

We have seen the relation of personal and interpersonal variables to group cohesiveness. The performance of the group as a whole has considerable influence as well; success fosters cohesiveness. The mutuality of concern for the group's task, which provides the focal point for group process along the task dimension, becomes socially rewarding when the task is completed successfully. Here we can see another example of the interrelatedness of the task and social dimensions. Reaching a particular goal thus provides a common, rewarding experience for all of the group members. This commonality, or shared field of experience, further sets the group apart from other groups.

Communication and Cohesiveness

None of the factors described so far is enough, in and of itself, to build a cohesive group. Rather, it is the *interaction* of these variables which determines the degree of cohesiveness in a group. Communication is the vehicle through which this interaction takes place. Through communication, individual needs are met and tasks are accomplished. In other words, "the communication networks and the messages that flow through them ultimately determine the attractiveness of the group for its members."[13]

We've devoted most of this book to the study of how communication affects small group process. Our earlier discussion of defensive and supportive communication, for example, suggests some ways in which we can adjust our communicative behavior to improve group cohesiveness. But in addition to the *quality* of communication, the *amount* of communication in the group also affects cohesiveness. Homans suggests: "If the frequency of interaction between two or more persons increases, the degree of their liking for one another will increase, and vice versa."[14] Highly cohesive groups are characterized by free and open communication. The more we interact with one another, the more we reveal ourselves to others and the more they reveal themselves to us. Through communication, we negotiate group roles, establish goals, reveal similarities and differences, resolve conflict, and express affection. It makes sense, then, that as the frequency of communication increases, so does the group's cohesiveness.

COMMUNICATION NETWORKS

Another influence on group climate is the **communication network:** Who talks to whom? If you think about the group meetings in which you participate, it may seem that while some people talk more than others, most of their communication is addressed to the group as a whole. Next time you're in a group, note *who* is talking to *whom.* You will find that relatively few comments are addressed to the group as a whole and that we direct most of what we say in groups toward specific persons. In some groups, we find that communication tends to be distributed equally among the group members. Figure 5–1 represents such a distribution.

In some groups most comments are addressed to one central person, perhaps the designated leader or chairperson of the group. Figure 5–2 represents this type of communicative pattern.

Other patterns may emerge, such as the circular patterns in which we talk primarily to the persons sitting next to us, or linear patterns in which we communicate in a kind of chain reaction. These patterns may be built into the structure of the group from the outset or they may emerge spontaneously. Either way, networks tend to stabilize over time. Once we establish channels of communication, we continue to use these same channels. This network of channels influences group climate as well as group productivity.

A review of research suggests that, in general, "groups in which free communication is maximized are generally more accurate in their judgments, although they may take longer to reach a decision."[15] We tend to feel more satisfied in groups where we participate actively. When interaction is stifled or discouraged, we have less opportunity to satisfy our needs through communication. There is no doubt that groups with a centralized communication network (see Figure 5–2) are more efficient. That efficiency enhances group cohesiveness, but there is considerable evidence which suggests that the free and open communication networks which include everyone in the group (see Figure 5–1) are more likely to lead to more accurate group judgments as well as to a more attractive group climate and greater individual satisfaction.

Figure 5-1   Equal Distribution of Communication

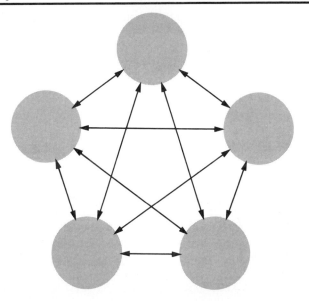

Figure 5-2   Leader-Addressed Communication

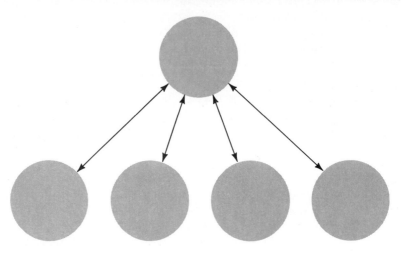

ANOTHER FACTOR: GROUP SIZE

We have stated that there is a positive relationship between the level of our participation and the degree of our individual satisfaction. Obviously, as the size of the group increases, our opportunity to interact with other members decreases. What size should a group be in order to achieve maximum cohesiveness and productivity? Three heads are better than one, but are twenty heads better than three?

We don't know the precise number of people which will maximize the effectiveness of your group, but we can share some observations which may provide guidance. As group size increases, we witness the principle of "diminishing returns." Imagine a long rope attached to a heavy weight. By yourself, using all of your strength, you may not be able to move that weight. As more people join you in your effort, the weight begins to move and the task becomes easier. But as the group size increases, *each individual uses a smaller and smaller percentage of his total strength.*[16] One study found that cohesiveness is positively related to the opportunity for interaction afforded by group size: as group size increases, the opportunity for interaction decreases.[17] As we shall soon see, cohesiveness is also related to productivity. What, then, is the optimum size?

Herbert Thelen has suggested the principle of "least group size." Clearly we want our groups small enough to encourage maximum participation yet large enough to generate the maximum number of ideas. Thelen says that "the group should be just large enough to include individuals with all the relevant skills for problem solution."[18] While this principle gives us no firm rule about group size, it does at least provide a guideline. In small group communication, bigger is not necessarily better. It has been our experience that groups of six to eight members are just about right; or, to paraphrase one of our former professors, twelve is just about the right size for a small group . . . if four people don't show up.

GROUP CLIMATE AND PRODUCTIVITY

Thus far in this chapter we have discussed many variables which affect group climate—defensive behavior, confirming and disconfirming responses, group cohesiveness, group size—and we have made some suggestions about how to improve the climate of your groups. As we have suggested, when there is free and open communication and when everyone participates, we tend to feel more attraction toward the group and consequently receive more personal satisfaction. Another reason for developing and maintaining a positive group climate is that *climate affects productivity.*

When the group has a trusting, open atmosphere and a high level of cohesiveness, group members "do not fear the effects that disagreement and conflict in the task dimension can have on their social fabric. *Cohesive groups have strong enough social bonds to tolerate conflict.*"[19] In Chapters Seven and Nine we will explore the function of conflict. For our purposes here, it is enough to say that through constructive conflict, groups deal with the difficult issues confronting them. When there is no conflict, it is usually because people do not trust one another enough to assert their individuality. Avoiding the issues does not lead to clarity concerning those issues. An absence of clarity does not help the group reach the most effective solutions.

It is a mistake to view positive group climate or group cohesiveness as a condition in which everyone is "nice all the time." Quite the contrary. In a highly cohesive group, members know that they will not be rejected for their views and, therefore, are more willing to express them—even though such expression may provoke disagreement.

> At a point where someone in a cohesive group would say, "You're wrong!" or "I disagree!" an individual in a less cohesive group will say, "I don't under-stand," or "I'm confused." Members of groups with little cohesion have yet to create much of a common social reality.[20]

This common "social reality" which includes group roles and group norms gives us the freedom to assert our individuality within a predictable context. In a cohesive group we already know that we are accepted in the group.

Another aspect of this social reality is the degree to which each group member makes the group's goal her or his own. In highly cohesive groups, individuals personally commit themselves to the group's well-being and to the accomplishment of the group's task. In part, we can attribute this personal commitment to the feeling we may have that *this particular group* meets our needs better than *any other group.* When this is the case, as it often is in a cohesive group, there is a degree of *dependence* on the group. This dependence increases the *power* the group has over us. To put this in a less intimidating way, "There can be little doubt that members of a more cohesive group more readily exert influence on one another and are more readily influenced by one another."[21] These factors—mutual personal commitment to the group, personal dependence on the group, group power over individuals within the group—come together in a positive group climate. The result is that *cohesive groups work harder than groups with little cohesiveness,* regardless of outside supervision.[22]

With few exceptions, building a group climate in which cohesiveness can grow results not only in greater individual satisfaction but in greater group productivity as well.

IMPROVING GROUP CLIMATE: PUTTING PRINCIPLE INTO PRACTICE

In this chapter we have taken a foray into some of the dynamics which contribute to group climate, examining variables which can make the group experience either stimulating and rewarding or stifling and frustrating. We've presented material that ranges from case studies to discussions of scholarly research:

- Jack Gibb found that we often communicate in ways which arouse *defensive* responses in others. When people are busy defending themselves, they cannot give much of themselves to the group effort. Conversely, we can communicate in ways which others perceive as *supportive.* To the extent that you engage in supportive communication, you will foster a positive group climate in which people are free to focus their attention on the group and its task.

- Sieberg identified patterns of communicating with responses that are either *confirming* (causing the others to value themselves more) or *disconfirming* (causing the others to value themselves less). If you can develop a sensitivity to your own confirming and disconfirming behaviors, you can become more confirming in your group behavior, thus contributing to a more positive group climate.

- *Listening* is an active process of selecting, attending, understanding, and remembering. Effective listening is crucial to maintaining a positive group climate. Only by listening attentively can we gain the understanding necessary to respond accurately, appropriately, and supportively to others. To do this, we need to overcome the barriers of prejudging and inner rehearsal.

- *Group cohesiveness* is measured by the degree of attraction which group members feel toward one another and the group. Cohesiveness is the result of the interaction of a number of variables including the group's composition, individual benefits derived from the group, and task effectiveness and communication. Being aware of these factors can help foster group cohesiveness.

- Communication networks—patterns of interaction within a group—tend to stabilize over time. Keeping open the channels of communication between all group members improves group cohesiveness and the quality of group decision making. While such a network is usually desirable, it is less efficient (in terms of time alone) than communication networks in which all communication passes through one centralized person (e.g., a chairperson).

- We tend to have more positive feelings toward a group when we participate actively in that group. Therefore, there is a point of diminishing returns when it comes to group size. If you are forming a group, include just enough people to ensure the presence of all of the relevant skills for problem solution . . . and no more.

- A positive group climate is essential if you are to reach your maximum potential as a working group. A trusting and open climate allows each of us the freedom of being ourselves: to agree or disagree, or to engage in conflict without fear of rejection. The ability of a group not only to withstand but to benefit from constructive conflict is crucial to a group's productivity.

We hope that you can use this information in ways that will contribute positively to the climate in *your* group.

PRACTICE

Confirmation/Disconfirmation

In your discussion group, stage a discussion in which group members attempt to use all of the disconfirming responses listed in this chapter. Choose a familiar topic about which everyone has something to say. Have observers keep a record of the number and type of disconfirming responses and the reactions (especially nonverbal) to them. Now repeat the discussion, covering as many of the same topics as possible, but this time concentrate on using only confirming responses. Again, have observers keep records. When you have completed both rounds of discussion, have group members discuss their reactions and have observers report their findings.

Group Climate Self-Assessment[23]

How does your behavior affect group climate? The following questions may provide some insight. Circle the number of the response which describes most accurately your behavior in groups.

1. I try to clarify the ideas of others.

7	6	5	4	3	2	1
Always	Usually	Frequently	50% yes 50% no	Occasionally	Seldom	Never

2. I plan what I am going to say while others are speaking.

1	2	3	4	5	6	7
Always	U	F	50/50	O	S	N

3. I tend to tell others when their ideas are irrelevant or inappropriate.

1	2	3	4	5	6	7
A	U	F	50/50	O	S	N

4. It is extremely important to me for the group to adopt my point of view.

1	2	3	4	5	6	7
A	U	F	50/50	O	S	N

5. My responses to others' comments are direct and supportive.

7	6	5	4	3	2	1
A	U	F	50/50	O	S	N

6. I express my ideas without concern for others' previous comments and personal feelings.

1	2	3	4	5	6	7
A	U	F	50/50	O	S	N

7. I make frequent contributions to a group discussion.

7	6	5	4	3	2	1
A	U	F	50/50	O	S	N

8. In a group I feel free to share my feelings about the group's task and other group members.

7	6	5	4	3	2	1
A	U	F	50/50	O	S	N

9. I encourage my group to confront problems as they arise.

7	6	5	4	3	2	1
A	U	F	50/50	O	S	N

10. I praise others for their good ideas.

7	6	5	4	3	2	1
A	U	F	50/50	O	S	N

Add up the circled numbers to determine your score. Compare your score with other group members. Discuss the results.

Variation: Complete this exercise as you believe other group members would respond. To what degree do your perceptions and theirs coincide? Why are there differences?

Notes

1. As we do not wish to leave the reader in suspense as to the outcome of all this, the relationship is still alive and well. We have all learned from the experience and have discussed it many times.

2. Jack R. Gibb, "Defensive Communication," *Journal of Communication* 11 (September 1961): 141.

3. Alvin Goldberg and Carl Larson, *Group Communication: Discussion Processes and Applications* (Englewood Cliffs, New Jersey: Prentice-Hall, Inc., 1975), p. 105.

4. Evelyn Sieburg and Carl Larson, "Dimensions of Interpersonal Response," (paper delivered at the annual conference of the International Communication Association, Phoenix, April 1971): 1.

5. Goldberg and Larson, pp. 103–4.

6. Allan A. Glatthorn and Herbert R. Adams, *Listening Your Way to Management Success* (Glenview, IL: Scott, Foresman and Company, 1983).

7. Ibid., p. 1.

8. Ibid., p. 2.

9. Ibid., p. 2.

10. Ibid., p. 3.

11. A. Paul Hare, *Handbook of Small Group Research,* 2nd ed. (New York: Free Press, 76), p. 10.

12. Ibid., p. 171.

13. Ernest G. Bormann, *Discussion and Group Methods: Theory and Practice,* 2nd ed. (New York: Harper & Row, Publishers, Inc., 1975), pp. 162–63.

14. George C. Homans, *The Human Group* (New York: Harcourt Brace, 1950), p. 112.

15. Hare, p. 343.

16. W. Moede, "Guidelines for a Psychology of Achievement," *Industrielle Psychotechnik* 4: 193–209.

17. Stanley Seashore, *Group Cohesiveness in the Industrial Work Group* (Ann Arbor: University of Michigan Press, 1954).

18. Herbert A. Thelan, "Group Dynamics in Instruction: Principle of Least Group Size," *School Review* 57 (1949): 139–48.

19. Bormann, p. 145.

20. Ibid., pp. 144–45.

21. Dorwin Cartwright and Alvin Zander, *Group Dynamics: Research and Theory,* 3rd ed. (New York: Harper & Row, Publishers, Inc., 1968), p. 104.

22. Hare, p. 340.

23. We extend our gratitude to our colleague Norman H. Watson for his assistance in developing this questionnaire.

6 Nonverbal Group Dynamics

After studying this chapter, you should be able to:

■ Explain why nonverbal communication is important to the study of groups.

■ Define emblems, illustrators, affect displays, regulators, and adaptors.

■ Identify three dimensions of ascribing meaning to nonverbal behavior.

■ Apply research findings about body posture and movement, eye contact, facial expression, vocal cues, territoriality and personal space, personal appearance, and communication environment to small group communication.

Nonverbal Group Dynamics

The scene is Paris, 1968. As the world holds its breath, delegates from the United States, South Vietnam, North Vietnam, and the National Liberation Front gather to negotiate an end to the long Vietnam conflict. All sides seem willing to compromise. But the talks come close to ending before they begin when bitter disagreement erupts over the seemingly trivial matter of seating arrangement. Newspaper headlines announce: "NEGOTIATORS DISAGREE OVER SEATING ARRANGEMENT—PEACE TALKS POSTPONED." Who sat where would have reflected the status of the conferees, and on that issue they were *not* prepared to compromise. It took eight months before the negotiators agreed on a round table, *a la* King Arthur, so that all representatives could be at an equal distance from one another. The initial squabble over seating arrangement had an unproductive effect on the talks. In this case, the individuals involved represented governments. But similar nonverbal dynamics come into play in corporate boardrooms, group conferences, and other situations involving small groups of people communicating together.

What is nonverbal communication? Just what is involved in nonverbal group dynamics? Scholars have yet to arrive at a consensus regarding these questions. For our purposes, we find the following definition of **nonverbal communication** useful: *Nonverbal communication consists of communicative behavior that does not rely on a written or spoken linguistic code, but creates meaning intrapersonally, or between two or more individuals.* In the context of a small group, this definition includes such behaviors as body posture and movement, eye contact, facial expression, seating arrangement, tone of voice, spatial relationship, and personal appearance.

Much of the research about nonverbal group behavior summarized in this chapter is not based on studies that have specifically examined nonverbal communication in small groups because relatively few studies of this nature have been conducted. The reason is that researchers have found it difficult to observe and classify nonverbal cues in a group where each person emits a myriad of nonverbal cues simultaneously. Yet, despite the lack of research examining nonverbal group dynamics in small groups, understanding how you display and respond to nonverbal cues should help you become more sensitive to the effects of nonverbal behaviors in groups. We have noted that communicating with several people in a small group can result in anxiety and uncertainty. We may not know how to solve the problem confronting the group, what role to assume, and how to maintain a cohesive group so that all members will be satisfied with the outcome. Learning about what types of nonverbal behavior occur in small group discussions and some effective methods for sending and processing nonverbal information can reduce much of the uncertainty that frequently surfaces during problem-solving group discussions.

We have also noted that every message contains both a content and a relationship dimension. Nonverbal messages are often the prime source of information about the nature of interpersonal relationships. Facial expression and vocal cues are particularly important sources of information about the nature of one's relationships. The nonverbal message thus plays an important **metacommunication** function. Metacommunication literally means communication about communication. The nonverbal aspect of the message communicates information about the verbal aspect of the message.

The purposes of this chapter are (1) to state why nonverbal communication is important to the study of small groups, (2) to identify two general frameworks for describing nonverbal communication, and (3) to discuss the application of nonverbal communication research to small groups.

THE IMPORTANCE OF NONVERBAL COMMUNICATION TO GROUP COMMUNICATION

Have you been involved with a small-group student project or served on a committee for a club or organization in which you felt uncomfortable or out of place? While you couldn't specifically identify why you felt odd, you knew something was wrong. You felt uneasy, not because of what was being said, but perhaps because of something *unspoken.* Maybe it was the apathetic facial expressions or the unenthusiastic vocal qualities exhibited by other group members. Or maybe it was the room in which your meeting was being held. Was it hot and stuffy or unattractively decorated? While you may not have realized it at the time, the nonverbal dynamics of that unexciting, uncomfortable meeting probably played a part in creating the unproductive group climate. On the other hand, you can probably remember some small group discussions that were positive experiences because other group members were sensitive to both the verbal and nonverbal group processes. Group members' body posture and eye contact may have suggested that they were involved in the discussion. Perhaps you met in a comfortable room. In short, the group meeting seemed interesting, exciting, and productive. While it would not be accurate to suggest that *all* unexciting group discussions are the result of poor nonverbal communication, nonverbal variables do dramatically affect a group's climate and the individual group members' attitudes toward the group.

There are at least three reasons why nonverbal communication variables are so important to small group communication. First, group participants spend more time communicating nonverbally than they do verbally. Second, nonverbal communication cues are more believable than verbal messages. And third, emotions are communicated primarily by nonverbal cues.

1. *People in groups spend more time communicating nonverbally than they do verbally.* In a small group discussion, usually only one person speaks at a time. But the rest of the group members can be emitting a host of nonverbal cues which influence the group deliberations. Eye contact, facial expression, body posture and movement—some cues are controlled consciously, others are emitted less intentionally—occur even when only one person is speaking. Since group members are usually within just a few feet of one another, most of the nonverbal cues can be easily observed. Viewing nonverbal communication from the broadest perspective, we can agree with the adage, "You cannot *not* communicate."

2. *Nonverbal messages are more believable than verbal messages.* Nonverbal communication affects how others interpret our messages. Nonverbal cues are so important to the communication process that when the verbal message (either spoken or written) contradicts the nonverbal message, you will be more inclined to believe the nonverbal message. The group member who sighs and, with a sarcastic edge to his voice, says, "Oh, what a great group this is going to be," communicates just the opposite meaning of his verbal message. Nonverbal cues are so vital to understanding that one researcher estimates sixty-five percent of the social meaning of messages is communicated nonverbally.[1]

Perhaps we often have more faith in the validity of the nonverbal message than we do the verbal message because nonverbal messages are more difficult to fake. We can easily monitor our speech—we *hear* what we are saying. But we are not always *aware* of what we are doing nonverbally. As you read this page, are you constantly aware of your posture? Are you moving your hands or your feet? Are you aware of the facial expression you are wearing? Sigmund Freud, in noting the validity of nonverbal messages, wrote, "He that has eyes to see and ears to hear may convince himself that no mortal can keep a secret. If his lips are silent, he chatters with his fingertips; betrayal oozes out of him at every pore."[2] Actions do speak louder than words.

3. *Emotions and feelings are communicated primarily by nonverbal cues.* If a group member is frustrated with the group or disenchanted with the discussion, more than likely you will detect his feelings by observing his nonverbal behavior—even before he verbalizes his frustration. If a group member seems genuinely interested in the discussion and pleased with the group's progress, this, too, can be observed through nonverbal behavior. Albert Mehrabian and some of his colleagues devised a formula that suggests

how much of the total emotional meaning of a message is based on verbal components and how much on nonverbal components.[3] According to his research, only 7 percent of the emotional meaning of a message is communicated through its verbal content. About 38 percent of the impact of the emotional content is derived from the voice (from such things as the rate, pitch, quality, and volume). But the largest source of emotional meaning, 55 percent, is the speaker's facial expression. Generalizing from this formula, we find that approximately 93 percent of emotions are communicated nonverbally. Mehrabian's research also suggests that when there is an inconsistency between an individual's verbalized emotional state and his true emotion expressed nonverbally, the nonverbal cues carry more clout in determining how the receiver will interpret the speaker's emotion.

An understanding of nonverbal communication, then, is vital to even a cursory understanding of the communication process in general and of group communication in particular. As you become a more skillful observer of nonverbal behavior, you will come to understand more thoroughly the way people interact in small groups.

FRAMEWORKS FOR DESCRIBING AND ANALYZING NONVERBAL CUES

To better observe nonverbal behavior in small groups, you need a basic vocabulary which will help you describe the behavior you see. Researchers have developed various systems for classifying nonverbal behavior. While these approaches have not been devised specifically for small groups, an understanding of two of these basic frameworks should help you analyze nonverbal behavior and interpret the meaning of nonverbal messages.

First, we will discuss a very basic category system devised by Ekman and Friesen that will help you *describe* nonverbal messages in small groups.[4] We will also discuss a framework developed by Mehrabian that will help you *assess* the meaning of nonverbal messages.[5]

Categories of Nonverbal Communication

Ekman and Friesen have identified five major types of nonverbal behavior: (1) **Emblems,** (2) **Illustrators,** (3) **Affect Displays,** (4) **Regulators,** and (5) **Adaptors.**

Emblems. Emblems are nonverbal cues which have a specific verbal counterpart and are shared by all group members. Emblems often take the place of spoken words, letters, or numbers. A group leader who wants the group to quiet down and places her index finger vertically in front of her lips uses a nonverbal emblem to take the place of the words, "Shhhh, let's be quiet now." A hitchhiker's raised thumb and a soldier's salute are other examples of emblems. A group member who points to his watch to indicate that the group should "get on with it" because time is running out, and a group member who uses her index finger and thumb to signify all is "OK," also depend on nonverbal emblems to communicate their messages.

Illustrators. Illustrators are nonverbal behaviors that accompany spoken communication. In a group you may see a gesture illustrating emphasis. Several researchers have observed that we synchronize many of our body movements to our speech.[6] A blink of the eyes, a nod of the head, and a shift in body posture accent our spoken messages. A nonverbal illustrator might contradict what someone is saying. The group member who stares out the window with an apathetic facial expression and says, "Sure, I'm interested in working in this group," nonverbally illustrates boredom and apathy. Or the group member who emphasizes his point by shaking his fist in the face of another group member illustrates conviction and determination.

Affect Displays. Although, as mentioned before, the *facial area is the primary source of emotional display,* research suggests that the *body indicates the intensity of the emotion, or affect, that is being expressed.* For example, a group member's face may indicate that he is bored with the meeting. If he is also slouched in his chair, he is probably more than just moderately apathetic about the discussion. Or if you've seen a television game show in which a young woman has just won a new sports car, you've noticed that her face tells you she's happy and that by jumping up and down and by hugging and kissing the MC, she is communicating the intensity of her ecstasy.

Regulators. Regulators, the fourth category of nonverbal behavior, help control the flow of communication between ourselves and others. Regulators are very important to small group discussions because we rely on them to know when we should talk and when we should listen. They also provide cues to when other group members want to contribute to the discussion. Eye contact, posture, gestures, facial expression, and body position all help regulate the communication in a group discussion. Generally, large groups operate with a rather formal set of regulators; discussion participants raise their hands so that the chairperson will recognize them before they speak. In a less formal discussion, group members rely on direct eye contact (to indicate that the communication channel is open), facial expression (raised eyebrows often signify a desire to talk), and gestures (such as a raised index finger) as clues to regulate the flow of communication.

Adaptors. This final category includes those nonverbal acts that satisfy personal needs and help us adapt to our immediate environment. Adaptors are also important as we learn to get along with other people and to respond to certain situations. Generally, we are not aware of most of our adaptive nonverbal behavior. Self-adaptors, for example, refer to things we do to our own

Nonverbal messages, often evident in the movement of the face and hands as demonstrated above, can enhance verbal messages.

bodies, like scratching, rubbing, or touching ourselves. Researchers have noted that when we become nervous, anxious, or upset, we will often display more self-adaptive behaviors.[7]

Dimensions of Nonverbal Meaning

Ekman and Friesen's five-category framework helps us describe more accurately the nonverbal behavior we observe in groups and in other interpersonal communication situations. Mehrabian, another researcher interested in nonverbal communication, has developed a three-dimensional model which identifies how we *respond* to nonverbal messages. Again we note that even though Mehrabian's approach was not designed exclusively for small groups, useful applications of his framework can be made to nonverbal group dynamics. By identifying the kinds of information which people receive from nonverbal messages, Mehrabian's framework helps us assign meaning to specific nonverbal behaviors. His research suggests that we ascribe meaning to nonverbal behavior along three dimensions: (1) **Immediacy,** (2) **Potency,** and (3) **Responsiveness.**

Immediacy. As defined by Mehrabian, immediacy refers to whether we like or dislike others. The immediacy principle states, "People are drawn toward persons and things they like, evaluate highly, and prefer; and they avoid or move away from things they dislike, evaluate negatively, or do not prefer."[8] According to Mehrabian's research, such nonverbal behaviors as touching, leaning forward, reducing distance and personal space, and maintaining direct eye contact can communicate liking or positive feelings. Based on the immediacy principle, group members who consistently sit closer to you, establish greater amounts of eye contact with you, and, in general, "are drawn toward you" probably like you more than the group members who generally don't look at you and regularly select seats away from you.

Potency. Potency, Mehrabian's second dimension of meaning, refers to the communication of status or power. Persons of higher status generally determine the degree of closeness permitted in their interactions. A person of higher status, for example, generally has a more relaxed body posture when interacting with a person of lower status.[9] During weekly sales meetings, the sales manager may feel quite comfortable leaning back in a chair with feet propped on the desk, while salespeople with considerably less status probably maintain more formal postures in the presence of their boss.

Responsiveness. Responsiveness refers to whether we perceive others as active or passive, energetic or dull, fast or slow. Body movement, facial expression, and variation of vocal cues (such as the pitch, rate, volume, and quality of the voice) all contribute to our perceptions of others as responsive or unresponsive. The group leader who communicates energy and enthusiasm would be rated highly responsive.

APPLICATIONS OF NONVERBAL COMMUNICATION RESEARCH

Nonverbal cues do not operate independently from other communication cues (e.g., message content, language style, and message organization) to create meaning. Also keep in mind that at this point in the development of nonverbal communication theory, there is much we do *not* know about nonverbal communication. After reading the research conclusions reported here you may be tempted to interpret someone else's "body language," but there are several principles that you should remember when ascribing meaning to the posture and movement of others.

1. *Nonverbal behavior must be interpreted in the context in which it occurs.* Just as you can misunderstand the meaning of a sentence taken out of context, so can you make an improper, inaccurate inference about a nonverbal behavior when it is interpreted out of context. Simply because a group member sits with crossed legs and folded arms does not necessarily mean that she doesn't want to communicate with others or that she is a "closed person." Other variables in the communication system may be affecting her posture and position.

2. *People respond differently to different stimuli.* For example, not all people express emotions in the same manner. It may take considerable time

before you can understand the unique, idiosyncratic meaning underlying specific nonverbal behaviors that another person exhibits.

3. *People respond nonverbally in a manner appropriate for the culture from which they learned the behavior.* Several researchers have documented cultural differences in posture, movement, personal space, territorial claims, facial expression, and the uses of time.[10] Each group to which you belong may adopt certain normative nonverbal behaviors. They may develop behaviors acceptable in that group which may not be appropriate in another group. For example, in a group of students it may be acceptable to sit on the floor with your legs crossed. In a group that includes faculty and administrators, a more formal seating posture would be expected.

These three principles point to a key conclusion: nonverbal messages are considerably more ambiguous than verbal messages. No dictionary exists with the definitive meanings for nonverbal behaviors. Exert caution, then, when you attempt to interpret the nonverbal behavior of other group members.

Our objective is to describe some of the research so that you can become more sensitive to your own nonverbal behavior and to the role nonverbal communication plays in the dynamics of a small group discussion. Specifically, we will discuss nonverbal communication research as applied to small group communication in the following areas: (1) body posture and movement, (2) eye contact, (3) facial expression, (4) vocal cues, (5) territory and personal space, (6) personal appearance, and (7) communication environment.

Body Posture and Movement

Perhaps you have seen the cover of Julius Fast's bestselling book, *Body Language*. If you have, you've seen the female model with a black miniskirt, legs crossed at the knee, a cigarette poised between the fingers of her right hand, and eyes seductively peering at you, while she flashes a faint Mona Lisa smile. The caption on the book cover reads, "Does her body say that she's a loose woman? Does her body say that she's a manipulator? . . . is she a phony? . . . is she lonely?"[11] We infer that by "reading" another person's body language (and by reading Fast's book, of course), we will be able to answer those questions. Unfortunately, the sophistication of nonverbal communication theory does not permit us to make conclusive statements about a person's personality and habits based solely on nonverbal information. We do know, however, that body posture and movement are sources of information regarding status, intensity of attitudes, warmth, and search for approval. Thus, a group member who is sensitive to the body posture and movement of other group members is probably in a better position to evaluate the overall mood and climate of the group.

Mehrabian has done extensive testing to identify what types of nonverbal postures and movements contribute to others' positive perceptions of you. As noted when we discussed Mehrabian's immediacy principle, an open position of our arms and body, a forward lean, postural relaxation, and touching may increase perceived liking.[12] We may often exhibit greater immediacy behaviors (e.g., more eye contact, more direct body orientation, more forward lean, and closer distance to others) when attempting to persuade others.[13] We may also be more successful at changing attitudes if we elicit more nonverbal immediacy cues.[14] During your next small group discussion, when one member tries to persuade another, see if you can detect increased immediacy displayed on the part of the group member advocating his or her point.

Mehrabian has also associated body posture and movement with status. In summarizing the results of Mehrabian's research regarding status, Knapp concludes that:

> [High-status individuals] are associated with less eye gaze; postural relaxation; greater voice loudness; more frequent use of arms akimbo; dress ornamentation with power symbols; greater territorial access; more expansive movements and postures; greater height; and more distance.[15]

If there are status differences among group members in groups to which you belong, try to identify the nonverbal behaviors that may enhance the high-status positions in the group.

Do you think you can tell whether someone is lying by observing his nonverbal cues? Several researchers have investigated how our nonverbal behaviors betray our efforts to conceal our thoughts. Ekman and Friesen found that feet and legs often reveal our true feelings.[16] They theorize that while we consciously manipulate our facial expression to hide deception, we are not so likely to monitor our feet. Our anxiety, then, may more readily be detected by observing nervous movement of the feet and legs than by looking for clues in the face or other areas of the body that we are likely to control consciously. Consider the following description of nonverbal behaviors which could indicate lying or deception:

> . . .liars will have a higher pitch, less gaze duration and longer adaptor duration, fewer illustrators (less enthusiastic), more hand-shrug emblems (uncertainty), more adaptors—particularly face play adaptors; and less nodding, more speech errors, slower speaking rate and less-immediate positions relative to their partners.[17]

Keep in mind that simply because a group member may exhibit one or more of these nonverbal behaviors does not mean that he or she is attempting to deceive other group members. While the cues listed above may be exhibited by an individual attempting to conceal or lie, not everyone who displays such behavior is deceptive. The ambiguity of nonverbal cues prevents us from drawing such definitive conclusions about the motives of another based on nonverbal cues alone.

Yet another avenue of research has attempted to identify which nonverbal cues are correlated with leadership. O'Connor discovered that frequency of gestures was highly correlated with individuals who were perceived as leaders in small groups.[18] In a follow-up study, Baird found that shoulder and arm gestures were used to a greater degree by group members who were rated by other group members to be group leaders.[19] While leaders may gesture more frequently than followers, it does not mean that frequency of gestures *causes* a person to emerge as a leader. The correlation evidence does not suggest a cause and effect relationship.

If someone in a small group is trying to persuade others, are there certain nonverbal cues that he may be likely to use during his attempts to persuade? Mehrabian and Williams found that persuasive communicators exhibit more animated facial expressions, use more gestures to emphasize their points, and nod their heads more.[20] Another team of researchers found that a person trying to project a warm, friendly image will be more likely to smile, not fidget with his hands, and shift his posture toward the other person.[21]

A final interesting line of research into body posture and movement suggests that in social situations our movement and posture are synchronized to the movement, posture, and speech of others. For example, at the end or beginning of a sentence spoken by another, you may nod your head or display a facial expression to agree or disagree with the comment. Condon, using slow motion films, documented a distinct relationship between facial expression, head movements, and speech.[22] Kendon is another researcher who observed that we may shift our body position in response to a verbal message.[23] Navarre and Emihovich report similar evidence that group members may respond in synchrony to the movement and posture of others.[24] These authors suggest that we may adapt a pose similar to that of those we like or agree with during group interactions. Thus, coalitions of group members may be identified not only by their verbal agreement, but also by their synchronized nonverbal behavior. It is probably more than just coincidence that group members consistently fold their arms and cross their legs in the same way. Just as religious services use singing and group litanies to establish unity and a commonality of purpose, small groups may unwittingly utilize common nonverbal behaviors to foster cohesiveness. In an effort to help a client self disclose, counselors report it helpful to adopt a body posture similar to that of their client. By synchronizing body position, counselors feel they can better empathize and establish a rapport with their client. In your small group discussions, observe the similarity and dissimilarity of group members' posture, positions, and gestures. Such cues may reveal interesting insights about group climate, leadership, and cohesiveness.

Collectively, the studies of body posture and movement suggest how you will be perceived by other group members in terms of status, deception, leadership, and persuasiveness.

Eye Contact

Have you ever felt uncomfortable because the person with whom you were talking seemed reluctant to establish eye contact? Maybe you've wondered, "Why doesn't she look at me when she's talking to me?" Or perhaps you've had just the opposite experience—the person with whom you were talking seemed to stare constantly at you. We become uneasy in these situations because they constitute a violation of eye-contact norms. While you may feel that you do a pretty good job of establishing eye contact with others, researchers estimate that we look at others only between 30 and 60 percent of the time.[25]

There are several factors that determine when eye contact will occur. Based upon a summary of the literature, Knapp provides a good review of the factors that generally encourage and discourage eye contact in interpersonal situations.[26] You are *more* likely to engage in eye contact with others when:

> *you are physically distant from your partner.*
>
> *you are discussing easy, impersonal topics.*
>
> *there is nothing else to look at.*
>
> *you are interested in your partner's reactions—interpersonally involved.*
>
> *you are interested in your partner—that is, like or love the partner.*
>
> *you are trying to dominate or influence your partner.*
>
> *you are from a culture which emphasizes visual contact in interaction.*
>
> *you are an extrovert.*
>
> *you have high affiliative or inclusion needs.*
>
> *you are dependent on your partner (and the partner has been unresponsive).*
>
> *you are listening rather than talking.*
>
> *you are female.*

You would be *less* likely to look at others when:

> *you are physically close.*
>
> *you are discussing difficult, intimate topics.*
>
> *you have other relevant objects, people, or backgrounds to look at.*
>
> *you are not interested in your partner's reactions.*
>
> *you are talking rather than listening.*
>
> *you are not interested in your partner—that is, dislike the partner.*
>
> *you are from a culture which imposes sanctions on visual contact during interaction.*
>
> *you are an introvert.*

If you maintain direct eye contact with your group while speaking, you can instantly monitor member feedback.

you are low on affiliative or inclusion needs.
you have a mental disorder like autism, schizophrenia, and the like.
you are embarrassed, ashamed, sorrowful, sad, submissive, or trying to hide something.

When eye contact *does* occur in a small group setting, it may serve one or more of these important functions: (1) cognitive function, (2) monitoring function, (3) regulatory function, and (4) expressive function.[27]

Cognitive function. This function of eye contact operates when eyes indicate thought processes. For example, some people look away when they are thinking of just the right words to say. Perhaps some individuals look away just before they speak so that they will not be distracted by the person to whom they are talking.

Monitoring function. Monitoring is concerned with the way in which we seek feedback from others when we are communicating with them. While addressing a small group, you determine how effectively or ineffectively you are expressing yourself by looking at the members of the group and monitoring their feedback. If you say something with which other group members disagree, you may observe a change in facial expressions, body postures, or movements. You may then decide that you need to spend more time developing and explaining your point.

Regulatory function. Our use of eye contact plays a vital role in regulating the back-and-forth flow of our communication with others. We can invite interaction simply by looking at others. For example, assume the chairperson of a committee asks for volunteers for an assignment. If you don't want to be "volunteered" for the task, you probably will not establish eye contact with the chairperson, just as you do not establish eye contact when the teacher of a class asks a question and you don't know the answer. Direct eye contact may be interpreted as an open communication channel, meaning that you would not mind being called on for the answer.

Expressive function. While eyes generally do not provide clues about a specific emotion, the immediate area around the eyes provides quite a bit of information.

Eye contact, then, reveals thought processes, provides feedback, regulates communication channels, and expresses emotions. In addition to these functions, eye contact may provide clues about the status and leadership roles in a small group. In the next small group meeting you attend, determine who receives the most eye contact in the group. Where do group members look for information and guidance? They probably look at the group leader. If, as in many groups, several group members share the leadership role, discussion participants may look toward any one of those who can provide leadership, depending upon the specific problem or level of uncertainty facing the group. For example, Alex may function as procedural leader. When the group needs help in how to proceed or wonders what the next step in the discussion process is, they look at Alex to indicate that they need his assistance. Phyllis may be the group leader who is the most knowledgeable on the discussion topic. When the group needs information, they look at Phyllis. Carolyn plays the role of tension reliever. When the group needs someone to help relieve tension, they look at Carolyn. Thus, eye contact can indicate leadership and other roles within the group. Watch for it.

Facial Expression

As discussed before, the face is the most important revealer of emotions. Sometimes we can cleverly mask our emotional expression, but the face is usually the first place we look to determine someone's emotional state. Facial expressions are particularly significant in interpersonal and small group communication situations because of the close proximity of communicators to one another. When emotions are displayed (affect displays) on the face, they are readily detectable. Even though some researchers estimate that the face can produce over twenty thousand different facial expressions, Ekman has identified six primary emotions displayed on the face: happiness, anger, surprise, sadness, disgust, and fear.[28]

Ekman has also developed a method of identifying which areas of the face play the most important roles in communicating emotions.[29] According to his research, we communicate happiness with the area around our eyes and with a smile and accompanying raised cheeks. We reveal disgust with a raised upper lip, a wrinkled nose, lowered eyelids and lowered brow. The most important area for communicating fear is around the eyes, but our mouth is also usually open when we are fearful. When we are angry, we are likely to lower our eyebrows, and have an intense stare. We communicate surprise with raised eyebrows, wide open eyes, and often an open mouth. We communicate sadness in the area around the eyes and mouth.

Group members' facial expressions are an important source of information about a group's emotional climate, particularly if several group members are expressing similar emotions. Their faces might suggest that they are bored with the discussion or that they are interested and pleased. But remember that group members may attempt to mask their facial expressions in an effort to conceal their true feelings.

Vocal Cues

"John," remarked a group discussion member, obviously upset, "it's not that I object to what you said; it's just the way you said it." The pitch, rate, volume, and quality of our voices (also called **paralanguage** cues) play an important part in determining the meaning of messages. Earlier in this chapter we noted that Mehrabian estimates that as much as 38 percent of the emotional meaning of a message is derived from vocal cues.

We may, then, make inferences about how a speaker feels about us from that individual's paralanguage cues. We may also base inferences about a person's competence and personality upon vocal cues. A speaker whose speech includes mispronunciations and vocal nonfluencies (like "uh" and "um") is probably going to be perceived as less credible than a speaker whose pronunciation is more articulate.[30] In addition to determining how nonfluencies affect a speaker's credibility, researchers have also been concerned with the communication of emotion via vocal cues.[31]

But while there may be times when emotional states can be detected from vocal cues, as a group discussion member you should beware of i..properly drawing inferences and derogatorily labeling someone's personality just because of vocal cues. As has been emphasized throughout this chapter, *nonverbal cues do not operate in isolation.* They should be evaluated in the context of other communication behaviors.

Territoriality and Personal Space

The next time you're sitting in class, note the seat that you have selected. Even though no one instructed you to sit in the same place, chances are that you tend to sit in about the same general area, if not in the same seat, during each class. Perhaps your family displays a similar norm of having each person sit at a certain place at the table. If someone sits in "your" chair, you feel that your territory has been invaded and you may try to reclaim your seat.

Territoriality is a term used in the study of animal behavior to note how animals stake out and defend a given area. Humans, too, consciously and, at other times, less consciously, feel duty bound to stake out and defend a given area.

Understanding territoriality may help you understand certain behaviors in a group. For example, the readiness of a group member to defend personal territory may provide insights about his or her attitudes toward the group and toward individual members of that group. During the next group meeting you attend, observe how the members attempt to stake out their territories. If the group is seated around a table, do the group members place objects in front of and around them to signify nonverbally that they are claiming the territory? Higher-status individuals generally attempt to claim more territory.[32] Notice how group members manipulate their posture and gestures should their space be invaded. Lower-status individuals generally permit greater territorial invasion. Note too how individuals claim their territory by leaving markers, such as books, papers, or a pencil, when they have to leave the group but expect to return shortly.

Several researchers have been interested in **small group ecology**—the consistent way in which people arrange themselves in small groups. As you interact with others in a small group, see if you can detect relationships between participants' seating arrangement and their status, leadership, and amount of communication directed toward others. Stenzor found that when group members are seated in a circle, discussants are more likely to talk to the person across from them than to those on either side.[33] Other researchers suggest that more dominant group members select seats at the head of a rectangular table or seats which maximize their opportunity to communicate with others.[34] On the other hand, people who sit in the corner seats of a rectangular table generally contribute the least amount of information to a discussion. Armed with this information, if you find yourself in a position to prepare the seating arrangement for a group discussion or conference, you should be able to make choices to maximize group interaction. If, for example, you know that Sue, who always seems to dominate the discussion, will be attending your next meeting, you may suggest that she sit in a corner seat rather than at the head of the table.

Did you know that an individual's position in a small group discussion can influence that person's chances of becoming the leader of the group? In a study by Howells and Becker, five people sat around a table, three on one side and two on the other. These two researchers discovered that there was a greater probability of the discussants' becoming leaders if they sat on the side of the table facing the three discussion members.[35] More direct eye contact with numerous group members, which can subsequently result in a greater control of the verbal communication, may explain why the two individuals who faced the other three group members emerged as leaders beyond chance expectations.

There is additional research to suggest that where you sit in a group may determine whether or not you initiate or receive information during group deliberations. One team of researchers who observed three-person groups in snack bars, restaurants, and lounges found that more visible group members tended to receive communication, while the more centrally located group members usually initiated communication.[36] Another research team came to a similar conclusion: group members who were visually central to other group members spoke most often.[37] As noted previously, eye contact seems to be an important factor in determining who speaks, who listens, and who has the greatest opportunity to emerge as group leader.

Other researchers have discovered that such variables as stress, sex, and personality characteristics also affect how we arrange ourselves in small groups. Some people prefer greater personal space when they are under stress.[38] If you know that an upcoming discussion will probably be an anxiety-producing meeting, it would be preferable to hold the meeting in a room which would permit the group members to have a bit more freedom of movement. This would assist group members in finding their preferred personal distance from fellow group members.

Sommer found that women tend to sit closer to others (either men or women) than men prefer to sit to men (i.e., men generally prefer greater personal space when sitting next to other men).[39] In a study to find out whether personality characteristics affect our preferred seating arrangement, Cook discovered that extroverts have a greater tendency to sit across from another person than do introverts.[40] Introverts generally prefer a seating arrangement which maximizes the distance between themselves and others. Collectively, these studies suggest that there is some consistency in the way we choose to arrange ourselves in small group discussions. A discussion leader who understands seating preferences should provide a comfortable climate for small group discussions.

Personal Appearance

How long does it take to determine whether or not we like someone? Some researchers claim that within seconds after meeting another person, we have completed our initial judgment of whether we should continue to communicate or try to politely excuse ourselves from the conversation. We base many of our initial impressions of another person primarily upon personal appearance. People's clothing (or lack of clothing), hair styles, weight, and height affect our communication with them.

Imagine that you are serving on a committee for a local civic organization. You arrive for your first meeting and find a slightly overweight, unshaven, and generally unkempt man; an attractive woman, dressed in the latest style; and an older gentleman, clad in overalls and a flannel shirt, and wearing a straw hat. Would the personal appearance of these people affect your ability to work with them in a task-oriented, problem-solving group? Would you be tempted to form stereotypical judgments about their personalities? According to recent research, you probably would.[41] Is it also possible that certain group members can be more persuasive and exert more leadership influence on the group because of their personal appearance? The results of several studies suggest that the answers to these questions is "yes."

Research suggests that females who are rated as attractive are more effective in changing attitudes than are females rated as less attractive.[42] In addition, more attractive individuals are often seen as having more credibility than less attractive people. They are also perceived to be happier, more popular, more sociable, and more successful than are those rated as being less attractive. Even the general shape and size of your body affects how you will be perceived by others.[43] Fat and round silhouettes (called endomorph body types) are consistently rated as older, more old-fashioned, less good looking, more talkative, and more good-natured. Athletic, muscular figures (mesomorph body types) are rated as more mature, better looking, taller, and more adventurous. Tall and thin silhouettes (ectomorph body types) are rated as more ambitious, more suspicious of others, more tense and nervous, more pessimistic, and quieter. Even though the research reported here was not conducted in the context of a small group, it is reasonable to conclude that perceived attractiveness and body type can affect how group members perceive one another. Such perceptions may have an impact on interaction, decision making, problem solving, overall group climate, and member satisfaction.

Research supports the assumption that personal appearance can affect the social influence you exert on others. As a participant in small group discussions, pay close attention to *your* personal appearance; the contribution you make to the group may depend on it.

Communication Environment

A group of five students has been assigned to work together on a project for their group communication class. Their task is to formulate a policy question and solutions to it. But their first problem is finding a place to meet. Apparently, the only available place is a small, vacated office in Smythe Hall, the oldest building on campus. No one seems too happy about the prospect of holding meetings in the old office, but they are relieved to have found a place to meet. When they arrive for their first meeting, they find a dirty, musty, paint-peeled room, with only three hardback wooden chairs and a gray metal desk. The ventilation is poor, and half of the light bulbs have burned out. Such a dismal environment affects the group's ability to work.

A classic study by Maslow and Mintz examined whether room decor has an effect upon the occupants of the room.[44] These researchers "decorated" three rooms. One was refurbished to fit the label of an "ugly room." It resembled a drab, cluttered, janitor's storeroom and was rated as "horrible" and "repulsive" by observers assigned to examine the room. The second room used in this study was decorated to look like an "average room," described as looking "similar to a professor's office." The third room was decorated with carpeting, drapes, tasteful furniture and room decorations, and labeled a "beautiful room." After the rooms were decorated, subjects were assigned to one of the three rooms and were given the task of rating several facial photographs. The results indicated that the environment had a significant effect upon how the subjects rated the faces. Facial photographs were rated higher in the "beautiful room" than in the "ugly room." Subjects in the "ugly room" also reported that the task was more unpleasant and monotonous than did subjects who were assigned to the "beautiful room." Finally, subjects assigned to the "ugly room" attempted to leave sooner than subjects assigned to the "beautiful room."

People can generally do a better job of comprehending information and solving problems in a more aesthetically attractive environment. Research does not suggest, however, that there is one best environmental condition for all group communication situations. The optimal environment depends on the specific task, as well as the needs and expectations of group members. Perhaps you are the type of person who must have absolute quiet while reading or studying, yet a friend of yours may be quite productive and maintain effective comprehension while listening to music. As a member or leader, you should attempt to find the best environment for your particular group based on the needs of your group and the type of task confronting your group. Ask members which type of environment they would prefer. If your group must solve a difficult problem that requires considerable thought, energy, and creativity, a quiet, comfortable room might be best. For groups meeting over a long period of time, comfortable chairs and pleasant decor are essential.

NONVERBAL GROUP DYNAMICS: PUTTING PRINCIPLE INTO PRACTICE

In this chapter we have noted that nonverbal communication variables have a profound impact on the dynamics of a small group. Group members send more messages nonverbally than they do verbally—we cannot *not* communicate. Nonverbal cues affect the meaning of messages; they are generally more believable than verbal messages. And nonverbal cues are particularly important in the communication of emotions.

We have discussed several applications of nonverbal communication research to small groups. Consider the following suggestions.

Interpreting Nonverbal Behavior

- Observe the nonverbal behavior of others, but beware of trying to read a group member's behavior like a book. Remember to consider that (1) the context of the nonverbal cue is important, (2) people respond differently to different situations, and (3) differences in culture affect how we react to others' nonverbal cues.

Body Posture and Movement

- You may be more effective in persuading others when you use eye contact, maintain a direct body orientation, and remain physically close to others.
- You can often identify high-status members of a group (or at least those who perceive themselves as having high status) by such nonverbal cues as postural relaxation, high vocal volume, territorial dominance, expansive movements, and sometimes, more distance from others.
- When someone is lying, he often exhibits a higher pitched voice, less eye contact, less enthusiasm, more hand shrugs, less nodding, slower speech with more errors, and a less-immediate posture.
- Group leaders may gesture more than followers.
- Observing the similarity of group members' posture and gestures can reveal insights about group climate, leadership, and cohesiveness.

Eye Contact

- People sometimes interrupt eye contact with others, not because they are disinterested, but because they are trying to think of the right words to say.
- When talking with others in a small group, be sure to look at all of the group members so that you can respond to the feedback they are providing.
- You can sometimes draw a person into the conversation just by establishing direct eye contact.
- You may be able to quiet a very talkative member by avoiding eye contact, because eye contact signals whether the communication channel is open or closed.
- By noting who looks at whom in a small group, you can get a good idea of who is the leader of the group. Group members usually look at their leader more than they look at any other member (assuming that they respect their leader's ideas and opinions).

Facial Expression

- Look at group members' facial expressions to find out the emotional climate in the group.

Vocal Cues

- You may find that you do not like a group member, not because of what he or she says, but because of vocal quality, pitch, or speech rate. Individuals' vocal cues affect our perceptions of them.

Territoriality and Personal Space

- Early on in the group gatherings, members will probably stake out their territory or personal space.
- When group members' territories are invaded, they will probably respond nonverbally (via posture or territorial markers) to defend their territories.
- Since most small group meetings take place in what one researcher calls the "social distance category" (four to twelve feet), a group leader should try to see that the distances between small group participants fall within this range.
- In a group, we are more likely to talk to someone across from us than to someone sitting next to us.
- If you know that a group member generally monopolizes the conversation, try to get that member to select a corner seat rather than a seat at the head of the conference table.
- You are more likely to emerge as the leader of a group if you are situated so that you can establish eye contact and direct body orientation with most of the group members.
- Since people prefer greater personal space when they are under stress, you should make sure that the group members are afforded plenty of territory if you know that a meeting is going to be stressful.

Personal Appearance

- Your personal appearance will affect the way other group members perceive you. Your appearance can also influence your ability to persuade others.

Communication Environment

- Make the physical environment for a group meeting as comfortable and attractive as possible; environment can affect a group's satisfaction and productivity.

PRACTICE

Receiving Nonverbal Reinforcement

Pair up with another student and take turns telling one another about an important idea, feeling, or experience. Your partner should give no indication of nonverbal attention while you are speaking: no smiles, head nods, "um-hums," postural orientation, facial expressions. After each person talks for 3 to 5 minutes, your instructor will lead you in a discussion of what it felt like (a) to receive no nonverbal attention and (b) to give no nonverbal attention. After you have discussed the importance of nonverbal communication, talk with your partner, this time providing genuine nonverbal feedback. Your instructor will lead you in a discussion of the differences between receiving and not receiving nonverbal reinforcement.

Nonverbal Group Observation

If you are working on a group project, videotape one of your group meetings or videotape your group attempting to solve a case study, such as the "Hurricane Preparedness" case or the "Bomb Shelter" case in Chapter Nine. Replay the video recording with the sound turned off.

1. Notice group members' use of emblems, illustrators, affect displays, regulators, and adaptors.
2. Observe how nonverbal cues regulate the flow of communication.
3. How does body posture and movement communicate the group members' status and attitudes?
4. Try to identify the four functions of eye contact in your group.
5. Do group members communicate much emotion with their faces?
6. Note relationships between territoriality behavior, seating arrangement, and leadership, status, and verbal interaction in the group.
7. If your group had to meet in a special room to videotape the session, how did the change in environment affect the group?

Small Group Ecology

Five people have been assigned by their instructor to work on a small group project for their group communication class. All of their meetings will take place in a room approximately twenty feet by twenty feet. One large rectangular table stands in the center of the room. There are also several chairs in the room. Shoved up into a corner is a small circular table.

Based on the small group ecology research, what do you think would be the ideal seating arrangement for this group? Justify your arrangement with the practices and principles presented in this chapter.

Consider these personality profiles of the five members:

Herbert: You worked with Herbert on a small group project last semester. You know from experience that he likes to be the
leader. However, he usually does not pull his weight when it
comes to getting the job accomplished. He likes to feel that
he is in control of the group. Most group members were not
satisfied with his leadership ability last semester. Chances
are, Herbert will try to assume leadership and control of this
group if you give him the opportunity.

Jane: Jane is extremely intelligent. She has made the Dean's List
each semester, and others usually respect her opinions. However, Jane only participates in a group's discussion when she
is encouraged to do so. She is very shy. She does not enjoy
group projects.

Nell: Nell is very outgoing. When there is a party or celebration,
Nell is the first to volunteer to help make the arrangements.
She enjoys working with people and people enjoy working
with her. She is well liked by most students.

Bill: Bill has real leadership potential. He has a talent for organizing people and accomplishing jobs. Although he is a very
hard worker, he usually does not like to be considered a
leader. He doesn't want people to think that he is just after
the status and prestige of being a leader. He can be a real
asset to a small group, but sometimes he must be encouraged to participate.

Barbara: Most people don't enjoy working with Barbara because she
is very pessimistic. She usually fears the worst will happen.
She is not a very hard worker because she thinks that the
group probably will not successfully complete the project.
She is intelligent and is a good researcher. But she usually
does't volunteer to work very hard unless she is encouraged
by other group members.

Notes

1. R. L. Birdwhistell, *Kinesics and Context* (Philadelphia: University of Pennsylvania
Press, 1970).
2. Sigmund Freud, "Fragment of an Analysis of a Case of Hysteria (1905)" *Collected Papers,* Vol. 3 (New York: Basic Books, Inc., Publishers, 1959).
3. Albert Mehrabian, *Nonverbal Communication* (Chicago: AVC, Inc., 1972): 108.
4. P. Ekman and W. V. Friesen, "The Repertoire of Nonverbal Behavior: Categories, Or-
igins, Usage, and Coding," *Semiotica* 1 (1969): 49–98.
5. Mehrabian, *Nonverbal Communication,* pp. 178–79.
6. W. S. Condon and W. D. Ogston, "Soundfilm Analysis of Normal and Pathological
Behavior Patterns," *Journal of Nervous and Mental Disease* 143 (1966): 338–47.

7. P. Ekman and W. V. Friesen, "Hand Movements," *Journal of Communication* 22 (1972): 353–74.

8. Albert Mehrabian, *Silent Messages* (Belmont, California: Wadsworth Publishing Company, Inc.): 1.

9. Mehrabian, *Nonverbal Communication,* p. 30.

10. E. T. Hall, *The Hidden Dimension* (Garden City, New York: Doubleday & Company, Inc., 1966); R. Shuter, "Proxemics and Tactility in Latin America," *Journal of Communication* 26 (1976): 46–52.

11. Julius Fast, *Body Language* (New York: M. Evans & Company, Inc., 1970).

12. Mehrabian, *Nonverbal Communication,* p. 30.

13. Ibid.

14. Albert Mehrabian and M. Williams, "Nonverbal Concomitants of Perceived and Intended Persuasiveness," *Journal of Personality and Social Psychology* 13 (1969): 37–58.

15. Mark L. Knapp, *Nonverbal Communication in Human Interaction* (New York: Holt, Rinehart & Winston, 1978): 228.

16. Paul Ekman and W. V. Friesen, "Nonverbal Leakage and Clues to Deception," *Psychiatry* 32 (1969): 88–106.

17. Knapp, *Nonverbal Communication,* p. 229.

18. J. O'Connor, "The Relationship of Kinesics and Verbal Communication to Leadership Perception in Small Group Discussion," unpublished Ph.D. dissertation, Indiana University, 1971.

19. John Baird, "Some Nonverbal Elements of Leadership Emergence," *Southern Speech Communication Journal* 40 (1977): 352–61; also see: Laurence M. Childs et al., "Nonverbal and Verbal Communication of Leadership," Paper presented at the Annual Meeting of the American Psychological Association, Los Angeles, 1981, ED210720.

20. Albert Mehrabian and M. Williams, "Nonverbal Concomitants of Perceived and Intended Persuasiveness," *Journal of Personality and Social Psychology* 14 (1969): 37–58.

21. M. Reece and R. Whitman, "Expressive Movements, Warmth, and Verbal Reinforcement," *Journal of Abnormal and Social Psychology* 64 (1962): 234–36.

22. W. S. Condon and L. W. Sander, "Neonate Movement Is Synchronized with Adult Speech: Interactional Participation and Language Acquisition," *Science* I (January 1974): 99–101; W. S. Condon and W. D. Ogston, "Soundfilm Analysis of Normal and Pathological Behavior Patterns," *Journal of Nervous and Mental Disease* 143 (1966): 338–47.

23. A. Kendon, "Some Relationships Between Body Motion and Speech: An Analysis of an Example," in A. W. Siegman and B. Pope (eds.) *Studies in Dyadic Communication* (Elmsford, NY: Pergamon Press, 1972).

24. Davida Navarre and Catherine A. Emihovich, "Movement Synchrony and the Self-Analytic Group," paper presented at the Eastern Communication Association, Boston, 1978.

25. M. Argyle and A. Kendon, "The Experimental Analysis of Social Performance" in *Advances in Experimental Social Psychology* 3, L. Berkowitz, ed. (New York: Academic Press, Inc., 1967): 55–98.

26. Knapp, *Nonverbal Communication,* p. 313.

27. A. Kendon, "Some Functions of Gaze-Direction in Social Interaction," *Acta Psychologica* 26 (1967): 22–63.

28. P. Ekman and W. V. Friesen, *Unmasking the Face* (Englewood Cliffs, New Jersey: Prentice-Hall, Inc., 1975).

29. Paul Ekman, W. V. Friesen and S. S. Tomkins, "Facial Affect Scoring Technique: A First Validity Study," *Semiotica* 3 (1971): 37–58; P. Ekman and W. V. Friesen, *Unmasking the Face* (Englewood Cliffs, NJ: Prentice-Hall, 1975).

30. K. K. Sereno and G. J. Hawkins, "The Effect of Variations in Speakers' Nonfluency upon Audience Ratings of Attitude Toward the Speech Topic and Speakers' Credibility,"

Speech Monographs 34 (1967): 58–64; G. R. Miller and M. A. Hewgill, "The Effect of Variations in Nonfluency on Audience Ratings of Source Credibility," *Quarterly Journal of Speech* 50 (1964): 36–44.

31. J. R. Davitz, *The Communication of Emotional Meaning* (New York: McGraw-Hill Book Company, 1964).

32. Albert Mehrabian, "Significance of Posture and Position in the Communication of Attitude and Status Relationships," *Psychological Bulletin* 71 (1969): 363.

33. B. Stenzor, "The Spatial Factor in Face to Face Discussion Groups," *Journal of Abnormal and Social Psychology* 45 (1950): 552–55.

34. F. Strodtbeck and L. Hook, "The Social Dimensions of a Twelve Man Jury Table," *Sociometry* 36 (1973): 424–29; A. Hare and R. Bales, "Seating Position and Small Group Interaction," *Sociometry* 26 (1963): 480–86.

35. L. T. Howells and S. W. Becker, "Seating Arrangement and Leadership Emergence," *Journal of Abnormal and Social Psychology* 64 (1962): 148–50.

36. Ronald L. Michelini, Robert Passalacqua, and John Cusimano, "Effects of Seating Arrangement on Group Participation," *The Journal of Social Psychology* 99 (1976): 179–86.

37. C. Harris Silverstein and David J. Stang, "Seating Position and Interaction in Triads: A Field Study," *Sociometry* (1976): 166–70.

38. M. Dosey and M. Meisels, "Personal Space and Self Protection," *Journal of Personality and Social Psychology* 11 (1969): 93–97.

39. R. Sommer, "Studies in Personal Space," *Sociometry* 22 (1959): 247–60.

40. M. Cook, "Experiments on Orientation and Proxemics," *Human Relations* 23 (1970): 61–76.

41. J. Kelly, "Dress as Non-Verbal Communication," Paper presented to the annual conference of the American Association for Public Opinion Research, May 1969; M. Lefkowitz, R. Blake, and J. Mouton, "Status Factors in Pedestrian Violation of Traffic Signals," *Journal of Abnormal and Social Psychology* 51 (1955): 704–6; J. Mills and E. Aronson, "Opinion Change as a Function of the Communicator's Attractiveness and Desire to Influence," *Journal of Social Psychology* 1 (1965): 73–77.

42. J. E. Singer, "The Use of Manipulative Strategies: Machiavellianism and Attractiveness," *Sociometry* 27 (1964): 128–51.

43. W. H. Sheldon, *Atlas of Man: A Guide for Somatyping the Adult Male at All Ages* (New York: Harper and Row, 1954).

44. A. H. Maslow and N. L. Mintz, "Effect of Esthetic Surroundings," *Journal of Psychology* 41 (1956): 247–54.

7 Conflict Management in Small Groups

After studying this chapter, you should be able to:

■ Explain why conflict occurs in small groups.

■ Describe the negative impact conflict has on group communication.

■ Identify strategies for managing different types of conflict.

■ List three myths about conflict.

■ Define the concept *groupthink.*

■ Identify six symptoms of groupthink.

■ Apply techniques for reducing groupthink.

■ Define consensus.

■ Apply techniques for managing conflict and reaching consensus in small groups.

Conflict Management in Small Groups

Social psychologists tell us it is inevitable: people disagree and experience conflict when they interact. Neither centuries of peace propaganda nor applications of the most recent principles of human behavioral research have been able to eliminate disagreement and full-fledged conflict. At any given moment in history, people have been involved in conflicts ranging from family feuds to international wars. Whether the group objective is negotiating international trade or deciding how to best repave a company parking lot, groups experience disagreement.

Our goal in this chapter is to give you some ideas about the causes of conflict and to present some strategies for *managing* it. We don't attempt to teach you how to eliminate group conflict; our aim is to help you understand conflict and the importance of conflict in your group deliberations.

In this chapter we will examine the role of conflict in small group discussions. First, we will define conflict and note why it occurs so often. Second, we will examine three types of conflict. Third, we will look at three common myths regarding the function of conflict in small groups. Fourth, we will discuss groupthink, a phenomenon that occurs when there is too little disagreement or controversy in a small group. And finally, we will talk about reaching consensus, or unanimous group agreement. We will also present several suggestions for fostering consensus in groups. Our prime objective in this chapter is to help you understand how conflict can be both useful and detrimental to group decision making.

WHAT IS CONFLICT?

Conflict occurs when there is a disagreement over two or more of the options that a group can take in trying to resolve a problem. Conflict also occurs when an individual's goal is perceived to be incompatible with the goals of others. Folger and Poole define conflict as "the interaction of interdependent people who perceive incompatible goals and interference from each other in achieving these goals."[1]

If a group experienced no conflict, discussion would be limited because there would be little to discuss. One easily recognizable value of conflict is that it causes a group to test and challenge ideas. But conflict can also be detrimental to group interaction and group decision making. Conflict has a negative impact on a group when it: (1) keeps the group from completing its required task, (2) interferes with the quality of the group's decision or productivity, or (3) threatens the existence of the group.[2]

What causes conflict in groups? Why does it exist? Conflict results from differences between group members—differences in personality, perception, information, and amount of power or influence. Because people are unique, different attitudes, beliefs, and values will inevitably surface and cause conflict. Each person has a distinct personality—your voice, mannerisms, and responses to stimuli differ from others'. No matter how much we try to empathize with others, we still have our individual perspectives of the world. We also differ in the amount of knowledge we have on various topics. As you participate in groups, you soon realize that some group members are more experienced or more widely read. This difference in information contributes to different attitudes. We also differ in the amount of power, status, and influence we have over others—differences that can increase conflict. A person with power often tries to use that power to influence others. And most people do not like to be told what to do or think.

MANAGING DIFFERENT TYPES OF CONFLICT

Miller and Steinberg have identified three common types of conflict: **simple conflict, pseudo-conflict,** and **ego-conflict.**[3] They suggest that by identifying the existing type of conflict, you will be in a better position to develop methods for managing it. Let's take a look at these three types of conflict in the context of a small group.

Simple conflict occurs when two individuals each know what the other person wants, but neither can achieve his own goal without also keeping the other from achieving his goal. "Simple conflict involves one person saying, 'I want to do X,' and another saying, 'I want to do Y,' when X and Y are incompatible forms of behavior."[4] While the conflict may seem far from "simple," it is called simple conflict because the issues are clear and each party understands the nature of the problem confronting it. For example, in a corporation with only a limited amount of money to invest in new product expansion, one board member may want to invest in real estate, while another member may want to spend the resources for capital improvements. The issue is clear; the individuals simply differ in the course of action to be taken. Miller and Steinberg suggest keeping the discussion focused on the issues, rather than letting the discussion degenerate into personal attacks. If it is not possible to

Conflict in small groups can be constructive, provided it does not degenerate into personal attacks.

postpone the decision until tensions are reduced, it is better to gather addition-al facts and evidence than to rely on group members' opinions.

In the other types of conflict we mentioned, the issues are not as clear-cut. Pseudo-conflict occurs when individuals agree but, because of inaccurate com-munication, they think they disagree. "Oh, I see," said Mark after several minutes of heatedly defending a position he suggested to the group, "I just misunderstood you. I guess we really are in agreement." Often just asking for additional information or clarification will resolve pseudo-conflicts. The key strategy is to make sure all group members clearly understand the question under consideration. Good listening and feedback skills as discussed in Chap-ter Three are important assets in managing conflicts which result from misun-derstandings.

Of the three types of conflict under discussion, ego-conflict is the most difficult type to manage. Ego-conflict occurs when individuals become defen-sive about their positions because they feel they are being personally attacked. As we noted in our discussion of supportive and defensive communication in Chapter Five, defensive reactions from one individual often result in others becoming defensive as well. "Just because you're the chairman of the group doesn't give you the right to railroad decision making," snaps Frank. "Well, you're just jealous. You think *you* should have been elected chairperson," retorts Ed.

An exchange such as this suggests that the conflict is less over a substantive issue than it is over ego defense. When egos are involved, simply using well-practiced feedback techniques or trying to clarify the issues is not easy. As Miller and Steinberg suggest, the first thing to do in managing ego-conflict is to

> ... give people a chance to bring out relevant concerns and then stop. The parties should not be prevented from expressing primary concerns, even if they are highly emotional, but they should be discouraged from escalating the conflict into violent personal attacks and counter attacks. When an ego-conflict looms stormily on the horizon, take control of the communication situation and let each person have his say, but do not allow either one to carry on too far.[5]

Giving individuals an opportunity to air their grievances gives them some feeling that their opinions are being acknowledged. Perhaps the best strategy is to suggest a cooling off period after individuals have had a chance to make their point. After this period of reflection, attempt to deal with the conflict of issues, not the conflict of personalities. The key is to break the cycle of defensiveness. In essence, try to change ego-conflict into simple conflict so that facts, rather than personal opinions, become the primary evidence used to support or defend a position. Ego-conflict often results from a struggle for power in the group. One person may feel ignored or he may simply want to be more assertive. Such a problem is not easily dismissed and its management requires the best efforts of all concerned. Conflicts which stem from ego defense and personality clashes are seldom resolved quickly, if ever; attempting to manage the tension so that it exerts minimal effect on the group process may be the optimal goal when dealing with complex ego-based conflict.

Let's consider some misunderstandings that you may have about the presence of conflict in small groups. The more alike group members are (in attitudes, beliefs, values, experiences, education, power, and so forth), the less likely serious conflict will occur. Yet, we work in small groups so that we can benefit from individual differences. A diversified group of people should expect and should try to use their differences in experience and perception to enhance the quality of their group's decision.

Myths About Conflict

Many small group communication textbooks published just a few years ago included few references to conflict. While some texts did offer suggestions for reaching group agreement, few specifically discussed the functions or positive aspects of group member disagreement. Conflict management is a relatively new area of communication research, and, as a result, there are misunderstandings about the nature and function of conflict.

People have several misconceptions about the role of conflict in commu-

Table 7-1 Summary of Three Conflict Types

	Simple Conflict	Pseudo-Conflict	Ego-Conflict
Source of conflict	Individual disagreement over which course of action to pursue.	Misunderstanding individuals' perceptions of the problem.	Defense of ego. Individual believes he or she is being attacked personally.
Suggestions for managing conflict	1. Keep discussion focused on the issues. 2. Use facts rather than opinions for evidence. 3. Look for alternatives or compromise positions. 4. Make the conflict a group concern, rather than an individual concern. 5. If possible, postpone the decision while additional research can be conducted. This delay also helps tensions to diminish. 6. Make sure issues are clear to all group members.	1. Ask for clarification of perceptions. 2. Employ active listening.	1. Let members express their concerns but do not permit personal attacks. 2. Employ active listening. 3. Call for a cooling-off period. 4. Try to keep discussion focused on issues (simple conflict). 5. Encourage parties to describe, rather than explain, the conflict; be descriptive, rather than evaluative and judgmental.

nication because they have the overall feeling that conflict is bad and should be avoided. With higher rates of divorce, crime, and international political tensions, it is understandable that conflict is generally viewed negatively. We will examine some of the feelings you may have about conflict and determine whether a different attitude can improve the quality of your group discussions.[6]

Myth #1: During group discussion, conflict should be avoided at all costs. Do you feel uncomfortable when conflicts occur in a group? You may feel that "good groups" should not experience conflict, but should experience harmony and interpersonal tranquility. People often view conflict as unnatural. There is a general feeling that if people express conflicting points of view, efforts should be made to squelch the disagreement. Conflict, however, is a natural by-product of communication; unless you are participating in a group in which each participant shares the same attitudes, beliefs, and values (an unlikely situation), there will be some conflict. Of course, individual group members may privately disagree with other group members, but because they regard disagreement as inappropriate, they may not admit their negative feelings. Several researchers have discovered that conflict is an important, indeed useful, part of the group communication.[7] As discussed in Chapter Eight, in the process of a group's efforts to solve a problem, the members experience conflict and tension. The eruption of conflict in a group becomes frustrating for group members who believe that conflict is unnatural and unhealthy. Realize that conflict probably *will* occur and that it is *not* an unnatural or unhealthy part of the group communication process.

Myth #2: All conflict occurs because people do not understand each other. Have you ever been in a heated disagreement with someone and then shouted, "You just don't understand me!"? It is easy to assume that all conflict occurs because the other person does not understand your position. Even though some conflict occurs because of misunderstandings (pseudo-conflict), not all conflict occurs because of a communication inaccuracy. You may believe that if others *really* understood they would agree with you. But, as Robert Doolittle observed,

> . . . many conflicts result from more than mere misunderstandings. Indeed, some of the most serious conflicts occur among individuals and groups who understand each other very well but who strongly disagree.[8]

While it may be true that conflict can result from not understanding another group member's message, some conflicts intensify when the other's point is clarified. For example, Mayor Johnson wanted to rezone a certain area in the city. Potter, a member of city council, opposed the rezoning; he felt the master zoning plan developed by the city three years ago was a good one. Johnson and Potter had several heated arguments about the rezoning controversy. But when Potter realized that Johnson wanted to rezone the land for industrial development, Potter became even more entrenched in his position. He *understood* the mayor's position on the issue, but he simply *disagreed*. A further clarification of the issue would not resolve the conflict. The two needed to discuss the reasons for their discrepant viewpoints. Not all conflict occurs because people misunderstand each other's viewpoint; conflict can occur because they *do* understand. If you experience such conflict, remember to discuss the evidence and the validity of the arguments and not just restate your position.

Myth #3: If there is conflict, it can be resolved. Perhaps you consider yourself an optimist. You like to think that if there is a problem, it can be solved. You may also feel that if a conflict arises, it is just a matter of reaching a compromise to resolve it. At the risk of being overly pessimistic, however, you should realize that not all conflicts can be resolved. Realistically, many disagreements are not as simple as we would like to make them. Fundamental differences between evangelist Billy Graham and atheist Madaline Murray-

O'Haire would probably not be resolved easily, if at all. Some ideologies are so far apart, so discrepant, that resolving the conflict is unlikely. This does not mean that whenever a conflict arises in your group you should despair, "Oh, well, no use trying to solve this disagreement." That position also oversimplifies the conflict-management process. But because some conflicts cannot be resolved, the group may have to focus on those differences over which they are most likely to reach agreement.

If you find yourself arbitrating a conflict in a small group, first decide which issues are most likely to be resolved. If you make the faulty assumption that all conflict can be resolved just by applying the right techniques, you may get frustrated. But, on the other hand, you must be wary of the self-fulfilling prophecy effect, too. If you hastily reach the conclusion that the conflict cannot be resolved, you may behave in a way that fulfills your prediction.

Consider, for example, the hypothetical, but very possible, case of Bob and Freda. Bob has lived in a large industrial city for several years. Freda has lived in a small rural community. When the two of them were recently disagreeing about how to reduce the level of crime in the United States, Bob unabashedly announced at the outset of the conflict, "There is no use continuing this discussion. A girl from the country just can't understand the problems of a large urban metropolis." With an attitude like that, Bob did not make much headway in his discussion with Freda. His mind was made up and the conflict could not be resolved. You must take time to understand all of the conflicting points of view before you can decide whether a conflict is unresolvable. While it is true that not all conflicts can be resolved, do not dismiss a disagreement as unsolvable too quickly.

GROUPTHINK

Frank Baxter, chairperson of the board of Eastern Oil Company, was meeting with other members of the board of directors. The agenda was to decide whether Eastern Oil would merge with Southern Oil Company. Baxter called the meeting to order. After the preliminary reading and approval of the minutes from the last meeting, Baxter stated that he thought the merger between Eastern and Southern Oil Companies would benefit both companies. As soon as Baxter finished presenting his opinion, other board members quickly chimed in, offering their support of the merger. None of the board members stated any objections to the deal; they supported Baxter's decision 100 percent. One member, however, felt that the merger might violate antitrust legislation by creating a monopoly in the southeastern United States. He also noted that the government would probably oppose the merger. But other board members quickly tried to gloss over the potential problem. One member confidently stated, "The government should not have any power to affect how we run our corporation. After all, it's *our* company."

After a few additional supportive comments from other board members, the group voted to approve the merger between Eastern and Southern Oil Companies. After the meeting, one member commented, "I wish all the group meetings I participated in would go as smoothly as our board meetings. We always seem to get along so well together. Baxter does a great job as chairperson."

"Yes," observed another member, "he certainly has our respect. We always support what he has to say."

Upon first analysis of this board of directors meeting, you might think it is a good example of an effective group meeting. There is little uncertainty and the chairperson appears to have the support of his group. All seems well. But by analyzing the meeting more closely, we see that the group is not functioning as well as it should; it is not taking advantage of the benefits of working together. This board of directors is a victim of **groupthink.**

Groupthink occurs when a group strives to minimize conflict and reach a consensus at the expense of critically testing, analyzing, and evaluating ideas. A lack of critical thinking results when a group reaches decisions too quickly, without properly considering the implications of their decisions. Sociologist Irving Janis feels that many poor governmental decisions and policies formulated in recent years are the result of groupthink.[9] After studying minutes of meetings and transcripts of conversations, he concluded that a lack of healthy disagreement contributed to inept decisions such as the Bay of Pigs invasion in 1962. The Kennedy administration's decision to attack Cuba was the product of a group of presidential advisors who were reluctant to voe their private doubts about invading Cuba. Janis has also noted that the Watergate break-in was ultimately the result of a group plagued by groupthink. Members of the Committee to Reelect the President believed that they needed information that was kept at the Democratic headquarters in the Watergate office complex. Again, even though some members privately felt that breaking into the Democratic headquarters to take the information was wrong, they did not raise their objections and the burglary took place. *The pressure for consensus resulted in groupthink.*

Groups most prone to experiencing groupthink have leaders who are held in high esteem. Since these leaders' ideas are often viewed as sacrosanct, few people disagree. A group may also exerience groupthink if its members consider themselves highly cohesive. They take pride in getting along so well with one another and try to provide support and encouragement to other members' ideas.

Symptoms of Groupthink

Can you identify groupthink when it occurs in groups to which you belong? Do you know how to guard against an overly dependent attitude toward consensus? Can you help reduce the likelihood that groupthink will occur in your group? Here are some of the common symptoms of groupthink.[10] See if you can think of some group communication experiences that exemplify groupthink.

Critical thinking is not encouraged or rewarded. If you are working in a group and disagreement or controversy is openly labeled as counterproductive, the chances are that groupthink is alive and well. One of the prime advantages of working in groups is having the opportunity to evaluate ideas so that the best possible solution can be obtained. If group members seem overly proud of the fact that peace and harmony prevail at their meetings, groupthink is likely to occur.

Group members feel that their group can do no wrong. Members of the Committee to Reelect the President did not consider the possibility of failing to obtain information from the Democratic headquarters. They felt their group was invulnerable. This sense of invulnerability is a classic symptom of groupthink. Another symptom is when members dismiss a potential threat to the group goal as a minor problem. In our opening example with the Eastern Oil Company merger, the potential problem of government intervention was quickly dismissed. The group had the feeling that their decision was a good one and that no outside threat could interfere with their plans. If your group feels a consistent spirit of overconfidence in dealing with problems that may interfere with the stated goals, conditions are ripe for groupthink.

Group members are overly concerned about justifying their actions. Groups who experience a high degree of cohesiveness like to feel that they are acting in the best interest of their group. Therefore, a group that experiences groupthink likes to rationalize its position on the issues. Group members are particularly susceptible to feelings of tension and dissonance. If the group's position is attacked, the group may respond in several ways to deal with the resulting tension and conflict. First, a group may try to destroy the credibility of the one who makes the attack. For example, a group of students working on a group project for a small group communication class received some negative feedback about their progress from their instructor. The group responded by saying that the instructor was not a good teacher and would not know a good group if he saw one. The group tried to rationalize its poor performance by attacking the credentials of the person who stated the criticism. A group may also avoid information that is contrary to the opinion of the group. The star of a Broadway production received poor reviews from one of the local papers. She responded by refusing to read the rest of the review and vowed never to read that particular paper again. Similarly, if a group receives criticism from someone, it may not seek advice from that person again. Finally, a group may listen only selectively to less-than-positive information about a decision it has reached. If a group is criticized, it may rationalize the criticism to diminish the impact of the comments. Groups susceptible to groupthink are overly concerned about convincing themselves that they have made proper decisions in the past and that they will make good decisions in the future.

Group members apply pressure to those who do not support the group. Have you ever voiced an opinion contrary to the majority opinion and quickly realized that other group members were trying to pressure you into going along with the rest of the group? Groups prone to groupthink have a low tolerance for members who do not go along with the group. Controversy and conflict injected by a dissenting member threaten the *esprit de corps.* Therefore, a person voicing an idea different from the group's position is often punished. Sometimes the pressure is subtle, taking the form of a frown or grimace. Group members may not socialize with the dissenting member. Or group members may not listen attentively to the dissident. Usually their first response is trying to convince this member to reconsider his or her position. Members may try to persuade the dissident to conform; but, if the member still does not agree with the others, he or she may be expelled from the group. Of course, if a group member is just being stubborn or unfairly obstinate, the others should try to reason with the dissenter. But don't be too quick to label someone as a troublemaker simply because he or she maintains an opinion different from that of most other group members.

Group members often believe that they have reached a true consensus. A significant problem in groups whose members experience groupthink is that the members are not aware that groupthink is occurring. They feel that they have reached a genuine consensus—that a spirit of unity prevails. For example, suppose you and a group of your friends are trying to decide which movie to see on Friday night. Someone suggests, "Why don't we see *Gone with the Wind?*" Even though you have seen the movie on television, you don't want to inject a note of contention so you agree with the suggestion. Other group members also agree.

After your group has seen the movie and you're coming out of the theatre, you overhear another one of your friends say, "I enjoyed the movie better when I saw it on television." After a quick poll of the group, you discover that most of your friends have already seen the movie! They agreed to see it only because they did not want to hurt anyone's feelings. They *thought* everyone else was in agreement. While it appeared that the group had reached consensus, there were actually only a few people who agreed with the decision. Therefore, even if you feel that the rest of the group agrees and that you are the only person who feels that a different solution would be best, your group could still be experiencing groupthink. Just because your group seems to have reached a consensus does not necessarily mean that all of the members truly agree.

Group members are overly concerned about reinforcing the leader's beliefs. Leaders of small groups often emerge because they suggest some of the best ideas, motivate group members, or devote themselves to the goals of the group more than anyone else. But if group members place too much emphasis on the credibility or infallibility of their leader, there's a good chance that groupthink will occur. Leaders who like to be surrounded by people who will always agree with their ideas lose the advantage of working in small groups. Most of us do not like criticism. We do not like to be told that our ideas are inept or inappropriate. Therefore, it is easy to see why group leaders would be attracted to those who agree with their positions. But testing the quality of solutions requires different opinions. A leader who is sensitive to the problem of groupthink will try to solicit and tolerate all points of view from the group.

Suggestions to Reduce Groupthink

While we have identified six symptoms of groupthink, you still may be asking yourself, "So what?" You may agree that groupthink, which is characterized by a lack of conflict or controversy, should not occur in an effective task-oriented group, but what you really want to know is, "How can I reduce the chances of groupthink occurring in my group?" We expect theory to do more than just describe what happens; it should also suggest ways of *improving* communication. To help prevent groupthink, consider the following specific suggestions which are based on the initial observation made by Janis, as well as on the theory and research of other small group communication research-ers.

The group leader should encourage critical, independent thinking. We noted that one characteristic of groupthink is that the group members general-ly agree with the group leader. The leader of a small group can help alleviate the groupthink problem by encouraging members to think independently. The leader should make it clear that he or she does not want the group to reach an agreement until each member has critically evaluated the issues. Most group leaders want to command the respect of their groups. But, insisting that the group always agree with the leader does not constitute respect; instead, it may demonstrate a fear of disagreement. Thus, if you find yourself in a leadership role in a small group, you should encourage disagreement not just for the sake of argument, but for the purpose of eliminating groupthink. Even if you are not in a leadership position, you can encourage a healthy discussion by voicing any objections that you have to the ideas being discussed. Don't permit instant, uncritical agreement in your group.

Group members should be sensitive to status differences that may affect decision making. Imagine that you are a young architect assigned to help design a new dinner theater for a large futuristic shopping center. When you first meet with the other architects assigned to the project, the senior member of your firm presents to the group a rough sketch of a theater patterned after a mid-1800s American opera house. While the design is both practical and attractive, you feel that it is incongruous with the ultramodern design of the rest of the center. Because of the status difference between the younger archi-tects and the senior architect, you and your contemporaries are tempted to laud the design and keep your reservations to yourselves. Doing so would result in groupthink. Groups should not yield to status differences when evaluating ideas, issues, and solutions to problems. Instead, they should consider the merits of the suggestions, weigh the evidence, and make a decision about the validity of the idea without becoming overly concerned about the status of the person making the suggestion. Of course, we realize that this is easier to suggest than it is to implement. Numerous studies suggest that a person with more credibility is going to be more persuasive.[11] Cereal companies utilize this principle when they hire famous athletes to sell breakfast food. The message is, "Don't worry about the quality of the product. If this Olympic gold medal winner eats this stuff, you'll like it, too." When analyzing the impact of the famous athlete, we realize that the athlete's fame and status do not necessarily make the cereal good. Yet we still might buy the cereal. We make a decision based on emotion rather than on fact. Group members sometimes make decisions this way too. Be on your guard to avoid agreeing with a decision just because of the status or credibility of the person making the suggestion. Evaluate the quality of the solution on its *own* merits.

Invite someone from outside the group to evaluate the group's decision-making process. Sometimes an objective point of view from outside the group can help avoid groupthink. Many large companies hire consultants to evaluate the decision making that occurs within the organization. But you don't have to be part of a multinational corporation to ask someone to analyze the process of your group's decisions. If you are working on a group project or on a committee, ask someone from outside the group to sit in on one of your group meetings. At the end of the meeting, ask the guest observer to summarize the observations and evaluations he or she has made about the group. Inviting someone from outside your group may make some members uncomfortable, but, if you explain why the visitor is present (or, better yet, if the group can reach an agreement that an outside observer would help improve the decision-making process), the group will probably accept the visitor and eagerly await the objective observations. Sometimes an outsider can identify unproductive group norms more readily than a group member can. Chapter Eleven identifies additional criteria for observing and evaluating small group communication.

Assign a group member the role of the devil's advocate. If a pattern of no disagreement develops in a group, members may enjoy the satisfaction of "always getting along" with each other and may never realize that their group suffers from groupthink. If you find yourself in a group of pacifists, it may be useful to play the role of the devil's advocate by trying to raise objections and potential problems. Or, you might ask someone else to play the role. If someone periodically assumes the role of "disagreer," the group is more likely to consider the available alternatives.

The Peterson Plastics Company has been steadily losing employees to its competitor, Wilson Plastics, Inc. A group of management executives met to discuss how to ensure greater employee retention. The vice president for personnel strongly advocated offering a substantial pay bonus to employees after six months, one year, and five years, arguing that employees about to receive such a bonus will probably not change jobs. Several of the junior executives in the group know, however, that money is not really an issue in this case. Peterson is losing employees because its plant is neither air conditioned nor well ventilated, while Wilson offers employees an air-conditioned working environment. But the junior executives hesitated to introduce contention by countering the vice president's proposal. Because of groupthink, they reached a less than satisfactory decision to offer pay bonuses. If the management group had considered the negative consequences of its decision by having someone play the devil's advocate, it might have opted for a better way to retain employees. Again, the myth that conflict and disagreement have a negative influence on a group's productivity results in a poor quality solution. Assign someone to consider the negative aspects of a suggestion *before* it is implemented. It could save the group from groupthink and enhance the quality of the group's decision.

Ask group members to subdivide into small groups (or to work privately) and to consider potential problems with the suggested solutions. The larger the group the less likely that all group members will be able to voice their objections and reservations. Most of the work conducted by the Congress of the United States is done in small committees. The members of Congress realize that in order to hear and thoroughly evaluate bills and resolutions, small groups of representatives must work together in committees. If you are working in a group too large for everyone to discuss the issues, suggest breaking up into groups of two or three people, each to compose a list of objections to the proposals. The lists could be forwarded to the secretary of the group who could then weed out the duplicate objections and identify the common points of contention. Even in a group of seven or eight members, it may be useful to form two subcommittees to evaluate the recommendations of the group. The principles here are to permit group members to participate frequently a·ˉ to encourage them to evaluate the issues carefully. Individuals could also ᴜ asked to write down their personal objections to the proposed recon..nendations and then present the list to the group.

The previous clues for identifying and correcting groupthink should help improve the quality of your group's decisions by capitalizing on opposing points of view. But a textbook summary of a few suggestions for dealing with groupthink may lead you to the false assumption that the groupthink problem can easily be corrected. It cannot. It may seem like we have overemphasized how to avoid groupthink. But, because of the prevalent attitude that conflict should be avoided, we feel it necessary to provide some specific guidelines for identifying and avoiding groupthink. In essence, *be critical of ideas, not people.* Some controversy is useful. Ideally, groups should strive for an optimum amount of controversy so that they will not be lulled into groupthink. But the group should not make extra efforts to create conflict. An important goal of a decision-making group is to obtain the best unanimous decision possible—to reach consensus. In the last section of this chapter we will turn our attention toward managing conflict in the search for consensus.

CONSENSUS: A GOAL OF TASK-ORIENTED SMALL GROUPS

We have noted that some conflict is inevitable in most groups. Because of our individuality, we often disagree with others. But this does not mean that *all* group discussions are doomed to end in disagreement and conflict. Conflict can be managed. **Consensus**—when all of the group members agree with and are committed to the decision—can occur. We're not talking about a false sense of consensus, like groupthink, but about *honest, unanimous* agreement. Even if a group does not reach consensus on the key issues, the group is not necessarily a failure. Very good decisions can certainly emerge from groups whose members do not all completely agree on the decision. The Congress of the United States, for example, rarely achieves consensus, but that does not necessarily mean that its legislative process is ineffective.

After our discussion of conflict, you may be skeptical about whether a group of people can agree on anything. And it is true that many, if not most, groups do not reach total agreement. But it *can* be achieved. While conflict and controversy can improve the quality of group decision making, it is worthwhile to aim for consensus. Ideally, there is an optimum level of tension that can improve the quality of a group's decisions. Somewhere between groupthink and total disagreement lies the proper balance of managed conflict. A few words about the nature of consensus may help you form more realistic expectations about working together in small groups. We will also suggest some specific ways to help your group try to reach agreement.

Nature of Consensus

Consensus should not come too quickly. If it does, your group is probably a victim of groupthink. Nor should consensus come easily. Sometimes group agreement is built on agreements about minor points raised during the discussion. To enhance the possibility of consensus, group members should try to emphasize these areas of agreement. This can be a time-consuming process and some group members may lose patience before they reach agreement. Regardless of whether consensus comes quickly or develops over a period of several meetings, agreement generally results from careful and thoughtful interpersonal communication between discussion members.

In order to have complete consensus, some personal preferences must be surrendered for the overall well-being of the group. Group members must

Group members may not always reach consensus; however, members must be able to compromise on specific issues.

decide, both individually and collectively, whether they can achieve consensus. If two or three members are adamant in their positions and refuse to change their minds, the rest of the group may decide that reaching complete consensus is not worth the extra time. Some group communication theorists suggest that it may be better to postpone the decision if consensus is unattainable. Such postponement may be wise, particularly if the group *making* the decision will also be *implementing* the decision. If several group members are not in favor of the solution, they will be less anxious to put it into practice. Ultimately, if consensus cannot be attained, the group should abide by the decision of the majority.

Suggestions for Reaching Consensus

Communication researchers agree that it usually takes considerable effort and patience before all members of a decision-making or problem-solving small group reach consensus. There are, however, guidelines that may help members foster consensus in small group meetings.[12] Consider these specific suggestions for managing conflict and reaching consensus.

Avoid always arguing for your own position. It is normal to defend a solution or suggestion just because it is your own. But here's a suggestion that may help you develop a more objective point of view: If you find yourself becoming overly defensive or emotionally involved in an idea that you suggested, assume that your idea has now become the property of the group. The idea no longer belongs to you. Present your position as clearly as possible; then listen to the other members' reactions and consider them carefully before you push for your point. Just because people disagree with your idea does not necessarily mean that they respect you less.

Don't assume that someone must "win" and someone must "lose." When discussion becomes deadlocked, try not to view the discussion as "us" versus "them," or "me" versus "the group." Try not to view communication as a game in which someone wins and the others lose. Be willing to compromise and modify your original position. Of course, if compromising means finding a solution that is just marginally acceptable to everyone but does not really solve the problem, then it may be better to seek a better solution.

To be most effective, a group should try to cooperate and work together. The National Training Laboratories describes this type of group behavior as *integrative*—the group tries to integrate their individual goals into the group goal. Members who strive for integrative approaches to conflict management display the following attributes:

1. They attempt to pursue a common goal rather than individual goals.
2. They are open and honest in their communication with other group members.
3. They do not try to use strategy to manipulate the group.
4. They do not use threats or bluffs to achieve their individual goals.
5. They try to accurately understand themselves and the needs of others.
6. They evaluate ideas and suggestions on their own merits.
7. They try to find solutions to problems.
8. They strive for group cohesiveness.[13]

Don't change your mind too quickly just to avoid conflict. While compromise may be needed to reach agreement, beware of changing your mind too quickly just to reach a consensus. In short, beware of groupthink. When agreement seems to come too fast and too easily, be suspicious. Make certain that other alternatives have been explored and that everyone accepts the solution for basically the same reasons. The principle here is to beware of the tendency to avoid conflict. Remember our earlier discussion regarding common misunderstandings about the role and function of conflict in group discussion. Of course, we do not advocate producing conflict just for the sake of conflict, but don't be overly upset if disagreements arise. Reaching consensus takes time and often requires compromise. Be patient.

Avoid easy conflict-reducing techniques. It may be tempting just to flip a coin or to take a simple majority vote when a disagreement cannot be resolved. Resist that temptation. If possible, avoid making a decision until the entire group can agree. Of course, there will be times when a majority vote is the only way to resolve the conflict. Just be certain that the group explores other alternatives before it makes a hasty decision to avoid conflict. Consensus through *communication* is best.

Seek out differences of opinion. Remember that disagreements may help improve the quality of the group's decision. With a variety of opinions and information, there is a better chance that the group will find a better solution. Also remember that there is seldom just one solution to a complex problem. Perhaps more than one of the suggestions offered will work. Actively recruit opposing viewpoints if everyone seems to be agreeing without much discussion. As suggested previously in our discussion of groupthink, you could appoint someone to play the role of the devil's advocate if members are reluctant to offer criticism. Of course, don't belabor the point if you feel that, after considerable discussion, the group members genuinely are in agreement. Do try to test ideas that the group accepts *too* eagerly.

Try to involve everyone in the discussion; be a frequent contributor to the group. Again, we stress the principle that *the more varied the suggestions, solutions, and information, the greater the chance that the quality of solutions will improve and that consensus will result.* Encourage less talkative members to contribute to the group. Several studies suggest that group members will be more satisfied with e group solution if they have an opportunity to express their opinions and to offer suggestions.[14] Remember not to dominate the discussion. Good listening is important too, and you may need to encourage others to speak out and assert themselves.

Use group pronouns rather than self-oriented pronouns. Harry liked to talk about the problem as *he* saw it. He often began sentences with phrases like, *"I* think this is a good idea," or, *"My* suggestion is to. . . ." Studies suggest that groups that reach consensus generally use more group-referent pronouns like *we, us,* and *our,* while groups that are less likely to reach consensus use more self-referent pronouns like *I, me, my,* and *mine.*[15] Using group-oriented words can foster group cohesiveness.

Use metadiscussional phrases. Metadiscussion literally means "discussion about discussion." In other words, a metadiscussional statement focuses on the discussion process rather than on the topic under consideration.[16] Examples of metadiscussional statements include, "Aren't we getting a little off the subject?" or "John, we haven't heard from you yet. What do you think?" or "Let's summarize our areas of agreement." These statements contain information and advice about the problem-solving process, rather than about the issue at hand. Several studies show that groups whose members help orient the group toward its goal by (1) relying on facts rather than on opinions, (2) making useful, constructive suggestions, and (3) trying to resolve conflict, are more likely to reach agreement than groups whose members do not try to keep the group focused on its goal.[17]

Orient the group toward its goal. Many groups fail to reach consensus because they lose sight of their objective. If, however, group members continually try to communicate in such a way that they make constructive suggestions supported by factual evidence, there is a greater likelihood that they will agree.

Avoid opinionated statements that indicate close-mindedness. Communication scholars consistently find that opinionated statements and statements that suggest a low tolerance for a dissenting point of view often inhibit agreement. This phenomenon is especially apparent when the opinionated person is the discussion leader. A group with a less opinionated leader is more likely to reach agreement. Of course, with many of the suggestions that we have made, it is easier to *realize* that opinionated statements hamper consensus than it is to solve the problem. Remember that using facts and relying on information obtained by direct observation is probably the best way to avoid being overly opinionated.

Make an effort to clarify misunderstandings in meaning. We have discredited the myth that *all* conflicts and disagreements arise because the conflicting parties do not understand one another. But misunderstanding another's meaning does sometimes create conflict and adversely affect group consensus. The procedure for dealing with misunderstanding is simple but often not practiced. Ask a fellow group member to explain a particular word or statement that you do not understand. Constantly solicit feedback from your listeners. One feedback technique is to repeat the previous speaker's point before you state your position on the issue. While this procedure can be overused, time-consuming, and possibly stilted and artificial, it can help when misunderstandings about *meanings* arise. It may also be helpful for you to remember the principle that *meanings are in people, not in words.* Stated another way, the meaning for a word comes from a person's unique perspective, perception, and experience.

CONFLICT MANAGEMENT IN SMALL GROUPS: PUTTING PRINCIPLE INTO PRACTICE

Conflict can have both positive and negative effects on a group. Conflict occurs because people are different; we each have our own ways of doing things. These differences affect the way we perceive and approach problem solving.

Groupthink

The absence of conflict or a false sense of agreement is called groupthink. It occurs when group members are reluctant to voice their feelings and objections to issues being discussed.

To help reduce the likelihood of groupthink, review the following suggestions:

- The group leader should encourage critical, independent thinking.
- Group members should be sensitive to status differences that may affect decision making.
- Invite someone from outside the group to evaluate the group's decision-making process.
- Assign a group member the role of the devil's advocate.
- Ask group members to subdivide into small groups to consider potential problems with the suggested solutions.

Consensus

Consider applying the following suggestions to help reach consensus and to help manage the conflicts and disagreements which arise.

- Avoid always arguing for your own position.
- Don't assume someone must "win" and someone must "lose."
- Don't change your mind too quickly just to avoid conflict.
- Avoid easy conflict-reducing techniques.
- Seek out differences of opinion.
- Try to involve everyone in the discussion; be a frequent contributor to the group.
- Use group pronouns (e.g., *us, we, our*), rather than self-oriented pronouns (e.g., *I, me, mine*).
- Use metadiscussional phrases.
- Orient the group toward its goal.
- Avoid opinionated statements that indicate close-mindedness.
- Make an effort to clarify misunderstandings in meaning.

PRACTICE

Agree-Disagree Statements About Conflict

Read each statement once. Mark whether you agree (A) or disagree (D) with each statement. Take five or six minutes to do this.

————   1. I think most people find an argument interesting and exciting.

————   2. In most conflicts someone must win and someone must lose. That's the way conflict is.

————   3. The best way to handle a conflict is simply to let everyone cool off.

————   4. Most people get upset at a person who disagrees with them.

————   5. Most "hidden agendas" are probably best kept hidden to ensure a positive social climate.

————   6. If people spend enough time with one another, they will find something to disagree with and eventually become upset with one another.

————   7. Conflicts can be solved if people will just take the time to listen to one another.

————   8. Conflict hinders the work of the group.

————   9. If you disagree with someone in a group, it is usually better to keep quiet than get the group off the track with your personal difference of opinion.

————   10. When a group can't reach a decision, members should abide by the decision of the group leader if the leader is qualified and competent.

————   11. To compromise is to take the easy way out of conflict.

————   12. Some people seem to produce more conflict and tension than others. These people should be restricted from group decision-making situations.

After you have marked the above statements, break up into small groups and try to agree or disagree unanimously with each statement. Especially try to find reasons for differences of opinion. If your group cannot reach agreement or disagreement, you may change the wording in any statement to promote consensus. Assign one group member to observe your group interactions.

After your group has attempted to reach consensus, the observer should report how effectively the group used the guidelines suggested in this chapter.

The River Story[18]

Read the following story and then privately rank the five characters in the story from the most offensive character to the least objectionable. The character you find most reprehensible is the first on your list, and the least objectionable is the last. After you have had time to make a decision, your instructor will ask you to work in a group with four or five other people to reach agreement on the rank of the characters in the story. When your group has reached an agreement or your instructor concludes the discussion, use the rating sheet provided to evaluate your group's skill in reaching consensus.

The River

Once there was a girl named Abigail who was in love with a boy named Gregory. Gregory had an unfortunate mishap and broke his glasses. Abigail, being a true friend, volunteered to take them to be repaired. But the repair shop was across the river, and during a flash flood the bridge was washed away. Poor Gregory could see nothing without his glasses, so Abigail was desperate to get across the river to the repair shop. While she was standing forlornly on the bank of the river, clutching the broken glasses in her hands, a boy named Sinbad glided by in a rowboat.

She asked Sinbad if he would take her across. He agreed to on the condition that while she was having the glasses repaired she would go to a nearby store and steal a transistor radio that he had been wanting. Abigail refused to do this and went to see a friend named Ivan who had a boat.

When Abigail told Ivan her problem he said he was too busy to help her out and didn't want to be involved. Abigail, feeling that she had no other choice, returned to Sinbad and told him she would agree to his plan.

When Abigail returned the repaired glasses to Gregory she told him what she had had to do. Gregory was appalled at what she had done and told her he never wanted to see her again.

Abigail, upset, turned to Slug with her tail of woe. Slug was so sorry for Abigail that he promised her he would get even with Gregory. They went to the school playground where Greg was playing ball and Abigail watched happily while Slug beat Gregory up and broke his glasses again.

Consensus Evaluation Form

1. Group members always argued for their own position.
    strongly agree   agree   undecided   disagree   strongly disagree

2. Group members assumed that someone must win and someone must lose an argument.
    strongly agree   agree   undecided   disagree   strongly disagree

3. Group members did not change their minds just to avoid conflict.
    strongly agree   agree   undecided   disagree   strongly disagree

4. As a group, we avoided easy conflict-reducing techniques like flipping a coin or taking a quick vote.
    strongly agree   agree   undecided   disagree   strongly disagree

5. Group members sought out differences of opinion.
    strongly agree   agree   undecided   disagree   strongly disagree

6. All group members were involved in the discussion.
    strongly agree   agree   undecided   disagree   strongly disagree

7. Group members used group-oriented words ("we," "us," "our") more than they used self-oriented words ("I," "me," "mine").
    strongly agree   agree   undecided   disagree   strongly disagree

8. Group members used metadiscussional phrases.
    strongly agree   agree   undecided   disagree   strongly disagree

9. Group members tried to orient the group toward the goal.
    strongly agree   agree   undecided   disagree   strongly disagree

10. Group members avoided opinionated statements and were generally open-minded.
    strongly agree   agree   undecided   disagree   strongly disagree

11. Group members made an effort to clarify misunderstandings in meaning.
    strongly agree   agree   undecided   disagree   strongly disagree

Win As Much As You Can[19]

This activity is designed to explore the effects of trust and conflict on communication. Your instructor will explain how this exercise is to be conducted.*

Directions: For ten successive rounds you and your partner will choose either an "X" or a "Y". The "pay-off" for each round depends on the pattern of choice made in your cluster.
Strategy: You are to confer with your partner on each round to make a *joint decision.* Before rounds 5, 8, and 10 you confer with the other dyads in your cluster. There are three key rules:

1. Do not confer with the other members of your cluster unless you are given specific permission to do so. This applies to nonverbal as well as verbal communication.

---

*The *Instructor's Manual* explains how this activity should be conducted.

4 X's: Lose $1.00 each
3 X's: Win $1.00 each 1 Y: Lose $3.00
2 X's: Win $2.00 each 2 Y's: Lose $2.00 each
1 X: Win $3.00 3 Y's: Lose $1.00 each
4 Y's: Win $1.00 each

2. Each dyad must agree on a single choice for each round.
3. Make sure that the other members of your cluster do not know your dyad's choice until you are instructed to reveal it.

The Case of Johnny

Read the following case study about Johnny, a youth with several problems. Following the case study are a range of possible solutions to Johnny's problem. Your task is to decide, as a group, on the best solution to his problem. Strive for total group agreement. After a given amount of time, your instructor* will lead you in a discussion of your group's ability to reach consensus.

Round	Time Allowed	Confer with	Choice	$Won	$ Lost	$ Balance	
1	2 min.	partner					
2	1 min.	partner					
3	1 min.	partner					
4	1 min.	partner					
5	3 min. 1 min.	cluster partner					Bonus Round pay is multiplied by 3
6	1 min.	partner					
7	1 min.	partner					Pay is multiplied by 5
8	3 min.	cluster					
9	1 min.	partner					
10	3 min.	cluster					Pay is multiplied by 10

*Note to instructor: The *Instructor's Manual* explains how this activity should be conducted.

Johnny was born in a large midwestern industrial city. There were already nine other children in Johnny's family when Johnny was born; one more child, David, came after Johnny. His family lived in one of the worst slums in the city, known for its high rate of crime and juvenile delinquency. It was a neighborhood of factories, junk yards, poolrooms, cheap liquor joints, and broken homes.

By the time Johnny's father died, four of the older children had married and moved away. What was left of the family continued in its dismal course; the children were getting into one difficulty after another and Johnny's mother, sick and confused, was tired of trudging from school to police station to court, listening to complaints about them. Of the remaining children only Georgie, the oldest, assumed any responsibility toward the others. When the rest of the children got out of hand, he beat them brutally.

Johnny's mother tried to pacify landlords by keeping her screaming children out of the house and on the streets as much as possible. Five of Johnny's brothers, starting in childhood, ran up police records covering charges of disturbing the peace, breaking and entering, larceny, perjury, assault and battery, and malicious injury.

"I was in the police station, too, plenty," Johnny says. "Saturdays they had kids' day. We'd be in this long corridor, there'd be all little kids sitting down. They'd bring us in and those jerks, the cops, they'd be sitting there and this cop here, he was always insulting us. 'You little creep,' he'd tell me, and he'd belt me."

He was a trial to his teachers. They complained that he was "nervous, sullen, obstinate, cruel, disobedient, disruptive." "Teachers can stand him for only one day at a time," one said. "He talks to himself. He fights. When in Ms. Clark's room, he attempted to kick her. He isn't going to be promoted. He knows this and refuses to study."

With every new failure he was compelled to some new misbehavior. Once, at the beginning of a new semester, he told his teacher, "I wasn't promoted. O.K.! This year I'm going to make plenty of trouble." With every new punishment Johnny's conviction grew that his teachers, like everybody else, were "against him." Johnny had been seeing his parole officer, Mr. O'Brien, for some time now.

During the months of Mr. O'Brien's friendship with Johnny, his teachers found that he was making a tremendous effort to behave himself but that he was "like a kettle of boiling water with the lid about to blow off." Johnny managed to get through that term of school without too much trouble and was promoted, but school had not been out long before he fell into trouble with the police again, this time for breaking into a house and stealing fifty dollars' worth of jewelry. Before Johnny appeared in court, Mr. O'Brien visited him. Johnny, O'Brien reported, seemed "unhappy, but stolid and apathetic, though, once or twice as we talked, he verged on tears."

Johnny didn't deny the theft and, as his confession poured out, Mr. O'Brien asked, "Even when I thought you were being a good boy, Johnny, were you stealing all the while?" Johnny, verging on tears, replied. "Yes, sometimes. But lots of times I didn't steal because I thought of you."

Suggested Solutions: Love-Punishment Scale

1. Love, kindness, and friendship are all that are necessary to make Johnny a better kid. If he can be placed in a more agreeable environment such as a warm, friendly foster home, his trouble will clear up.

2. Johnny should be put into surroundings where most emphasis will be placed on providing him with warmth and affection, but where he will be punished if he really gets out of hand.

3. Johnny should be sent into an environment where providing him with warmth and affection will be emphasized, but where discipline and punishment will be frequent if his behavior warrants it.

4. Johnny needs an equal measure of both love and discipline. Thus, he should be placed in an atmosphere where he will be disciplined and punished if he does wrong but rewarded and given affection if he behaves himself, and where equal emphasis will be placed on both love and discipline.

5. Though they should not be too strong and frequent, punishment and discipline should be more emphasized than kindness and affection. Johnny should be placed in an atmosphere where he will be seriously disciplined but where he will also be allowed opportunities for warmth and kindness.

6. Johnny should be sent into surroundings where the most emphasis will be placed on discipline and punishment, but where there is the possibility for praise and kindness if he really behaves himself.

7. There's very little you can do with a kid like this, but put him in a very severe disciplinary environment. Only by punishing him strongly can we change his behavior.

Notes

1. Joseph P. Folger and Marshall Scott Poole, *Working Through Conflict: A Communication Perspective* (Glenview, IL: Scott, Foresman and Company, 1984), p. 4.

2. Michael Burgoon, Judee K. Heston, and James McCroskey, *Small Group Communication: A Functional Approach* (New York: Holt, Rinehart & Winston, 1974), p. 76.

3. Gerald R. Miller and Mark Steinberg, *Between People: New Analysis of Interpersonal Communication* (Chicago: Science Research Associates, Inc., 1975), p. 264.

4. Ibid.

5. Ibid., p. 269.

6. Portions of the following discussion of myths about conflict were adapted from Robert J. Doolittle, *Orientations to Communication and Conflict* (Chicago: Science Research Associates, Inc., 1976), pp. 7-9.

7. See Fred E. Jandt, ed., *Conflict Resolution Through Communication* (New York: Harper & Row Publishers, Inc., 1973).

8. Doolittle, p. 8.

9. Irving L. Janis, *Victims of Groupthink* (Boston: Houghton Mifflin Company, 1973).

10. Adapted from Irving L. Janis, "Groupthink," *Psychology Today* 5 (November 1971): 43–46, 74–76.

11. See Kenneth Andersen and Theodore Clevenger, Jr., "A Summary of Experimental Research in Ethos," *Speech Monographs* 30 (1963): 59–78.

12. Portions of the following section on consensus were adapted from John A. Kline, "Ten Techniques for Reaching Consensus in Small Groups," *Air Force Reserve Officer Training Corps Education Journal* 19 (Spring 1977): 19–21.

13. *1968 Reading Book* of the National Training Laboratories Institute of Applied Behavioral Sciences.

14. See Henry W. Riecken, "The Effect of Talkativeness on Ability to Influence Group Solutions of Problems," *Sociometry* 21 (1958): 309–21.

15. See John A. Kline and James L. Hullinger, "Redundancy, Self Orientation, and Group Consensus," *Speech Monographs* 40 (March 1973): 72–74.

16. See Dennis S. Gouran, "Variables Related to Consensus in Group Discussions of Questions of Policy," *Speech Monographs* 36 (August 1969): 385–91; Thomas J. Knutson, "An Experimental Study of the Effects of Orientation Behavior on Small Group Consensus," *Speech Monographs* 39 (August 1972): 159–65; John A. Kline, "Orientation and Group Consensus," *Central States Speech Journal* 23 (Spring 1972): 44–47.

17. Gouran, pp. 385–91; Knutson, 159–65; Kline, pp. 44–47.

18. Sidney B. Simon, Leland W. Howe, and Howard Kirschenbaum, *Values Clarification: A Handbook of Practical Strategies for Teachers and Students.* (New York: Hart Publishing Company, Inc., 1972), pp. 292-293.

19. J. William Pfeiffer and John E. Jones, eds., *A Handbook of Structured Experiences for Human Relations Training,* vol. 2 (La Jolla, California: University Associates, 1974), pp. 62–67.

8 Understanding Problem Solving in Small Groups

After studying this chapter, you should be able to:

■ Differentiate between group problem solving and group decision making.

■ Formulate a question of fact, value, or policy for a problem-solving discussion.

■ Identify three criteria for a well-phrased policy discussion question.

■ Identify appropriate methods for researching group discussion questions.

■ Compare and contrast descriptive and prescriptive approaches to problem solving in small groups.

■ Identify the four phases of group process.

■ Discuss the three types of group activity tracks.

Understanding Problem Solving in Small Groups

Y ou're either helping solve the problem or you're part of the problem." Whether or not you agree with this statement, you probably do agree that you spend quite a bit of time and energy trying to solve problems. When you think about problem solving, perhaps you first think about the many problems that you have to solve each day, such as: "How can I finish my work by the deadline?" or "How can I pay off my charge card bill?" You may also remember times when you were part of a group or committee responsible for deciding "What can be done to allocate more resources to the library?" or "What should be our campaign platform?" While this chapter may suggest some strategies for solving your personal, everyday problems, it primarily will focus on understanding *group* problem solving.

DECISION MAKING *vs* PROBLEM SOLVING

What is the difference between **decision making** and **problem solving?** While the two processes are related, decision making is really just part of the problem-solving process. When you make a decision, you are choosing from several alternatives. For example, when attempting to decide which college or university to attend, you probably first considered the available choices, your resources, and your educational goals. Based on these factors you made a decision and selected a school. Problem solving, on the other hand, is the process by which you attempt to overcome, work around, or manage an obstacle to achieve a desired goal. Problem solving is a multi-step process during which time decisions must be made. For many people, having a decision to make *seems* to be a problem. But usually making a single decision is part of a larger problem-solving process. Your choice of where to attend college is one decision that contributes to solving the larger problem of what you hope to do to support yourself during your adult life.

Brilhart identifies at least six methods of group decision making.[1]

Decision by Consensus: *As discussed in the last chapter, consensus occurs when all members of the group agree on a particular course of action. This method is time-consuming and difficult to achieve, but group members are usually satisfied with the decision. This method is desirable particularly if the group members must also implement the solution.*

Decision by Majority Vote: *Majority rule is a democratic procedure that can be used efficiently to make swift decisions but that can also result in an unsatisfied minority. The group may sacrifice decision quality and group cohesiveness for efficiency unless time is allotted to discuss the issues.*

Decision by Expert: *An expert decision occurs when a group member or an individual outside the group is invited to make a decision based on his or her expertise. While an expert may well produce a fine decision, the group loses the advantages of greater input and a variety of approaches if it abdicates its decision making to an expert.*

Decision by Leader: *This approach may or may not include group consent. This, too, can be an efficient decision-making method, but without adequate discussion the group may be less satisfied with the decision.*

Random Choice: *This method is not recommended for use by groups who take their decision-making task seriously. Flipping a coin or making a decision by lottery is usually a sign of desperation which negates the need for group discussion.*

Averaging Individual Rankings or Ratings: *While this method can be useful as a discussion starter to see where the group stands on a particular issue, it does not take advantage of group members' various talents and resources.*

All of these methods of group decision making have one element in common: group members are selecting the best choice from the available alternatives. Problem solving, on the other hand, involves a more complicated multi-step process.

THE GROUP PROBLEM-SOLVING PROCESS

A board of directors of a multinational corporation, the fund-raising commit-tee for the local PTA, and a group of students assigned to complete a project for a group communication class all have something in common—they have problems to solve. As we have just discussed, problem solving is the process of seeking a solution to a problem caused by an existing obstacle. But why does a group or committee usually form when there is a problem to be solved? Have you ever been involved in a group problem-solving meeting and thought to yourself, "If I weren't working in this silly group, I could probably be more productive"? As we discussed in Chapter One, despite the frustrations of group work, a small group of people has the potential of arriving at a better quality solution because people who work collectively have a larger pool of information from which to draw. This chapter, designed to help you manage some of your uncertainty about solving problems in small groups, describes how most groups grapple with the task of solving problems.

A group must first *decide on its purpose*. Sometimes a group specifically forms for a given task. For example, the president of the local Jaycees may appoint a committee to organize the Fourth of July celebration. Other groups decide on their specific purpose only after their group is formed. Several neighbors may congregate because they are mutually concerned about improving their neighborhood. They decide on their specific purpose only after they have met. Eventually, they may agree that a problem exists (such as a lack of security or lowered property values) and needs to be solved. If a group decides that its function is to solve a specific problem, it must next *define the problem*. For some groups, defining the problem will be easy; for other groups, agreeing on the exact nature of the problem will take considerable time and debate.

After determining and defining their problem, a group tries to *solve* it. With a group of four or five people, each of whom has different values, attitudes, and beliefs, problem solving can create *uncertainty*. Each person attempts to solve the problem based on his or her individual problem-solving strategy. No two group members may be approaching the problem from the same perspective. Sensing this disparity in approaches, each group member may become uncertain about his or her own strategy while not really understanding anyone else's. It takes patience, understanding, and effective communication to help resolve this uncertainty.

Even though we have made claims for the advantages of group problem solving, you must understand the problem-solving process to achieve these advantages. We've also noted that many groups must overcome the obstacle of defining their purpose. We will explain how formulating a discussion question will help you begin the problem-solving process. We'll discuss three different types of group discussion questions: questions of fact, value, and policy. We will also review basic procedures for gathering information and researching a group discussion question. In the last part of this chapter we will identify the descriptive and prescriptive approaches to problem solving, presenting the descriptive approach in some detail. In Chapter Nine we will elaborate on several prescriptive approaches to problem solving.

FORMULATING DISCUSSION QUESTIONS

Before most scientists begin an experiment or conduct scholarly research, they have some idea of what they are looking for. Some researchers start with a *hypothesis,* a guess based on previous theory and research about what they will find in their search for new knowledge. Other investigators formulate a *research question* that provides a direction for their research. Like scientific research, problem-solving groups seek answers to questions. It makes sense, then, for group members to formulate a question before searching for answers. By identifying a specific question that they must answer, members can reduce some of the initial uncertainty that accompanies their discussion.

Phrasing a discussion question should be done with considerable care. It is an important part of initiating and organizing any group discussion, particularly problem-solving discussions, since the quality and specificity of a question usually determine the quality of the answer. The better a group does in preparing a discussion question, the greater are their chances of having a productive and orderly discussion.

In some group discussions and conference situations, the question has been predetermined. Government committees and juries exemplify such groups. But usually groups are faced with a problem or need and are responsible for formulating a specific question to guide their deliberations. There are basically three types of discussion questions: **questions of fact, questions of value,** and **questions of policy.** To help you determine which type would be most appropriate for your various group discussions, we'll discuss each.

Questions of Fact

In summarizing the responsibilities of the jury during a criminal court case, the judge provides a very specific question of fact to help guide the jury in their discussion. "Your job," instructs the judge, "is to decide whether the defendant is guilty or innocent of the charges against him." A question of fact asks whether something happened or did not happen; its answer determines what is true and what is false.

A question of fact can ultimately be answered by one of two responses— either "yes" or "no" (although, of course, a "yes" or "no" response can be qualified in terms of the probability of its accuracy). The question, "Did the Royals win the World Series in 1980?" is a question of fact; either they did or they did not. "Is the Soviet Union expanding military operations in South America?" Again, the answer is either "yes" or "no," depending on the evidence. But questions of fact often appear deceivingly simple. In trying to answer a question of fact, it is important to define the critical words or phrases in the question. In the preceding question, for example, what is meant by "expanding military operations"? Does this mean building new missile bases or does it mean sending a few military advisors to a Latin American country? By reducing the ambiguity of a question's meaning, a group can save considerable time in agreeing on a final answer.

Another important consideration is whether or not your group should try to investigate a question of fact. You must consider your group's objective. If the group wants to determine what is true and what is false, then formulate a question of fact and define the key words in the question to give it greater focus and clarity. If the group intends to make a less objective value judgment or to suggest solutions to a problem, choose one of the following types of questions.

Questions of Value

A question of value generally produces a lively discussion because it concerns attitudes, beliefs, and values about whether an issue is good or bad, or right or wrong. Answering a question of value is more complicated than simply determining whether an event occurred or did not occur. "Are Democratic presidents better leaders than Republican presidents?" is an example of a question of value. Group members' responses to this question depend on their attitudes toward Democrats and Republicans.

A *value* is also often defined as an enduring conception of good and bad. Our values affect our perceptions of what is right and wrong. A *value is more resistant to change than an attitude or a belief.*

An attitude is a learned predisposition to respond to a person, object, or idea in a favorable, neutral, or unfavorable way. In essence, the attitudes you hold about your world determine whether you like or dislike what you experience and observe. If you have a favorable attitude toward Democrats, it will affect your response to the value question, "Are Democratic presidents better leaders than Republican presidents?"

A *belief* is the way in which you structure what is true and false. Put another way, it is the way you structure reality. If you say you believe in God, that indicates that you have structured your reality to include the concept "God"—that God does exist. If you claim that you do not believe in God, then you have structured your perception of what is true and false so that God is *not* part of your reality.

What are your values? Which of your values have the most influence on your behavior? Because our values are so central to how we respond in our world, it may be difficult for us to quickly come up with a tidy list of our most important values. While we may be able to list things we like and things we do not like *(attitudes),* or what we feel is true and not true *(beliefs),* our values are sometimes difficult to identify as the guiding forces affecting our behavior. Figure 8–1 shows values in the center of the diagram to indicate that they are *central* to our behavior; the next ring, *beliefs,* are influenced by our values. Finally, we hold the attitudes we do because of what we value and what we believe is true and false.

An understanding of the differences between attitudes, beliefs, and values should help you better understand what happens when a group discusses a value question because, as noted previously, we base our response to a value question on our own attitudes, beliefs, and values. You can be in a better position to understand the statements of other group members, as well as your own responses, if you can identify the underlying attitudes, beliefs, and values that influence the responses to a value question.

Questions of Policy

If you participate in a problem-solving group discussion, chances are that the discussion revolves around a question of policy. A policy question is phrased to help the group determine what course of action or policy change should be implemented to solve a problem or reach a decision. "What should be done to improve the quality of education in colleges and universities in the United States?" and "What can the Congress do to reduce America's dependence on foreign oil?" are examples of policy questions. Policy questions can be easily identified because the answer to the question requires a change of policy or procedure. Discussion questions including phrases such as, "What should be done about . . .?" or "What could be done to improve . . .?" are policy questions. Most legislation in the U.S. Senate and House of Representatives is proposed in response to a specific policy question.

A well-worded policy question should imply that there is a specific problem that must be solved. The question "What should be done about UFO's?" is not an appropriate policy question for a group to consider because it does not provide enough direction to a specific problem. Do not confuse a *discussion topic* with a *discussion question.* To say that your group is going to discuss unidentified flying objects indicates that your group has a topic, but it does not suggest that you are trying to solve a problem. The group could rephrase the discussion question to make it more oriented to policy: "What could be done to improve how the government handles and investigates UFO sightings in the U.S.?" The rephrased question more clearly implies that there is a problem in the way UFO sightings are investigated by the government. The latter question provides clearer direction for research and analysis.

Figure 8–1   Interrelationship of Values, Beliefs, and Attitudes

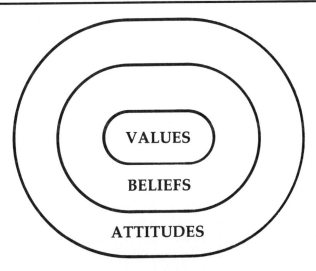

Secondly, *a good policy question is properly limited in scope.* Don't try to tackle a problem that is too complex unless your group has the time and resources to solve the problem. A group of students in a communication class were assigned the tasks of formulating a policy question, discussing it, and then reporting the results of their discussion to the class. The students had three weeks to analyze and suggest possible solutions to the problem they had chosen to investigate. The group decided to consider the question, "What should be done to deal with the federal deficit?" While the question clearly implies a specific problem, it lacked focus and specificity which frustrated the group's efforts. A better discussion question with a more limited perspective, such as, "What should be done to improve the tax base in our community?" would have been more manageable. It is better to consider a simple, clearly worded question which can be analyzed in the time period allotted to your group than to consider a question which would keep the Congress of the United States busy for several months. On the other hand, a group should *not* phrase a policy discussion question in a manner which demands only a "yes" or "no" answer, or which substantially limits the group's options for solutions. Given this criteria, "Should seat belt usage be required by law?" is a less satisfactory policy discussion topic than "What can be done to ensure greater highway safety?"

As a third important criterion, *a policy question should be controversial.* It should be an important issue worthy of discussion. An issue is a question about which individuals disagree. If the group considering the question disagrees about what policy should be formulated to solve the problem, such disagreement does not necessarily indicate that the group should select another issue. If the group were in agreement from the beginning of the discussion about how the problem should be solved, there would be nothing to discuss. As noted in Chapter Seven, conflict, controversy, and disagreement should not always be viewed negatively. The purpose of a group discussion is to consider *all* of the alternatives and to agree on the *best* alternative. Therefore, don't reject a discussion question because other group members may hold contrasting points of view. Your discussion will be more interesting and a better solution will probably emerge if the group examines *all* sides of the issue.

We have talked about three types of discussion questions: fact, value, and policy. It may appear that these three types of discussion questions do not overlap, but, as one researcher has observed, group members must concern themselves with questions of fact and value when considering a question of policy.[2] The research and evidence to be considered must be judged as true or false *(question of fact).* And certainly, group members' attitudes, beliefs, and values *(questions of value)* will influence the decisions that they make regarding policy changes *(questions of policy).* Thus, a discussion question serves a valuable function in providing direction to your group deliberations. Once the group devises a discussion question, however, don't feel that you cannot modify it if it is not exactly what your group should be discussing. Use it as a guide to orient your group's efforts toward its goal.

As issues confront your group, decide whether you are considering a question of fact, value, or policy. Identifying the type of question involved will help you understand the dynamics of the issue under discussion. If you realize that the question, "Should we legalize casino gambling?" involves value judgments, you will be less hasty to condemn group members whose beliefs and values cause them to disagree with you. While the basic disagreement may persist, frustration and defensiveness can yield to understanding and compromise. Remember too that even though a discussion question may be clearly identified as one of fact, value, or policy, it is likely that the discussion will include other types of questions. Once your group has a well-defined problem to discuss, group members should begin researching and analyzing the problem.

CONDUCTING RESEARCH: PREPARING FOR GROUP DISCUSSION

G.I.G.O. (which stands for "garbage in, garbage out") is an abbreviation that computer programmers use to illustrate that if you put the wrong information into a computer system, you will get the wrong information out of the computer. A problem-solving group discussion works much the same way. If the group members have not done their homework and have not researched and analyzed the issues of the discussion, the end product of the discussion will be less than satisfactory. An informed group solution doesn't just happen. It is the product of an informed group membership that has taken the time to gather the facts, examples, statistics, and opinions of others in order to reach the most informed and enlightened decision possible. Effective group discussions and conferences result from group members who come prepared to discuss the issues.

You have probably had lessons in how to gather information, conduct research, and make the best use of the library. But because conducting research for a group discussion is vital to an effective deliberation, we'll review some of the resources and techniques that are available to you when you research and analyze issues facing your group. We will also give you suggestions for conducting your own interviews and surveys.

LIBRARY RESEARCH

By far the majority of questions that lend themselves to group problem solving also lend themselves to library research. Even questions specific to a particular locale or institution can be discussed more intelligently by group members who have used library research to familiarize themselves with analogous situations. For example, even though a group discussing the issue "Should Oak Park Community College become a four-year institution?" might not find any library materials about their specific question, they might discover a recent magazine article that explores the advantages of a community college's offerings over those of a four-year college, or one that investigates another school's solution to the problem now facing Oak Park. Discussion participants exploring an issue of more widespread significance—say, almost any political, social, or ecological problem—will probably discover numerous sources of information in the library that directly pertain to their topic. In short, the library is as invaluable to a participant in a small group discussion as it is to an author of a research paper. The knowledge and skills needed to use the library are *essential* to anyone participating in group problem solving.

While each school's library is unique in some ways, college and university libraries do share common tools and materials. Among these are the card catalog, the stacks, periodical and newspaper indexes and holdings, the reference section, and government documents.

The Card Catalog

A library's *card catalog* usually consists of one or more rows of file cabinets which contain three-by-five-inch cards, at least one for every book and pamphlet housed in the library. Cards are arranged alphabetically by title, author, and subject, so most of the library's holdings are represented more than once in the card catalog.

The subject arrangement will probably be the most valuable to you as you search for information on a specific topic. Before you begin exploring the card catalog, take a few minutes to jot down headings under which you think you might find information related to your subject. Check each of these headings in turn; add to your list any subject headings listed on the library's own "See also" cards, which you may encounter when you locate your headings in the card catalog.

Each card in the catalog contains the vital information about the work to which it refers: the author's name, the title, the publisher, the date of publication, the number of pages, a note or brief outline of the work's contents, and other headings under which the work may be located in the catalog. Most important to the researcher trying to find a work is the call number, marked in the upper left-hand corner of the three-by-five card. Depending on the individual library's classification system, the call number may be either a Dewey Decimal number or a Library of Congress reference number; in either case, it serves as your key to finding the work on the library's shelves, and you should copy it as you prepare a bibliography.

Three-by-five-inch note cards provide an efficient way to record and later assemble your bibliography. Using one card per source, record the author's name, the title of the work, the publisher, the date of publication, and the call number. Unless you are instructed to record this information in a particular way, simply select and consistently adhere to a style which you find logical and easy to use. Remember, you may need to consult these cards several days or even weeks after first recording them; be sure your notations are consistent,

If members of a group first familiarize themselves with their problem through research, often their problem-solving discussion will be more productive.

legible, and meaningful. Once you have as large a bibliography as you desire, you may want to alphabetize the note cards by the authors' last names, thereby enabling you to quickly locate any given card.

Computer Access System

In addition to the card catalog, many libraries now use computer technology to help researchers locate library materials. Instead of going to a card filing system, the user (often with the assistance of a librarian) types in the research topic or author's name at the computer terminal. The bibliographic information needed is displayed and the user can then decide whether a printed copy of the information would be useful. The user may be charged for this service depending on the amount of information received. Ask your librarian if this service is available for your use.

The Stacks

The *stacks* are the library's holdings. A library may be either "open stack," in which *you* find the materials you want, or "closed stack," in which you present bibliographical information to a librarian or assistant, who then gathers your materials *for* you. Even in a "closed stack" library, some sections will probably be open to you. There may be an "open stack" undergraduate library of selected titles, a reference section, periodical and newspaper holdings, and government documents. If any part of the library you are using is "open stack," familiarize yourself with the library's floor plan before searching for materials. Most libraries offer floor plan sketches, tours, or both to their users. Keep in mind that materials in even very small libraries will be shelved according to call numbers, not according to alphabetical order by author or title.

Periodical and Newspaper Indexes and Holdings

Unless you are fortunate enough to remember the name and the date of a periodical or newspaper in which you chanced to read an article on your subject, you will probably need the assistance of one of the numerous periodical and newspaper indexes available. The most commonly used of these is the *Readers' Guide to Periodical Literature,* an index to articles appearing in approximately one hundred popular periodicals. The *Readers' Guide* provides an alphabetical listing of authors, subjects, and titles of articles. As with the card catalog, the most convenient approach for most researchers is to look up the subject. You may consult the same headings under which you looked in the card catalog. A typical *Readers' Guide* entry will include the title of the article, the periodical in which it appears, the volume and date of issue of the periodical, and the page on which the article begins. Abbreviations, used extensively in the *Readers' Guide,* may be deciphered by consulting the key at the front of each volume. Once you understand the symbols used, you can easily transfer the vital information from the *Readers' Guide* to your own bibliography cards.

Similar to the *Readers' Guide* are the *Social Sciences Index* and the *Humanities Index,* once combined as the *International Index to Periodicals* and later as the *Social Sciences and Humanities Index.* These works index scholarly journals and foreign periodicals not covered by the *Readers' Guide.* A number of more specialized periodical indexes also exist; among those you may find useful are the *Education Index,* which contains articles of interest to professional educators, and the *Public Affairs Information Service Bulletin,* which indexes articles relevant to such fields as business and finance, political science, and the social sciences.

Newspapers, like periodicals, are indexed. The most widely used newspaper index is the *New York Times Index.* Most college libraries will have back issues of the *Times* on microfilm, but even in those that do not, the *New York Times Index* will prove useful. Chances are good that a news story covered in the *Times* was also covered in other major national newspapers, at least one of which your library is likely to have. The *London Times,* the *Christian Science Monitor,* and the *Wall Street Journal* are also indexed. The format for all the newspaper indexes is similar to that of the periodical indexes.

Each library has its own system for housing periodical and newspaper holdings. Although very recent editions of newspapers may still be available in the library in their original newspaper form, back issues are usually kept on microfilm. Periodicals are frequently bound and may be shelved either together in one large section of the library or in various areas of the library's stacks, according to periodical subject matter.

The Reference Section

Most libraries have an "open stack" *reference section* which houses the library's encyclopedias; dictionaries; various book, periodical, and newspaper indexes; biographical aids, such as *Who's Who,* the *Dictionary of National Biography, The Directory of American Scholars;* and numerous specialized reference works. Whatever the field of your discussion question, there are likely to be reference works of potential value to you. Reference librarians usually are highly knowledgeable about their specialty and can be quite helpful to you. By all means seek their assistance in locating reference tools relevant to your subject.

Government Documents

Like reference works, government documents are usually found in one section of a library. Although government documents appear formidable to the inexperienced researcher, these holdings may serve as extremely valuable sources of information on many topics. Among the public documents available in most libraries are the *Congressional Record,* which records congressional debates and proceedings; various special reports and hearings of both the United States Senate and the House of Representatives; and bulletins and publications of various executive departments of the United States government. Available indexes that may help you locate relevant government publications include *The Catalogue of the Public Documents of Congress and of All Departments of the Government of the United States* and the *Monthly Catalogue of United States Government Publications.* In addition, libraries usually maintain special card catalogs for their government document holdings. As with books, periodicals, and newspapers, transfer bibliographical information to your own bibliography cards so that you have a permanent record of the sources you discover.

While our discussion here by no means presents an exhaustive explanation of the ways in which a library may assist you in researching a discussion question, it may serve to remind you of sources that you otherwise might not have consulted. Even small college libraries can offer you a wealth of resources if you are willing to explore them.

There are other approaches to researching a problem besides using the library. Some groups may need to administer a survey or conduct interviews to investigate their problems. Let's take a closer look at these two research approaches.

Survey Research

Survey research methods are useful when a group wants to sample several individuals' attitudes, beliefs, values, behavior, or knowledge of a given topic, event, or behavior. The main objective of survey research is to *describe,* rather than to *explain.* Surveys are particularly effective if you are researching a local problem and can find no existing research documenting it. Surveys are also valuable if you want to gauge how people respond to the solution of a given problem. A group interested in solving the problem of an inadequate tax base to support education may decide to survey individual attitudes toward several possible solutions. Before recommending a solution, the group may wish to determine how much of a tax increase would be endorsed by the community. A student and faculty group who decide to study revising the required curriculum may want to survey student attitudes and suggestions for modifying academic requirements. Surveys can also be useful in helping a group understand the seriousness of a problem. A group might also want to gather opinions about the probable causes, effects, and symptoms of the problem.

Bowers and Courtwright suggest that any individual or group that attempts to conduct a survey faces common problems, including: (1) developing clear, unbiased questions, (2) selecting a large enough sample to be representative of the entire population being sampled, (3) writing the questionnaire so that it is clear to the reader and efficient for the interviewer, (4) deciding on whether to interview people face-to-face, over the phone, or by mail, (5) making sure that the design of the questionnaire will answer the questions that need answers, and (6) testing the clarity of the questionnaire by administering a pilot study or mini-survey.[3]

First, the group must determine the objectives of the survey. In essence, what does the group want to know that it doesn't know now? Once the objectives have been determined, the group can then decide how best to ask questions that will give them clear answers. There are two basic types of questions. **Open-ended questions,** like an essay examination question, permit the respondent to answer freely without any choices or constraints. **Closed-ended questions** ask the respondent to choose answers from among several responses supplied by the interviewer. Multiple-choice and true-false questions, and questions which require respondents to rank items of importance or indicate agreement or disagreement are examples of closed-ended questions. It is easier to tabulate the results of closed-ended questions, but open-ended questions provide the flexibility for receiving a wide range of responses. The type of questions your group asks depends on what you want to know.

After developing and organizing questions, you need to decide on a survey method. If you primarily ask open-ended questions, it may be best to conduct face-to-face interviews so that you can probe and clarify respondents' answers. Interviewing requires skills in listening and recording. If you have the time and resources, you may want to mail the questionnaires. Including a self-addressed stamped envelope with each mailed questionnaire helps improve your response rate. You can also stop people in public places on campus or in your community to have them respond to a brief written questionnaire. It is wise, however, to make sure you have permission to do this from the appropriate individual or group who owns the property on which you distribute the questionnaires. In addition, most universities have rules about conducting research on campus. If you are working on a group project for a class, consult your instructor before making final decisions about survey methods and distribution.

Before administering your questionnaire, it is wise to survey a very small sample to make sure your questionnaire is clear. Have your instructor or other members of your class examine its format and wording to see that it makes sense to those who will respond to it. This step could save you time, energy, money, and embarrassment.

Sample Questions

Open-ended question:

1. What are your feelings about increasing property taxes to support local schools and other services?

Closed-ended questions:

1. Are you in favor of raising property taxes?

    _____ yes   _____ no

2. Local property taxes should be increased to support our local school. Circle your response.

    strongly agree   agree   undecided   disagree   strongly disagree

3. Select the statement that most closely reflects your feelings about tax increases.
    a. Property taxes should be increased to support local schools.
    b. Property taxes should not be increased to support local schools.
    c. I am uncertain whether property taxes should be increased to support local schools.
    d. Taxes other than the property tax should be increased to support local schools. (If you selected choice D, indicate which tax(es) should be increased to support local schools.)

4. Rank order the following sources of potential tax revenue increases to support local schools from most desirable (1) to least desirable (6).

Figure 8–1   Interrelationship of Values, Beliefs, and Attitudes

_____	property tax	_____	cigarette tax
_____	sales tax	_____	alcohol tax
_____	gasoline tax	_____	income tax

Once you have designed and tested the questionnaire, you must then make sure that you survey a broad sample of people to justify your conclusions. If, for example, you were interested in determining whether students would support an increase in university tuition by 5%, it would not be wise to ask only graduating seniors. A random sample of the entire population of students at your school would provide the most adequate basis for making a decision about the acceptability of a tuition increase. You would also need to ask _enough_ people to gauge the attitude of your entire student body. If you survey only 20 students out of a student population of 15,000, you have a greater potential for error.

TYPES AND TESTS OF EVIDENCE

Learning to efficiently utilize the library is important, but this skill in itself does not ensure effective research. You must also learn what to look for in the library sources that you discover. Specifically, you must know something about the various kinds of evidence and must be able to evaluate their usefulness. Four types of evidence are available: facts, examples, opinions, and statistics.

Facts

We define a _fact_ as any statement proven to be true. A fact cannot be a prediction about the future, as such a statement is not verifiable; it must be a report of something that has already happened or that is happening. "It will rain tomorrow" cannot be a fact because there is no way the statement can be verified. But, "The weather forecaster predicts rain" may be a fact if the weather forecaster has indeed made such a prediction; the accuracy of the forecast is irrelevant to the question of whether the statement is a fact. Ask yourself these questions to determine the factuality of a statement:

1. Is it true?
2. Is the source reliable?
3. Are there contrary facts?

Examples

An *example* is an illustration—a particular case or incident—and is of greatest value when used to dramatize and emphasize a fact. An example may be real or hypothetical. A *real example* may also be labeled a fact; it actually exists or has happened. A *hypothetical example* is of little use in *proving* a point but it can add color and interest to, or help explicate an otherwise dry or difficult factual presentation. Apply these tests to examples:

1. Is it typical?
2. Is it significant?
3. Are there contrary examples?

Opinions

The label *opinion* refers to any quoted comment. Those opinions most valuable as evidence are those made by an unbiased authority who bases opinion on fact. Like examples, opinions can enhance interest and help dramatize a point. Like examples, opinions too are most effective as proof when they are used in conjunction with facts or statistics. The following questions will help you determine the usefulness of opinions:

1. Is the source reliable?
2. Is the source an expert in the field?
3. Is the source free from bias?
4. Is the opinion consistent with other statements made by the same source?
5. Is the opinion characteristic of opinions held by other experts in the field?

Statistics

Because it is impractical or even impossible to present dozens of facts or examples in presentation that must occur within a given time limit, people often rely on statistics to express such quantities. A *statistic* is simply a number: 10,000 people, 132 reported cases of child abuse, 57 Western nations. All of these are statistics and may provide firm support for an important point. Pay special attention, though, to the tests of statistics that we list below. Statistics are probably the most frequently misgathered and misinterpreted type of evidence. Use these criteria for judging the quality of your statistics:

1. Is the source reliable?
2. Is the source unbiased?
3. Are the figures recent? Do they apply to the time period in question?
4. How were the statistics drawn? If from a sample, is the sample representative of the total population? Is the sample of adequate size?

5.   Does the statistic actually measure what it is supposed to measure?
6.   Are there contrary statistics?

Using Evidence Effectively

Once you have located and collected your evidence, you should keep in mind a couple of guidelines for applying it effectively. First, never take evidence out of context. Even if a statement seems to be exactly the evidence you need, don't use it if the next sentence says something like, "However, this idea has recently been proved false." Second, try to gather and utilize evidence from as great a variety of sources as possible. And finally, use many different types of evidence to support a point.

Having been given some direction in using the library and some guidelines for securing, evaluating, and applying evidence, you should now be able to understand the various aspects of a given discussion question and to gather needed support for points you may want to make during a problem-solving discussion. Such an informed discussion participant is far better able to help the group reach a rational, informed decision than is the group member who only relies on opinions.

TWO APPROACHES TO GROUP PROBLEM SOLVING

We have stressed that problem-solving groups must identify a clear point of departure. Groups need a statement of why they exist and what their problem is. Phrasing the problem as a policy-oriented discussion question is a very useful way for a group to approach its problem-solving task.

Let's consider two distinct approaches to problem solving, identified by Fisher as *descriptive* and *prescriptive*. According to Fisher:

> [A descriptive problem-solving approach] attempts to document not how groups should make decisions but how they do make decisions. As its name implies, a descriptive approach involves observing actual groups interacting for the purpose of social decision making. The descriptive method seeks to describe the interactive process that is common to those groups.[4]

A **descriptive problem-solving approach,** then, does not give you numerous guidelines and specific techniques for solving problems in groups; rather, it outlines how most groups go about solving problems. Fisher identifies two assumptions about the descriptive approach to group problem solving: (1) There is a "natural" or normal process of group problem solving, and (2) Groups will follow a normal problem-solving approach unless some external authority interferes with the group's freedom to solve its problem (e.g., an agenda is handed to the group, or a strong-willed leader within the group attempts to dictate how the group should approach the task at hand.)[5]

A **prescriptive problem-solving approach** is based on a different set of assumptions. A prescriptive approach uses a specific, predetermined agenda to help the group solve problems efficiently and effectively. As summarized by Fisher:

> [A prescriptive approach] provides guidelines, a road map, to assist the group in achieving consensus. In one way, such a prescriptive approach is based on an assumed "ideal" process.[6]

Fisher has also noted two assumptions which underlie the prescriptive approach to problem solving: (1) Group members are consistently rational, and (2) The prescribed agenda will result in an improved quality decision.[7] The key difference between the descriptive problem-solving approach and the prescriptive approach is that *the descriptive approach helps the group understand how groups usually solve problems, while the prescriptive approach offers specific suggestions for the development of a group agenda.*

Some scholars advocate the descriptive approach, pointing out that it does not constrain a group from its normal or natural process of solving a problem. Others contend that the prescriptive approach has the advantage of giving the group needed structure for solving problems. Each approach has unique advantages. We feel that it is useful both to understand how groups solve problems and to be acquainted with some techniques of organizing an agenda for problem-solving discussions. We have devoted the remainder of this chapter to an overview of the descriptive approach to problem solving in small groups. In Chapter Nine we will present several prescriptive approaches to group problem solving.

THE DESCRIPTIVE APPROACH

"Don't worry, Mom, I'm just going through a phase." Think back. Does this sound like something you may have said at one time? Apparently you were trying to alleviate Mom's concern by assuring her that your behavior was not at all uncommon and that it surely must pass in time. Implicit here is an assumption that we, as individuals, pass through several identifiable developmental stages, each of which leaves us at the door of the next. Problem-solving groups, like individuals, go through several identifiable stages in their development. With an understanding of these stages, you can learn to communicate in ways which expedite a group's passage from one stage to the next.

Several researchers have attempted to identify the phases of a problem-solving group. They have observed and recorded who speaks to whom and they have categorized the types of comments group members exchange. Even though the researchers have used various labels to describe these phases, they have reached similar conclusions. Table 8–1 illustrates the general pattern.

Table 8-1   Summary of Literature on Group Phases

	Phase 1	Phase 2	Phase 3	Phase 4
Thelen and Dickerman (1949)	Forming	Conflict	Harmony	Productivity
Bennis and Shepard (1956, 1961)	Dependence	Inter-dependence	Focused Work	Productivity
Tuckman (1965)	Forming	Storming	Norming	Performing
Fisher (1970, 1974)	Orientation	Conflict	Emergence	Reinforcement
Bales and Strodbeck (1951)	Orientation		Evaluation	Control
Schutz (1958)	Inclusion		Control	Affection

Of the various studies on developmental phases of groups, the most significant for the area of small group communication is the research of B. Aubrey Fisher who focused his attention primarily on *what was said* throughout the phasic development of his test groups. Therefore, we have adopted his terminology (**orientation, conflict, emergence,** and **reinforcement**) here. See Table 8-1 to compare these terms to the other researchers' terms.[8]

Phase One: Orientation

In the first phase of small group interaction "group members break the ice and begin to establish a common basis for functioning."[9] Earlier we mentioned the uncertainty that most of us feel when we join a new group. Our speech communication with one another during this phase tends to be oriented toward getting to know one another, sharing our backgrounds, and tentatively approaching the group's task. We are not likely to say anything that might prompt the rest of the group to reject us, such as aggressively asserting our point of view about the group's task. Fisher noted in his studies that "more ambiguous comments . . . are contained in phase one than in any other phase except the third, which is also characterized by ambiguity."[10]

If we examine all of the research on the *orientation phase,* we see that communication is directed at orienting ourselves toward (1) each other, and (2) the group's task (which can also be said about the other phases). What sets this phase apart from the others is *the degree to which the social dimension is emphasized and the tentative, careful way in which the task dimension is approached.*

Even the most efficient, task-motivated group will spend some time socializing and getting acquainted. Do not underestimate the importance of this type of interaction. Interpersonal trust—an essential ingredient for an effective working group—does not happen all at once. We begin slowly, with "small talk," to determine whether it is "safe" to move on to deeper levels of interaction. The orientation phase, then, triggers the development of trust and group cohesiveness which are so important for the group's survival in the second phase, *conflict.*

Phase Two: Conflict

During the first phase of orientation, group members begin to form opinions about their own position in the group and about the group's task. By the second phase they start asserting these opinions. They have "tested the water" in the first phase and now they are ready to jump in. On the process, or social level, this is a period in which individuals compete for status in the group. As we shall discuss in Chapter Ten, two or more potential group leaders may emerge with the support for each dividing the group into "camps." In a decision-making or problem-solving group this division is reflected along the task dimension as well. During the first phase, members were hesitant to speak about the group's task; but, in the second phase they begin to assert their individuality and respond favorably or unfavorably to the direction that the group's task proposals are taking. With such polarization of attitudes, disagreement or conflict naturally results.[11]

Communication during this *conflict stage* is characterized by persuasive attempts at changing others' opinions and reinforcing one's own position. Some group participants relish the idea of a good argument as an activity which allows them to sharpen intellectual skills in a spirit of healthy competition. Others have a very different point of view and see conflict as something to avoid at all cost. But avoiding conflict means avoiding issues which are relevant and even crucial to the group's success. Just as individuals need to assert their own points of view, so do groups need to investigate thoroughly all relevant alternatives in order to select the best solutions. A fuller discussion of the role of conflict in group communication appears in Chapter Seven.

The conflict phase is necessary at both the task and the process dimensions of small group communication. Through conflict, we begin to clearly identify the task issues which confront the group. It is also through conflict that we begin to clarify our own and others' roles. This clarification leads toward greater predictability (less uncertainty) and the establishment of group norms.

Phase Three: Emergence

In phase three we can observe new patterns of communication which indicate the *emergence* of the group from its conflict phase. If the group is going to function as a cohesive unit with any kind of group consensus, the conflict of phase two must first be resolved. Conflict, then, is still a part of phase three. But what sets the *emergence phase* apart from the preceding conflict phase is *a change in the way in which we deal with conflict.* This shift is most apparent in the *reappearance of ambiguity* in our task-related statements.

Think of a time when a group adopted a course of action which, at first, you had opposed. Did you support the group decision in the end? If so, you had to change your attitude along the way. How did that take place? Can you identify a point in time when you suddenly turned against your former position? Probably not. The change was most likely gradual, was characterized by creeping ambivalence, and took place during the third phase of group interaction. If we have argued strongly for a position in phase two, it is difficult to let go of that position all at once. Our egos simply won't stand for it. At the same time, we may feel a need to pull the group back together. We sense that "a house divided against itself cannot stand" and so we approach that division and try to bring the group back together. Task and process dimensions are interwoven at this stage. While there is divisiveness within the group, there is also clarity. Leadership patterns and group roles have been established. The issues and problems confronting the group have been identified. The need to settle differences and reach consensus has become apparent. Here *metadiscussion*—talking about the status of the group, acknowledging differences and the need for consensus—may be a turning point. At other times, the change may occur more subtly as proponents of various positions become less tenacious in their arguments. However the change takes place and ambiguity seems to be the means by which we can comfortably shift our positions toward group consensus.

Fisher noted that ambiguity in the third phase functions very differently from the way it does in the first phase. During the orientation phase, ambiguity serves as a tentative (and, therefore, safe) expression of attitudes.

> This explanation of ambiguity is not appropriate to the third phase . . . ; groups are no longer searching for attitude direction. This direction was plotted in the orientation phase and debated in the conflict phase. In the third phase, task direction is no longer an issue. . . . Ambiguity . . . functions in the third phase as a form of modified dissent. That is, the group members proceed to change their attitudes from disfavor to favor of the decision proposals through the mediation of ambiguity."[12]

In the emergence phase, then, we see the group settling on norms and moving toward consensus via ambiguous statements which gradually modify the dissenting positions. Such ambiguous statements might take the form of a qualifier or reservation to the previous position: "I still would like to see our company merge with the Elector Electronics Corporation, but maybe we could consider a merger later in the year. Such a merger may be more appropriate next fall." Such a statement allows us to "save face" while still permitting consensus to emerge.

Phase Four: Reinforcement

A spirit of unity characterizes the final phase of group interaction. In the preceding three phases the group has struggled through getting acquainted, building cohesiveness, expressing individuality, competing for status, and arguing over issues. The group eventually emerges from all of those struggles with a sense of direction, consensus of opinion, and a feeling of group identity. Having survived the struggles, it's little wonder that the fourth phase is characterized by an expression of positive feelings toward the group and the group's decisions. Finally, there's a genuine sense of accomplishment!

Reinforcement predominates as the pattern of communication:

> Jim: I may have been against it at first, but I've finally seen the light. We're going in the right direction now.
>
> Marilyn: Yes, but don't shortchange your contribution, Jim. If you hadn't opposed it so vehemently, we never would have developed the idea so fully. *(Laughter, backslapping, etc.)*

Fisher noted that ambiguous and unfavorable comments have all but disappeared in the fourth phase, being replaced by uniformly favorable comments and reinforcement of favorable comments. This is the time when all of the hassle of group decision making and problem solving seems worthwhile. It is a time when the group is at its most cohesive, individual satisfaction and the sense of achievement is high, and uncertainty is at an all-time low. Furthermore, it is a time to remember when we find ourselves in a new group with new problems.

A group in its initial stages of development is very different from that same group in its final phase. This metamorphosis can be followed and charted by carefully observing the communicative behavior of group members. Groups, like individuals, struggle through childhood and adolescence on their way to maturity.

The Phase Nature of Group Process

Fisher's research suggests a clear, coherent progression of steps which represent the way groups tend to solve problems. It would seem that one phase neatly and consistently follows another phase. Poole, however, suggests that the group problem-solving process, like any complex process, does not flow from one phase to the next with clear-cut divisions.[13] Rather than describing group decision making as a sequence of four distinct stages, Poole builds upon Fisher's research by suggesting that groups engage in three basic types of **activity tracks** that do not necessarily follow a logical step-by-step pattern. The three types of activities that Poole believes best describe group interaction are: (1) **task process activities,** (2) **relational activities,** and (3) **topical focus.**[14]

Let's take a closer look at each activity. *Task process activities* are "those activities the group enacts to manage its task,"[15] such as analyzing the problem, becoming oriented to the issues of the problem, establishing criteria, and evaluating the various solutions proposed. Answering such questions as, "What's the problem here?" "How can we better understand the problem?" and "How effective will our solution be?" are examples of task process activities.

Verbal or nonverbal communication that indicates who is liked and disliked can be categorized as *relational activity.* Relational activities include "those activities that reflect or manage relationships among group members as these relate to the group's work."[16] As we noted in Chapter Four, communication has both a task and a relationship dimension. The relational activities of group members deal with those communication behaviors that sustain or damage the quality of interpersonal relationships among group members. Criticism, conflict, praise, and encouragement give group members some feeling about their relationships with one another. Relational activities affect the group's working climate.

The third type of activity, *topic focus,* deals with the "general themes, major issues or arguments of concern to the group at a given point in the discussion."[17] Bormann and other researchers have noted that groups often focus their conversation on a given theme or topic.[18] Such themes or topics serve as the actual agenda for the group; they are what the group talks about. This third type of activity, then, deals with major topics that do not relate to the specific task of the group or to the member relationships. These three activity "tracks," as Poole calls them, do not all develop at the same rate or according to the same pattern. Some groups may spend a considerable portion of their time being concerned with group relationships before discussing the task in great detail. On the other hand, a very task-oriented group would devote considerable energy to completing the task, thereby letting the relationship activity play a minor role at various stages of the group's deliberations. A group switches activity tracks at various **breakpoints** which occur as the group switches topics, adjourns, or schedules a planning period. Another type of breakpoint, called a delay, occurs because of a conflict or an inability to reach consensus. The group is not sure how to proceed. Whereas the group may expect and schedule some normal breakpoints, delays are usually unscheduled. Poole notes, "depending on the nature of the delay and the mood of the group, [a] breakpoint can signal the start of a difficulty or a highly creative period."[19] A disruption is the third type of breakpoint which results from a major conflict or a realization that the group may not be effective enough to complete the task. A major disruption of the group's activity calls for flexibility while the uncertainty of the disruption is managed.

We include a discussion of Poole's analysis of group phases and group activity to emphasize the process nature of group communication. While several researchers have documented distinct chronological phases in a group's decision-making efforts, realize that the group's communication can also be described by the three activities of task process, relational activity, and topical focus. A descriptive approach to group communication can help you better understand and explain why certain types of statements are made in groups. With an understanding of the process, you should be in a better position to evaluate and improve your participation in group meetings.

In the next chapter we will present several prescriptive formats which are designed to help you organize group problem solving and decision making.

UNDERSTANDING PROBLEM SOLVING IN SMALL GROUPS: PUTTING PRINCIPLE INTO PRACTICE

The assumption underlying this chapter is that if you can understand how groups go about the task of solving problems, you will be better able to manage the problem-solving process in small groups. The following suggestions should help you apply the concepts presented in this chapter.

Formulating Discussion Questions

- Formulate a discussion question that focuses and directs your group deliberations.
- Formulate a question of fact if your group is trying to decide whether something is true or false, occurred or did not occur.
- Formulate a question of value if your group is trying to decide whether one idea or approach to an issue is better than another approach.
- Formulate a question of policy if your group is trying to develop a solution to a problem.

Conducting Research

- Consult the library (card catalog, stacks, periodical and newspaper indexes, reference section, government documents) to gather appropriate information to investigate your discussion question.
- Design a questionnaire to survey opinions if public acceptance of a solution is important to your group.
- Apply the various tests of evidence noted in this chapter when evaluating the evidence you have gathered.

Two Approaches to Group Problem Solving

- Adopt a descriptive approach to group problem solving if you understand the phases that a group goes through to reach a solution to a problem.
- Adopt a prescriptive approach to problem solving if your group needs the structure that a problem-solving agenda provides.

- Do not be overly concerned when your group takes time to orient itself to the problem-solving process. It is a normal part of group problem solving.
- Expect to experience some conflict and differences of opinions after the group has clarified its task and has passed through the orientation phase of group problem solving.
- Even though conflict may appear to impede the group's efforts to solve the problem, expect a decision to emerge after a thorough discussion and analysis of the issues.
- Do not overlook the importance of the reinforcement phase of group problem solving. Group members deserve to experience a sense of accomplishment after the group decision has emerged.

PRACTICE

Identifying Questions of Fact, Value, and Policy

Read the following narrative, then identify and phrase the following questions: (1) the main discussion question (and label it as fact, value, or policy), (2) at least one question of fact, and (3) at least one question of value.

> A new liberal divorce law has come up for discussion in the state senate. Senator Smith, who introduced the bill, has lobbied hard for its passage because she has found evidence to suggest that complications in the current law do not serve as a deterrent to divorce, but only result in lengthy delays and higher fees for divorce lawyers. Senator Williams also supports the new law; he was recently divorced and has experienced much frustration and aggravation in the process. Senator Schwartz, on the other hand, is happily married and quite conservative; he leads the opposition to the new law.

Hurricane Preparedness Case

Although you have idly watched local weathermen track Hurricane Bruce's destructive course through the Caribbean for several days, you have not really given any serious thought to the possibility that the number 3-rated storm might directly affect your coastal city. But at about 7 o'clock this morning the storm suddenly veered northward, putting it on course for a direct hit. Now the National Hurricane Center in Miami has posted a Hurricane Warning for your community. Forecasters are predicting landfall in approximately 9 to 12 hours. Having taken no advance precautions, you are stunned by the amount of work you now have to do to secure your three-bedroom suburban home, which is about ¼ mile from the beach. You have enough food in the house for two days. You also have a transistor radio with one weak battery and one candle. You have no other hurricane supplies, nor have you taken any hurricane precautions. Your task is to rank order the following items in terms of their importance for ensuring your survival and the safety of your property. Place number *1* by the first thing you should do, *2* by the second, and so on through number *13*. Please work individually on this task.

Fill your car with gas   ———

Trim your bushes and trees   ———

Fill your bathtub with water   ———

Construct hurricane shutters for your windows   ———

Buy enough food for a week   ———

Buy batteries and candles   ———

Bring in patio furniture from outside   ———

Buy dry ice   ———

Invite friends over for a Hurricane Party   ———

Drain your swimming pool   ———

Listen to TV and radio for further bulletins
before doing anything   ———

Make sure you have an evacuation plan   ———

Stock up on charcoal and charcoal lighter for
your barbecue grill   ———

Description of Group Process

Attend a public meeting such as a school board meeting, city council, or other public meeting in which problems are discussed and solutions are recommended. Prepare a written descriptive analysis of the meeting by attempting to identify phases in the group's discussions. Also, try to identify examples of the three activity tracks discussed in this chapter (task process, relational, topical). In addition, provide examples of breakpoints in the group discussion.

Notes

1. John K. Brilhart, *Effective Group Discussion* (Dubuque, Iowa: Wm. C. Brown Company Publishers, 1982), pp. 167-172.

2. Dennis S. Gouran, *Discussion: The Process of Group Decision-Making* (New York: Harper & Row, Publishers, Inc., 1974), p. 72.

3. John Wait Bowers and John Courtwright (Glenview, Ill.: Scott, Foresman and Co.)

4. B. Aubrey Fisher, *Small Group Decision Making: Communication and the Group Process,* 2nd ed. (New York: McGraw-Hill Book Company, 1980), p. 132.

5. Ibid.

6. Ibid., p. 130.

7. Ibid., pp. 130–31.

8. Stewart L. Tubbs and Sylvia Moss, *Interpersonal Communication* (New York: Random House, Inc., 1978), p. 266.

9. Ibid., p. 265.
10. B. Aubrey Fisher, "Decision Emergence: Phases in Group Decision-Making," *Speech Monographs* 37 (1970): 60.
11. Ibid., p. 61.
12. Ibid., p. 63.
13. Marshall Scott Poole, "Decision Development in Small Groups, III: A Multiple Sequence Model of Group Decision Development," *Communication Monographs,* Vol. 50 (December 1983): 321–341.
14. Ibid., p. 326.
15. Ibid.
16. Ibid.
17. Ibid.
18. See: Ernest G. Bormann, *Discussion and Group Methods* (New York: Harper & Row, Publishers, 1975).
19. Poole, "Decision Development," p. 330.

9 Small Group Problem-Solving Techniques

After studying this chapter, you should be able to:

■ Use the reflective-thinking problem-solving format in a small group discussion.

■ Apply the rules of brainstorming to a problem-solving group discussion.

■ Apply the ideal solution problem-solving method to a group discussion.

■ Apply the single question problem-solving approach to a group discussion.

■ Determine when participative decision-making methods such as buzz groups, nominal group technique, risk technique, or quality control circles will be useful.

■ Determine which problem-solving approach is most suitable for any given problem-solving group discussion.

Small Group Problem-Solving Techniques

Imagine that you have been appointed chairperson of a committee to help solve the problem of the deteriorating quality of education in your community. Students' scores on standardized achievement tests have declined in the past two years. The school administrators complain that they just do not have the funds to develop new programs or to increase the size of the faculty. It is the task of your committee to develop a plan to deal with the problem. In the last chapter we introduced the concepts of descriptive and prescriptive approaches to problem solving. As committee chairperson, you realize you could adopt a descriptive problem-solving approach by cluing in the other group members on some of the processes that groups experience when trying to solve a problem. Although giving your committee an understanding of the process may be beneficial, you feel you need to provide more structure to help the group efficiently organize its approach to solving the problem.

In this chapter we will identify some *prescriptive approaches* to problem solving that may help you organize a group's problem-solving attempts. We do not intend to convince you that there is one *best* way to solve problems in groups. Each group is unique. Each group member is unique. There is no single prescriptive problem-solving formula that always works. But this chapter will give you several suggestions for solving problems in groups, one of which should meet your specific group's need at any given time.

Research suggests that some method of group problem solving is better than no method at all.[1] Groups need some structure because of their relatively short attention span. In separate studies two researchers found that groups shift topics about once a minute.[2] As we noted in the last chapter, Poole argues that groups consider task process, relational concerns, and topical shifts with varying degrees of attention.[3] Thus, group members benefit from an agenda that helps reduce uncertainty by keeping the discussion focused on the group's task.

First, we will talk about the most traditional problem-solving method— **reflective thinking.** Second, we will present a creative problem-solving technique called **brainstorming.** This method may help you come up with ideas when the group seems to have run out of imagination. Third, we will discuss two problem-solving approaches based on answering questions: the **single-question format** and the **ideal-solution method.** These two formats help keep the group's energy focused on the processes necessary to solve the problem. Finally, we will discuss techniques for organizing group discussion which encourage all group members to participate.

In trying to make small group communication theory practical and useful, we will not only describe these four problem-solving approaches, but we will also give you some specific suggestions for applying the principles to your group discussions. Even though we will describe several approaches to problem solving, your group will not necessarily use any one of these methods exclusively. You may find several of these methods useful at various phases of the problem-solving process.

A TRADITIONAL APPROACH TO PROBLEM SOLVING: REFLECTIVE THINKING

In 1910 philosopher and educator John Dewey wrote a book called *How We Think.* He identified the steps most people follow to systematically solve a problem. In describing his problem-solving format, Dewey did not originally have a small group in mind.[4] But the format, called **reflective thinking,** has since been used by many groups as a way to provide structure and form for the problem-solving process. Some researchers and numerous group communication textbooks recommend the reflective-thinking format as a useful and productive way to organize group problem solving. However, many contemporary group communication theorists feel that it serves a more useful purpose as a description of the way *some* people solve problems rather than as an ideal way for *all* groups to solve problems. Dewey's reflective-thinking format consists of five steps.

Step One: Identify and Define the Problem

A group first has to recognize that a problem exists. This step may be a group's biggest obstacle. Before the PTA Fund-Raising Committee can effectively consider suggestions for raising money, the committee members must recognize that a specific need exists. Many groups don't bother to verbalize what problem is facing them; each person would rather begin by offering solutions to remedy his or her perception of the problem. But it is essential that the group clearly and succinctly agree on the problem facing it. The problem should be carefully limited so that all group members know its scope and size. After the members identify and limit the problem, they should define key terms so that they have a common understanding of the problem. The terms should be defined in context so that they are meaningful in light of the problem under consideration. For example, one student group recently decided to tackle the problem of solving what they perceived as student apathy on campus. They phrased their problem as a question: "What can be done to alleviate student apathy on campus?" They had identified a problem, but they soon discovered that they needed to decide what they meant by the term *apathy*. Does it mean a low student attendance at home football games? Or does it mean a sparse showing of students at the recent fund-raising activity, "Hit Your Professor with a Pie"? After a few additional efforts to define the key word, they decided to limit their problem area to low attendance at events sponsored by the student activities committee. Having a clearer focus on their problem, they were ready to continue with the problem-solving process. Consider the following questions when attempting to identify and define a problem for group deliberations:

1. What is the specific problem that we are concerned about?
2. Is the question we are trying to answer clear?
3. What terms, concepts, or ideas do we need to define?
4. Who is harmed by the problem?
5. When do the harmful effects of the problem occur?

Step Two: Analyze the Problem

During the analysis phase of group problem solving, group members need to research and investigate the problem. In analyzing the problem, a group may wish to consider the following questions:

1. What is the history of the problem? How long has the problem existed?
2. How serious is the problem?
3. What are the causes of the problem?
4. What are the effects of the problem?
5. What are the symptoms of the problem?
6. What methods do we already have for dealing with the problem?
7. What are the limitations of those methods?
8. How much freedom do we have in gathering information and attempting to solve the problem?
9. What are the obstacles that keep us from achieving our goal?
10. Can the problem be divided into subproblems for definition and analysis?

For the group to analyze the problem effectively, members need to acquaint themselves with the basic techniques for conducting research presented in Chapter Eight.

Another phase in the analysis step of the reflective-thinking process is to formulate criteria for an acceptable solution. **Criteria** are standards or goals that a good solution must meet. Formulating such criteria may prevent future uncertainties and misunderstandings and may help your group sort through the proposed solutions to arrive at the best possible one. Many groups are tempted to begin listing solutions before the problem has been properly analyzed or before adequate criteria have been identified. But if you adhere to the reflective-thinking format, you will identify the criteria before offering possible solutions. In listing criteria for a solution, you may wish to consider the following questions:

1. What philosophy should we adopt with respect to solving the problem?
2. What are the minimum requirements of an acceptable solution?
3. Which criteria are the most important?
4. How should we use the criteria to evaluate the suggested solutions?

Sample criteria for a solution may include the following:

1. The solution should be inexpensive.
2. The solution should be implemented as soon as possible.
3. The solution should be agreed on by all of the group members.

Step Three: Suggest Possible Solutions

After the group has analyzed the problem and selected criteria for a solution, the group should begin to list possible solutions. State solutions in tentative, hypothetical terms. Many groups brainstorm for solutions. *Brainstorming* simply involves suggesting many possible solutions without evaluating them. Brainstorming will be discussed in more detail in the next section of this chapter.

Step Four: Suggest the Best Solution(s)

After the group has compiled a list of possible solutions to the problem, the group should be ready to select the *best* solution. Group members should refer to the criteria that they proposed during the analysis stage of their discussion and should consider each of the tentative solutions in light of these criteria. The group should decide which of the proposed solutions best meets the criteria that the group has formulated. Often a group decides that a combination of several solutions is the best method for dealing with the problem. The following questions may be helpful in analyzing the proposed solutions:

1. What would be the long-term and short-term effects if this solution were adopted?

2. Would the solution really solve the problem?
3. Are there any disadvantages to the solution? Do the disadvantages out-weigh the advantages?
4. Does the solution conform to the criteria formulated by the group?
5. Should the group modify the criteria?

If group members agree, the criteria for a best solution may need to be changed or modified.[5]

Step Five: Test and Implement the Solution

Group members should be confident that the proposed solution is valid (i.e., will solve the problem). After the group has selected the best solution, the final step is to determine how it can be put into effect. You may wish to consider the following questions:

1. How can the group get public approval and support for their proposed solution?
2. What are some of the specific steps necessary to implement the solution?
3. How can we evaluate the success of our problem-solving efforts?

In many groups, someone else may be responsible for implementing the solution. If this is the case, those group members who selected the solution should clearly communicate why they selected it to the group members who will put the solution into practice. If they can demonstrate that the group went through an orderly process to solve the problem, they can usually convince the others that their solution is valid.

Applying Reflective Thinking

The rationale behind Dewey's steps of reflective thinking is that groups work best when the discussion is an organized process, as opposed to an unorganized, random discussion of the issues. Remember that *reflective thinking should be used as a guide, not as an exact formula for solving every problem.* As we noted earlier, several group communication researchers have discovered that groups do not necessarily solve problems in a neat, linear, step-by-step process.[6] Groups go through several phases of growth and development as its members interact.[7] The steps of reflective thinking are most useful in helping a group understand the phases of problem solving. As Bormann has noted, "Difficulties arise when [group] participants demand rationality from a group throughout its deliberations."[8] One researcher suggests that reflective thinking may work best if there is a limited range of possible solutions or courses of action to be taken.[9] To add flexibility to the reflective-thinking steps, the group may return to an earlier problem-solving step to help clarify

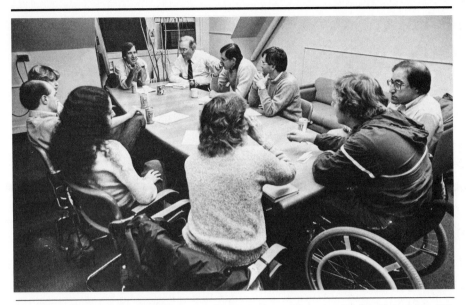

By using a problem-solving agenda to structure a meeting, a group can maintain its focus and will ultimately be more successful in achieving its goal.

the discussion. For example, after spending time researching and analyzing the problem, the group may decide to define the problem a little differently than they had previously. Or perhaps, after trying to apply the criteria to select the best solution, the group may decide that they need to revise the criteria. In short, the group's goal should not be to follow prescriptively the steps of reflective thinking; rather, *the group's goal should be to solve the problem.* In trying to apply the reflective-thinking process to group problem solving, consider the suggestions listed below.

1. *Be sure to clearly identify the problem you're trying to solve.* Make sure that you are not just discussing a topic. For example, one group decided to discuss the quality of the justice system in the United States. They selected a topic area, but they did not identify a problem. They should have focused clearly on a specific problem, such as "How can we improve the quality of the judicial system in the United States?" or "What should be done to improve the education and training of lawyers in the United States?"

2. *Phrase the problem as a question to help guide your group's discussion.* Identifying your group's problem as a question adds focus and direction to your deliberations. When formulating a problem-solving discussion question, keep in mind the guidelines we've discussed in Chapter Eight.

3. *Don't be too eager to start suggesting solutions until you have analyzed the problem.* Many group communication researchers agree that until your group has researched the problem, you may not have enough information and specific facts to reach the best solution.[10] You will be tempted to think of solutions to your problem almost as soon as you have identified it. By deferring the search for a solution, you will gain a greater understanding of the causes, effects, and symptoms of the problem.

4. *In the definition and analysis steps of reflective thinking, don't confuse the causes of the problem with the symptoms of the problem.* When a patient tells a doctor that he has a fever and a headache, the doctor realizes that those feelings of ill health are symptoms and not necessarily causes of the patient's discomfort. The cause may be a cold or flu virus, or a number of other things. The doctor tries to identify the cause of the symptoms by running tests and analyzing the patient's past medical history. In other words, the doctor needs to define, analyze, and solve a problem. You should try to clarify the differences between the causes and the symptoms (effects) of the problem. Perhaps your only goal is to alleviate the symptoms. However, you should be able to verbalize the differences between the causes and symptoms so you can better understand what your group is trying to accomplish.

5. *Constantly evaluate the group's problem-solving method.* When we took our first group discussion course, the only problem-solving method suggested to the class was reflective thinking. After attending many lectures and reading many pages about the value of reflective thinking as a problem-solving tool, we spent several weeks preparing for a group presentation. In all of our discussions we were expected to carefully follow the steps in the reflective-thinking process. Some communication theorists suggest, however, that for certain types of problems, there are alternative problem-solving methods that work just as well, if not better, than reflective thinking. If the main problem confronting the group is generating ideas, brainstorming may be a better format. In the remaining portion of this chapter we will discuss some of these other problem-solving strategies.

A CREATIVE APPROACH TO PROBLEM SOLVING: BRAINSTORMING

Imagine that your employer assigns you to a task force to try to increase the productivity of your small manufacturing company. Phrased as a question, the problem is: "What can be done to increase efficiency and productivity for our company?" Your group is supposed to come up with ideas to help solve the problem. Assume that your boss has clearly identified the problem for the group and has provided you with several documents analyzing the problem in some detail. Your group may decide that the reflective-thinking problem-solving format, which focuses on identifying and analyzing the problem, may not be the best process to follow. Your group needs innovative ideas and creative, original solutions. Perhaps your group could benefit by applying a few simple rules of brainstorming.

Brainstorming is a problem-solving approach designed to help a group generate several creative solutions to a problem. The brainstorming technique was first developed by Alex Osborn, an advertising executive who felt a need to develop a creative problem-solving technique that would rule out evaluating and criticizing ideas and focus instead on developing solutions that were imaginative and innovative.[11] The brainstorming technique has been employed by businesses, committees, and government agencies to improve the quality of group decision making. Although the method can be used in several phases of many group discussions, it may be most useful if the group needs to come up with original ideas or if the group just hasn't been producing many ideas at all. Here is a step-by-step description of how brainstorming works:

1. *Select a specific problem that needs solving.* Be sure that all group members can identify and clearly define the problem.
2. *Group members should be told to temporarily put aside all judgments and evaluations.* The key to brainstorming is ruling out all criticism and evaluation. Osborn suggests:
   - Acquire a "try anything" attitude.
   - Adopt a policy of no faultfinding to avoid stifling creativity.
   - Remember that all ideas are thought-starters.
   - Today's criticism may kill future ideas.
3. *After the group members have a clear understanding of the problem and they know the brainstorming ground rules, tell them to think of as many possible solutions to the problem as they can.* Consider the following suggestions:
   - The wilder the ideas, the better.
   - It is easier to tame ideas down than to think ideas up.
   - Think out loud and mention unusual ideas.
   - Someone's wild idea may trigger a good solution from someone else in the group.
4. *Make sure that the group understands that "piggybacking" off someone's idea is useful.* Combine ideas. Add to previous ideas. Adopt this philosophy: once an idea is contributed to the group, no one owns the idea. It now belongs to the group and anyone can modify it.
5. *Have someone record all of the ideas that are mentioned.* They could be recorded on a chalkboard or an overhead projector so that each group member can see the suggested solutions and can come up with new ideas. You could also use a tape recorder to record your conversations.

6. *Some groups have found it is better to evaluate ideas at a later session.* Consider these suggestions:
   - Approach each idea positively and give it a fair trial.
   - Try to make ideas workable.
   - If only a small percentage of the ideas generated by the group is useful, the session has been successful.

Applying Brainstorming

While you should now understand how brainstorming works, you may still have some questions about how you can apply this method of creative problem solving to your group discussions. Consider the following suggestions:

1. *Be certain each group member understands the specific problem that the group is trying to solve.* The problem must be clearly defined and understood. Problems must also be limited in size and scope. A broad, vaguely worded problem must be clarified before the group attempts to identify possible solutions.

2. *Brainstorming works best as part of an overall problem-solving strategy.* As with the reflective-thinking method, group members need to define and analyze the problem under consideration, provided it has not already been clearly identified for them. One difference between a creative problem-solving method like brainstorming and the traditional reflective-thinking pattern is that the criteria for solutions are applied after possible solutions have been generated. The reason is that an explicit statement of criteria may put a damper on group creativity. Solutions are evaluated after they are developed rather than being developed according to an established list of criteria.

3. *Make sure that each group member follows the brainstorming rules.* Brainstorming will be most effective if group members stop criticizing and evaluating ideas. Don't forget that a group member can criticize nonverbally through tone of voice, facial expression, or posture. Everyone in the group must feel completely free to communicate all ideas that may solve the problem. What should you do if there are a few members who just can't seem to stop evaluating the ideas that are suggested? You may have to: (1) courteously remind them to follow the rules, (2) ask them to remain quiet, (3) ask them to record the ideas of others, or (4) if all else fails, ask them to leave the group.

4. *If brainstorming doesn't work for your group, consider this alternative: Have each group member work individually.* One team of researchers has discovered that group members' creative talents may be restricted when others are present.[12] Group members may collect more solutions if they first work alone and then regroup. After they are together again, the group can modify, elaborate on, and evaluate the ideas.

5. *If you are serving as the group's leader, try to draw less talkative group members into the discussion and compliment them when they come up with good ideas.* Call people by name: "Curt, you look like you've got some good ideas. What do you suggest?" You can also compliment the entire group when the members are doing a good job of generating ideas: "Good job, group! We've got thirty ideas so far. Let's see if we can come up with thirty more."

6. *Set aside a definite amount of time for a brainstorming session.* It is often useful to decide, as a group, how much time you want to devote to brainstorming. Be sure to give yourself plenty of time—it's better to have too much than too little. Or, you may want to set a goal for a certain number of ideas that should be recorded: "We will stop brainstorming when we get sixty ideas."

7. *Make sure that a creative problem-solving format is what your group needs.* Brainstorming can help generate ideas. But if your group does not have a lot of time to devote to brainstorming, a simpler, more conventional problem-solving pattern (such as reflective thinking) may be best. Don't avoid the brainstorming approach when it may be useful as part of an overall problem-solving plan (e.g., it can be used to generate possible solutions in the third step of the reflective-thinking format).

Some researchers feel that an ideal size for a brainstorming group is five members. If the group is too large, members may feel inhibited and thus not contribute creative ideas. Therefore, make sure that brainstorming is the problem-solving format that your group needs.

QUESTION-ORIENTED APPROACHES TO PROBLEM SOLVING

As we discussed earlier, the main reason for suggesting that a group adopt a problem-solving format is so the group can organize its deliberations more efficiently to reach its goal. Thus far, we have discussed a traditional problem-solving format (reflective thinking) and a method to assist in generating creative ideas (brainstorming). A third general approach to problem solving requires that the group consider a series of questions to keep the group oriented toward its goal. Specifically, we will describe two such approaches, called the **ideal-solution format** and the **single-question format.** These two formats can help the group develop strategies for solving a problem. Both formats have the group consider a series of questions to help identify the critical issues that they need to resolve. The questions also provide an orderly sequence of thought to help the group formulate the best possible solution. After we discuss both of these formats, we will offer some specific suggestions for applying these approaches to your group discussions.

Ideal-Solution Format

Obviously, one main objective in problem-solving group discussions is identifying the best solution to a problem. In the *ideal-solution format,* the group answers a series of questions designed to help identify the ideal solution. Goldberg and Larson devised the following agenda of questions:

1. Do we all agree on the nature of the problem?
2. What would be the ideal solution from the point of view of all the parties involved in the problem?
3. What conditions within the problem could be changed so that the ideal solution might be achieved.
4. Of the solutions available to us, which one best approximates the ideal solution?[13]

This sequence of questions guides the group toward the barriers that the problem under consideration has created. The questions also encourage the group to analyze the problem's cause and to evaluate the proposed solutions. The advantage of the ideal-solution format over other problem-solving approaches is its simplicity in reducing the uncertainty of solving problems in groups. Group members simply consider each of the questions listed previously, one at a time. Brilhart recommends the ideal-solution format for discussions that involve groups of people with varied interests. He also feels that the ideal-solution pattern can work best when attitudes for acceptance of a solution are important.[14] Thus, the ideal-solution format performs the important function of enabling group members to see the problem from several points of view in the search of the best solution.

Let's consider a situation in which the ideal-solution format might prove valuable. Sean is the personnel director for the Barnette Chemical Company. Mr. Barnette, the company president, has assigned Sean the task of organizing a committee to investigate the problem of low morale among workers. Employee turnover has been high, and most employees are not satisfied with the working conditions at the chemical plant. Sean has asked the three foremen from the production line to serve on the committee. He also decides to organize the committee's agenda for problem solving using the ideal-solution format. Since each of the foremen probably has different ideas about how the problem can best be solved, Sean feels the ideal-solution format will be useful in keeping the committee members' discussion focused on their specific task. After explaining the purpose for the meeting, Sean asks, "Do we all agree on the nature of the problem?" This question encourages each of the foremen to talk about the problem from his own perspective while permitting the others an opportunity to hear each viewpoint. After considerable discussion, the committee agrees that the main cause of worker dissatisfaction is that the employees do not get much opportunity to participate in most of the important decisions affecting their work. The employees feel their opinions aren't respected. Following the ideal-solution format for problem solving, the group next considers, "What would be the ideal solution to this problem?" Since the group has already agreed on the probable cause of the problem, they soon agree that they need a job enrichment program that permits the company employees greater opportunity to convey their ideas and suggestions to their managers. Specifically, the group recommends that each foreman should have more time to talk with the employees on a one-to-one basis in order to listen to the suggestions employees have for solving problems and increasing productivity. The committee members agree that the employees need greater opportunity to be heard. After the ideal solution has been described, Sean then asks the committee, "What do we need to change about our present way of managing our employees so that the ideal solution that we have identified can be put into practice?"

Note that the group has considered each question in the ideal-solution format separately. The group has first agreed on the problem, then considered why the problem exists, and finally, noted how the problem can be solved. Now they are ready to consider a question that will help them formulate specific steps for implementing the ideal solution that they have identified. After considering all of the suggestions and recommendations made by the foremen, Sean asks them, "Which of the specific recommendations that we've made will best help us achieve the ideal solution that we've identified?" This question directs the group discussion toward specific practical suggestions that will enable the group to formulate a detailed set of recommendations for the company president.

While the ideal-solution format is similar to reflective thinking, its chief value is that it uses questions to help a group systematically identify and analyze the problem, pinpoint the best possible solution, and formulate specific methods for achieving the solution. Like the other problem-solving formats presented in this chapter, it helps a group, particularly one with varying viewpoints and experiences, focus on a problem and devise ways to solve it.

Single-Question Format

Like the ideal-solution format, the single-question format requires considering answers to a series of questions designed to guide the group toward a best solution. Goldberg and Larson suggest that the answers to the following five questions can help the group achieve its goal:

1. What is the question whose answer is all the group needs to know in order to accomplish its purpose?
2. What subquestions must be answered before we can answer the single question we have formulated?
3. Do we have sufficient information to answer the subquestions confidently? (If yes, answer them. If no, continue below.)

4. What are the most reasonable answers to the subquestions?
5. Assuming that our answers to the subquestions are correct, what is the best solution to the problem?[15]

A key difference between the single-question format and the ideal-solution format is that the single-question format requires that the group formulate a question to help gain information needed to solve the problem. The single-question format also helps the group identify and resolve issues that must be confronted before it can reach a solution. As noted by Goldberg and Larson, "An assumption of the single question form seems to be that issues must be resolved, however tentatively."[16] *Thus, the single-question format would probably work best if a group is capable of reaching reasonable agreement on the issues and is able to agree on how the issues can be resolved.* A group characterized by conflict and contention would probably not find the single question approach productive.

A school board is meeting to decide on next year's budget. Lucy Jones, chairperson of the board, thinks that the board can use the single-question format to agree on a budget. Because the board will have to consider many subquestions, she knows that they need a problem-solving plan that will help resolve those subissues. But she also knows that she must keep the discussion focused on the main problem at hand—agreeing on next year's budget. Another reason she thinks the single-question format would work well for the meeting is that she knows the board members generally work well together.

The budget is complex and controversial. The board must first agree on the budget requests from the numerous departments and divisions in the school system before they can agree on the final dollar figure. Chairperson Jones opens the meeting by saying, "If we can agree on our ultimate objective for this meeting, I think it would help keep our discussion on track. First, we really need to identify the specific question that we are trying to answer during this meeting. Remember, agreeing on our ultimate objective will help keep our discussions focused."

Boardmember Smith replies, "Our main objective is to agree on the budget for next school year. Phrased as a question, we want to know: 'What is next year's school budget?'"

Chairperson Jones then asks the board to consider the next question in the single-question format: "What subquestions must be answered before we can answer the single question we have formulated?"

"Well," responds member Brown, "we need to ask whether we can agree on the budget requests submitted to us from each of the departments and divisions. If we can agree on these individual budgets, then we will probably be able to agree on the total budget."

Chairperson Jones asks, "But do we have enough information to approve the individual department's budget requests?"

"Yes, I think we do," answers another member. "We've got the budget requests for the last five years. And we also have a record of the amount of money spent by each department."

The board then considers the budget requests of each department. After reaching consensus on the subquestions, the board is ready to consider the final phase of their problem-solving process. "Assuming that we are satisfied with the recommendations for individual department budgets, let's see if we can agree on the total budget for the coming year," says chairperson Jones. The group can now readily agree on the final budget for next year.

The success of the single-question format depends on the group agreeing on the subissues before trying to agree on the major issues. If you are working with a group that has difficulty reaching agreement, the single-question format may *not* be the best approach. The group may become bogged down arguing about trivial matters while the major issues go unanswered. Decide whether your group will be able to reach agreement on the minor issues before you decide to use the single-question format for solving problems. If your group can't reach agreement, the ideal-solution format or reflective-thinking format may be a better method of organizing your group's deliberations.

Applying Question-Oriented Approaches

You may have noticed some similarities between the single-question, the ideal-solution, and the reflective-thinking formats. All of these approaches suggest that the group should begin its deliberations by trying to define the problem or attempting to formulate a question that will provide focus to the discussion. After the group zeroes in on the key issues, members must next analyze the problem. The ideal-solution format suggests that the group formulate criteria to direct its search for a solution, while the single-question format asks the group to identify and answer subquestions to help formulate a solution.

By using questions to guide the group toward its goal, the ideal-solution and single-question formats help the group agree on minor issues before trying to agree on the best solution to the problem. Larson attempted to identify whether an ideal-solution format, single-question format, reflective-thinking format, or no pattern would produce better quality solutions.[17] Results from his study indicate that the ideal-solution format and the single-question format generated better quality solutions than did the reflective-thinking approach. All three approaches fared better than no approach at all. While just one laboratory study does not prove that the single-question and ideal-solution formats are superior to the reflective-thinking format, it does suggest that under certain conditions the goal-oriented approaches may have certain advantages. In Larson's study, when the groups were given alternatives and told to choose the best solution to a problem, their discussions lasted only about twenty minutes. Thus, by considering specific questions, members were able to efficiently orient themselves toward the goal of solving the problem. Maier also concluded that a problem-solving approach that has the group consider minor issues before major issues can enhance the quality of group decisions.[18] Clearly, additional research is needed before theorists can prescribe specific formulas that ensure absolute efficiency in group problem solving. If you are going to lead a group discussion, the following suggestions may help you apply the ideal-solution and single-question approaches to problem solving:

1. *If you are going to use the ideal-solution or single-question approach, provide the group members with copies of the questions which will guide your discussion.* Since each of these approaches relies on a series of questions to guide the discussion, you can reduce some of the uncertainty that occurs by making sure that each person has a personal copy of the questions. Tell the group to use the questions as a guide.

2. *Explain why you are using the format you have selected.* Most groups are willing to go along with a particular discussion agenda, especially if you give them a reason or two for having selected a specific approach. Tell the group that considering specific questions in a developmental format can keep the discussion on track. If your group has a specified time period in which to meet, you can explain that using questions to guide the discussion can help make the discussion more efficient.

3. *Keep the discussion focused on the specific question under consideration.* If you have provided copies of the questions for either the ideal-solution or single-question format, some group members may be tempted to skip a question or may want to discuss an unrelated issue. You may have to help orient the group toward the goal of solving the problem by focusing on one question at a time. Several studies suggest that groups whose members try to keep the other participants aware of the pertinent issues by summarizing the discussion and requesting clarification have a good chance of agreeing on a solution and of being satisfied with their discussion.[19]

Agendas for Participative Group Problem Solving

One of the key responsibilities of a problem-solving discussion leader is to encourage all group members to participate in the discussion. Several specific methods have been devised to encourage all individuals, particularly in larger groups or organizations, to become involved in the problem-solving process. Whether you have responsibilities as a corporate executive, church leader, or committee chairperson, the following agendas can help you maximize group participation. Specifically, we will consider (1) buzz sessions, (2) RISK technique, (3) nominal group technique, and (4) quality control circles.

Buzz Sessions

Have you ever been an audience member during a speech, symposium, or panel discussion and wished that you had had a greater opportunity to contribute to the discussion? Even during a public forum, which permits the audience to direct questions to a panel or speaker, there is often too little time

A buzz session not only encourages everyone to participate, but also allows for a wide variety of solutions to a problem.

to have to actively participate in the discussions. One technique that improves audience participation in the discussion is called the **buzz session.** This technique, frequently used in conferences and large group meetings, is really quite simple.

To conduct a buzz session, the leader or chairperson of a large gathering should make sure that everyone present has a general understanding of the problem or issue facing the group. The leader should pose a specific question for the group to address. The audience is then divided into small groups of about six people to respond to the question. One member of each small group should write down the suggestions developed. After a specific time period, the recorder of each group reports the results of the discussion to the large group. The results can also be written, either on paper to be distributed, or on a chalk-board for all to see and evaluate.

When given ample opportunity to participate in the decision process, an audience is more likely to produce, implement, and support a better quality decision. The buzz session technique fosters group member involvement whenever a large group of people assemble with the purpose of reaching a decision, recommending a solution, or striving for greater enlightenment.

RISK Technique

The Industrial Chemical Company is considering a change from a five-day to a four-day workweek. The company management feels that the four-day work-week would save energy, increase productivity, and reduce equipment mainte-nance costs. While statistics suggest that the four-day workweek would produce these desirable benefits, the company managers are uncertain about how the employees would react to the schedule change. In an effort to help the manag-ers reach a decision, a communication consulting firm has suggested that the **RISK technique** be used to assess employee reactions. Developed by group communication researcher Norman Maier, the RISK technique is designed to determine how proposed policy changes would affect company employees, government workers, or practically any group which may experience a change in procedure.[20] By encouraging those who may experience a change in policy to voice all concerns, risks, fears, and negative reactions to proposed changes, the RISK technique can estimate the impact of the changes on those who would be affected. In the case of the Industrial Chemical Company, employees could be placed in small groups and asked to list their concerns about switch-ing to a four-day workweek. John Brilhart suggests the following steps for implementing the RISK technique:

1. Present in detail the proposed change of procedure or policy to the group.
2. Explain the purpose and procedures to be followed in the RISK technique, being sure to describe the leader's nonevaluative role.
3. Invite and post all "risks," fears, problems, doubts, concerns, etc. The leader should allow no evaluation and make none himself, verbal or nonverbal, much as in brainstorming [*see* Chapter Nine]. The leader or other members of the group may clarify or simplify a member's risk statement, but never modify its intent. It is essential that the wording of the "risk" as posted be fully acceptable to the presenter. Allow plenty of time. Often the most significant items, the most threatening and disturb-ing to members, do not come until late in the session, often after periods of silence. The leader should keep encouraging the members to think of more risks. Members will be feeling out the leader and each other to determine if it is safe to express these, or if they might be in some way ridiculed or retaliated against.
4. After the initial meeting, reproduce and circulate the list to all partici-pants, inviting any additions that may have been thought of in the inter-im.
5. At the next meeting of the group, add any further risks mentioned.
6. Then, have the group decide if each risk is serious and substantive. No

risk should be considered as the property of its presenter, but of the entire group. Often the discussants can resolve many of each other's fears and concerns by sharing experiences, ideas, and points of view. All such doubts should now be removed from the list.

7. Remaining risks are now processed into an agenda.... Some can be resolved by obtaining information, but the problems remaining can now be dealt with one at a time in problem-solving discussions worked out by the group.[21]

Nominal Group Technique

One team of researchers suggests that sometimes it may be better to work on a problem individually, rather than collectively. They note that when one person starts to talk during a group discussion, other group members stop thinking and listen to the idea presented.[22] They also found that people work more diligently if they have an individual assignment than if they have a group assignment. As we noted in Chapter One, a disadvantage of group work is that it spreads responsibility, thereby increasing the probability that some group members will shirk their responsibilities. **Nominal group technique** is one procedure for overcoming these disadvantages. The group is nominal in the sense that members work on the problem individually in the presence of the group, rather than during sustained group interaction.

After group members have worked individually on a specific idea or question, they report their ideas to the group for discussion and evaluation. Group members then work individually to rank order the proposed solutions, followed by group discussion of the rankings. The following steps summarize the procedure:

1. Make sure all group members know the problem under consideration. Each member should be able to define and analyze the problem.
2. Working individually, group members should write possible solutions to the problem.
3. Have a round robin reporting of the individual solutions. Each idea should be noted on a chart, chalkboard, or overhead projector.
4. Discuss each idea as a group to make sure it is clear to all.
5. After discussing all proposed solutions, have individuals rank order the solutions. Tabulate the results.
6. Discuss the results of the rank ordering. If the first rank ordering is inconclusive, have individual group members rerank the options after additional discussion.

This technique has the advantage of involving all group members in the deliberations. It can be a useful method if you find some group members unwilling to or uncomfortable in making contributions because of status

differences in the group. Also, alternating discussion with individual deliberation, rather than sustaining group interaction, can be useful in groups plagued
by considerable conflict and tension. But because the method relies heavily
on individual work and not on group interactive work, some may feel it is not
really a group communication problem-solving approach.

Quality Circles: A Participative Decision-Making Agenda

Several organizations are using a method called **quality circles** to involve
employees in group problem solving and decision making. A quality circle
consists of a group of 5 to 15 employees who meet on a regular basis for the
purpose of improving productivity, morale, and overall work quality.[23] Specific
tasks of quality circles include:

Improving the quality of services or products
Reducing the number of work-related errors
Promoting cost reduction
Developing improved teamwork
Developing better work methods
Improving efficiency in the organization
Improving relations between management and employees
Promoting participants' leadership skills
Enhancing employees' career and personal development
Improving communication throughout the organization
Increasing everyone's awareness of safety

The concept of quality circles was developed in Japan in the late 1940s by W.
Edward Deming, a professor from the United States who was invited to Japan
to help improve industry. Based on the success of the program in Japan, it
eventually was implemented in the United States.

Employees trained in quality circle techniques receive basic information
about group communication theory and skills. Many of the concepts presented in this text, such as group relationships, cohesiveness, roles, consensus,
decision making, and problem solving are part of the training of quality circle
members. Members are also given training in statistics to help them analyze
production and quality.

Leaders of quality circles are given additional training in group leadership
and conflict management. The quality circle leader is primarily a procedural
leader in the sense that he or she is responsible for developing an agenda,
scheduling the meeting, and for ensuring equal participation by all group
members, encouraging quiet members to contribute.

The use of quality circles stems from the assumption that participative
decision making is one of the most valuable approaches to analyzing, managing, and solving problems in business and industry. The evidence suggests that

quality circles are effective if the employees are comfortable being involved in the decision-making process.

SMALL GROUP PROBLEM-SOLVING TECHNIQUES: PUTTING PRINCIPLE INTO PRACTICE

In this chapter we discussed several prescriptive approaches that a group can use to solve a problem. Groups often need some plan or structure to help members define, analyze, and solve a problem. We described eight different kinds of problem-solving formats: (1) reflective thinking, (2) brainstorming, (3) ideal solution, (4) single question, (5) buzz sessions, (6) RISK technique, (7) nominal group technique, and (8) quality control circles. Review the following suggestions for applying these problem-solving approaches to groups in which you participate.

Reflective Thinking

- To help your group define and limit the problem, phrase the problem as a question.
- Don't start suggesting solutions until your group has thoroughly analyzed the problem.
- Formulate criteria for a good solution before you begin suggesting solutions.
- Use the brainstorming technique to help your group generate possible solutions.
- If the other group members agree, you may need to change the criteria you have selected during the analysis phase of reflective thinking.
- Make sure that the reflective-thinking approach is the best method for your group; another problem-solving approach may work better.

Brainstorming

- Make sure all group members understand the ground rules for brainstorming. Don't evaluate the solutions until you have completed the brainstorming process.
- If group members do not follow the brainstorming rules, you may have to (1) restate the rules, (2) ask them to keep quiet, (3) ask them to record the ideas of others, or (4) ask them to leave the group.
- If brainstorming doesn't work, consider having each group member work individually.
- Try to draw less talkative group members into the discussion and compliment the group members when they come up with good ideas.
- Set aside a definite amount of time for a brainstorming session.
- Make sure that brainstorming is the best problem-solving approach for your group.

Ideal Solution and Single Question

- If you are the leader of the group, tell the group why you have selected either the ideal-solution format or the single-question approach to problem solving.
- Use the ideal-solution format to help the group agree on the nature of the problem.
- Use the single-question format if you are sure that your group is capable of reaching reasonable agreement on the issues and is able to agree on how the issues can be resolved.
- Provide the group members with copies of the questions used in the ideal-solution format or the single-question format; this will help keep your discussion on track.
- Remind group members to address only those questions and issues which are relevant to the discussion.

Participative Decision Making

- Use buzz groups to involve a large group of people in the problem-solving process.
- Use the risk technique to help manage uncertainty that occurs when new policy and procedures are suggested.
- Use the nominal group technique as a decision-making agenda when there are status differences, conflict, or stress that prohibits full group interaction.
- Consider using quality control circles in business and industry to improve productivity, morale, and overall work quality.

PRACTICE

The Bomb Shelter Case

Divide into groups of three to six people. Individually read the case study and follow the directions. Do not confer with anyone in your group until everyone has finished analyzing the case. After each person has analyzed the case study and made individual choices, discuss the case study as a group. Try to reach agreement. After a given amount of time your instructor will ask you to discuss your decision-making process. Which problem-solving techniques did you use? Did you formulate a discussion question? How could you and your group improve the problem-solving process?

   One evening two years from now you invite eight acquaintances to your home to talk with a psychologist whom you know personally. In the midst of your discussion you hear the air raid siren. You turn on the radio and the Civil Defense station broadcasts that enemy planes are approaching your city. Fortunately you have a well-equipped bomb shelter in your basement, so immediately you direct the psychologist, your eight companions, and a mechanic who has been repairing the air-conditioning unit to go downstairs. Shortly after you are all in the shelter, a terrific blast shakes the earth, and you realize that the bomb has fallen. For four frantic hours you get static on the radio in your shelter. Finally you hear the following announcement: "A bomb of great magnitude has hit ten miles from your city. Damage is extensive. Radiation is intense. It is feared that all those not in shelters have suffered a fatal dose of radiation. All persons in shelters are warned that it would be fatal to leave before at least a month. Further bombing is anticipated. This may be the last broadcast you will hear for some time."

Immediately you realize that you have eleven persons in a shelter which is equipped with food, water, and, most important, oxygen enough to last eleven people two weeks or six people a month. When you reveal this information, the group unanimously decides that in order for anyone to survive, five must be sacrificed. As it is your shelter, all agree that you must stay and choose the other five who are to be saved.

- *Mary,* a psychologist, is a few years older than the rest of the group. It has already become evident that the others respect her and recognize her ability to take control. Although she is rather cold and impersonal, she has helped quiet the group's nervousness and settled an argument between Don and Hazel. Even though no one seems close to her, you feel she would be valuable as an organizer and a pacifier.

- *Hazel* is studying home economics—nutrition and dietetics. She is a very attractive woman. One of the first things she did was to appraise the food supply. You realize that her training has given her practical knowledge of how to ration food to avoid waste; also, she is an imaginative cook who can fix even canned foods appealingly. She is efficient to the point of being domineering and bossy.

- *Alberta* is a brilliant woman who has been given a graduate assistantship to do research on radiation. She has been pampered all her life and is horrified at wearing the same clothes for a month, being unable to take a bath or wash her hair, and sleeping in a room with five other people.

- *Laura* is a literature major, has read extensively, and writes well herself. Already she has entertained and diverted the group by retelling one of the books she has recently read.

- *Nancy,* Chet's wife, has a pleasant personality generally. However, she has been the most nervous and upset of the group. Her temperamental mood is partially due to the fact that she is expecting a baby in two months.

- *Chet,* Nancy's husband, is a medical student. He has had two years of medical school, three summers in a camp as medical assistant, and a close association with his father, who is a doctor. You realize he would be a great aid; however, he refuses to stay unless Nancy also remains.
- *Jack,* the mechanic who had been working upstairs, also has a great deal of practical know-how. Although his education ended with high school, he has had experience with air-filtration systems, air purifiers, and oxygen supply. Despite his understanding of the technical aspects, he fails to grasp the necessity for self-control as far as the food and water supply is concerned.
- *Paul,* a young minister, is easy going. His calmness, optimism, and faith are an inspiration to the group. In an intangible way his presence is reassuring. He helped quiet Nancy's tearful outburst. He revealed that he has learned to remain calm, of necessity, because he is a diabetic.
- *Joe* is a clean-cut, husky football player, the star center of the college team. He is highly respected by everyone on campus. Joe was the only one able to lift by himself the heavy metal plate that had to be placed over the shelter door. At one point, when Chet took it upon himself to set the oxygen tank valve, Jack flew at him, shoved him out of the way, and reset the valve properly. A fist fight might have ensued had Joe not parted the two.
- *Don* is an incurable romantic. His smile, lively guitar music, and sense of humor have helped improve everyone's mood. He gets along well with everyone but offended Hazel already by being fresh. The others have also noticed his flirting eyes as he sings.

Evaluating Your Ability to Solve Problems in Groups

How effectively do you solve problems in small groups? Take this brief diagnostic test to rate yourself on the various skills needed to work in problem-solving groups. The results should give you a clearer understanding of how well or how poorly you perceive your problem-solving abilities. Keep in mind that there are no right or wrong answers.

1. I like to work with a small group of people to solve problems.
    often_____ usually_____ seldom_____ never_____

2. I do a good job of helping define and limit the problem that the group is discussing.
    often_____ usually_____ seldom_____ never_____

3. I enjoy doing a thorough job of conducting research to help solve problems.
    often_____ usually_____ seldom_____ never_____

4. I usually start thinking of possible solutions to the problem before the group has finished analyzing the causes and effects of the problem.

    often_____ usually_____ seldom_____ never_____

5. I do a better job analyzing the problem than suggesting solutions.

    often_____ usually_____ seldom_____ never_____

6. I like to assume some leadership responsibilities when I participate in a problem-solving discussion.

    often_____ usually_____ seldom_____ never_____

7. I am usually satisfied with my contributions to a problem-solving group discussion.

    often_____ usually_____ seldom_____ never_____

8. I try to encourage less talkative members to participate in the group problem-solving process.

    often_____ usually_____ seldom_____ never_____

9. I like to work in a problem-solving group when a specific agenda has been formulated and I am aware of the steps that the group is taking to solve the problem.

    often_____ usually_____ seldom_____ never_____

Do you note any consistent pattern in your responses to this brief questionnaire? What areas of group problem-solving ability do you need to improve? How might you improve your problem-solving ability?

The Kidney Machine

The people in your group represent a panel of doctors. Each of the patients listed below is in need of a kidney machine to do the work of their own failing organs. There are only 5 machines available at present because of the prohibitive cost of manufacturing them. No more machines will be available in time to save all of these patients. It is the job of your panel to decide, based on the information given, which patients will receive treatment and which will not. Those who do not receive treatment will die.

Mrs. Maria Vasquez:	27 years old. She is married and has 6 children who range in age from 2 to 10 years. Her husband is a printer who owns his own print shop in partnership with his brother-in-law.
Mrs. Mary Fortran:	31 years old. She is the director of foods research for N.A.S.A. She is a former Rhodes scholar with a Ph.D. in physics. At present she is working on a formula for a food capsule to be used in space travel. She is divorced and has no children.

Mike
Carbona:
39 years old. He is an ex-convict, was convicted for tax eva-
sion and served 7 years. He is active in local politics in New
Jersey. He is known as the spearhead behind the minority
rights program in his area. He is suspected of having Mafia
connections. The 9 Korean orphans he supports do not
know of his former crime involvement.

Peter
Maximo:
9 years old. He has an IQ of 160, but is severely mentally
disturbed at having witnessed the car accident which killed
two of his parents' friends. He has not spoken a word for
over two years.

Mrs. Terry
McBride:
27 years old. She is an instructor at a local university, working on her M.S. in communication. Her husband is partially
blind and is now receiving disability payments from the
army. They have no children. Their debts include some car
payments and a 30-year mortgage on the house.

Dick
Constable:
35 years old. He is a bachelor. He works as a federal narcot-
ics agent in Chicago, primarily arresting heroin dealers. He
is active in community youth organizations. He is also engaged to be married.

Father
Mussello:
53 years old. He is a Dominican friar who is the headmaster
of a parochial school. He is presently organizing missions to
help with Indian education in New Mexico. He specializes in
counseling young people and juvenile delinquents.

Thomas
Washing-
ton:
19 years old. He is a freshman at New York University in
New York. He and his family live in Harlem, a New York
ghetto. His father died when he was very little and his insurance money is paying for Thom's education. He is a member of a Black radical group whose avowed purpose is to
foster anarchy in America.

Using Problem-Solving Agendas

As a class identify a problem that needs to be solved. It could be a college/
university, local, state, or national problem. After the class has identified a
problem, divide into groups of five or six members. Each group should attempt to solve the problem using a different problem-solving format (e.g.,
reflective thinking, brainstorming, etc.). After the groups have deliberated,
have one member from each group summarize how the problem-solving
format worked for the group. Which format was the easiest to use? Did some
groups take more time than others to solve the problem? Did the problem-
solving format help or hinder the group's effort to solve the problem? Note
other differences and similarities about the group's problem-solving process.

Notes

1. Dennis S. Gouran, Candace Brown, and David R. Henry, "Behavioral Correlates of Perceptions of Quality in Decision-Making Discussion," *Communication Monographs* Vol. 45 (1978): 60–65; Linda L. Putnam, "Preference for Procedural Order in Task-Oriented Small Groups," *Communication Monographs* Vol. 46 (1979): 193–218.

2. David M. Berg, "A Descriptive Analysis of the Distribution and Duration of Themes Discussed by Task-Oriented Small Groups," *Speech Monographs* Vol. 34 (1967): 172–75; also see: Ernest G. Bormann and Nancy C. Bormann, *Effective Small Group Communication,* 2nd ed. (Minneapolis: Burgess Publishing Company, 1976), p. 132.

3. Marshall Scott Poole, "Decision Development in Small Groups III: A Multiple Sequence Model of Group Decision Development," *Communication Monographs* Vol. 50 (1983): 321–41.

4. See R. Victor Harnack, "John Dewey and Discussion," *Western Speech* Vol. 32 (Spring 1969): 137–49.

5. For evidence to support this modification of the reflective-thinking pattern, see John K. Brilhart, "An Experimental Comparison of Three Techniques for Communicating a Problem-Solving Pattern to Members of a Discussion Group," *Speech Monographs* Vol. 33 (1966): 168–77.

6. For example, *see* Robert F. Bales and Fred L. Strodtbeck, "Phases in Group Problem-Solving," *Journal of Abnormal and Social Psychology* 46 (1951): 485–95; Thomas M. Schiedel and Laura Crowell, "Idea Development in Small Groups," *Quarterly Journal of Speech* 50 (1964): 140–45; and B. Aubrey Fisher, "Decision Emergence: Phases in Group Decision-Making," *Speech Monographs* Vol. 37 (1970): 53–66.

7. Chapter Six discusses the phases of a group's growth and development in detail.

8. Ernest G. Bormann, *Discussion and Group Methods: Theory and Practice,* 2nd ed. (New York: Harper & Row, Publishers, Inc., 1975), p. 282.

9. John K. Brilhart, *Effective Group Discussion,* 3rd ed. (Dubuque, Iowa: Wm. C. Brown Company, Publishers, 1978), p. 145.

10. Norman R. F. Maier, *Problem-Solving and Discussions and Conferences* (New York: McGraw-Hill Book Company, 1963), p. 123.

11. Alex F. Osborn, *Applied Imagination* (New York: Charles Scribner's Sons, 1962).

12. Gerry Philipsen, Anthony Mulac, and David Dietrich, "The Effects of Social Interaction on Group Generation of Ideas," *Communication Monographs* 46 (June 1979): 119–25.

13. Alvin A. Goldberg and Carl E. Larson, *Group Communication: Discussion Processes and Applications* (Englewood Cliffs, New Jersey: Prentice-Hall, Inc., 1975), p. 149.

14. Brilhart, *Effective Group Discussion,* p. 146.

15. Goldberg and Larson, p. 150.

16. Ibid.

17. Carl E. Larson, "Forms of Analysis and Small Group Problem-Solving," *Speech Monographs* Vol. 36 (1969): 452–55.

18. Norman R. F. Maier, "An Experimental Test of the Effect of Training on Discussion Leadership," *Human Relations* Vol. 6 (1953): 166–73.

19. Dennis G. Gouran, "Variables Related to Consensus in Group Discussions of Questions of Policy," *Speech Monographs* Vol. 36 (1969): 385–91; Thomas J. Knutson, "An Experimental Study of the Effects of Orientation Behavior on Small Group Consensus," *Speech Monographs* Vol. 39 (1972): 159–65; John A. Kline, "Orientation and Group Consensus," *Central States Speech Journal* Vol. 23 (1972): 44–47; Steven A. Beebe, "Orientation as a Determinant of Group Consensus and Satisfaction," *Resources in Education,* Vol. 13, no. 10 (October 1978).

20. Norman R. F. Maier, *Problem-Solving Discussions and Conferences: Leadership Methods and Skills* (New York: McGraw-Hill Book Company, 1963), pp. 171–77.

21. Brilhart, *Effective Group Discussion*, p. 225.

22. Andre L. Delbecq, Andrew H. Van de Ven, and David H. Gustafson, *Group Techniques for Program Planning: A Guide to Nominal Group and Delphi Processes* (Glenview, Ill.: Scott, Foresman and Company, 1975), pp. 7–16.

23. *Positive Personnel Practices: Quality Circles' Participant's Manual* (Prospect Heights, Ill.: Waveland Press, 1982).

24. Ibid.

10 Leadership

After studying this chapter, you should be able to:

- Discuss three approaches to the study of leadership.

- Describe three styles of leadership.

- Explain the relationship between situational variables and the effectiveness of different leadership styles.

- Analyze a small group meeting and determine which leadership behaviors will move the group toward its goal.

- Describe your own style of leadership.

- Determine those situations in which you are most likely to be an effective leader.

- Be a more effective group leader and participant.

- Explain the purpose of simulation in leadership training.

- Manage meetings more effectively as designated leader.

Leadership

Before beginning this chapter, consider the following statements about leadership:

> Leaders are born and not made.
>
> An effective leader is always in control of the group process.
>
> A leader is a person who gets others to do the work.
>
> Leadership is a set of functions distributed throughout the group.
>
> The leader should know more than other group members know about the topic of discussion.
>
> An authoritarian leader is better than one who allows the group to function without control.
>
> It's best for a group to have only one leader.
>
> A person who has been appointed leader *is* the leader.

How do you feel about these statements? With which ones are you in agreement? Disagreement? If it hasn't happened already, be assured that one day you will find yourself in a leadership position—on a committee, in an organization, or perhaps in the military. In fact, *whenever you participate in a decision-making group your attitudes about leadership will affect your behavior, the behavior of others, and the effectiveness of the group.*

Our intent in this chapter is twofold: First, we will provide you with information about the nature of leadership in groups to help you become a more effective group participant; second, we will make some specific suggestions to help you become an effective leader.

WHAT IS LEADERSHIP?

When you think about the concept of "leadership," what comes to mind? A fearless commanding officer leading troops into battle? The president of the United States addressing the country on national t.v.? The president of the student body coordinating and representing student efforts? Perhaps you think of the chairperson of a committee you're on. Traditionally, the study of leadership has centered on people who are successful in leadership positions. It was argued that by looking at successful leaders we could identify those attributes or individual *traits* which best predicted good leadership ability. Identification of such traits would be tremendously valuable to those in business, government, or the military who are responsible for promoting others to leadership positions.

TRAIT PERSPECTIVE

Over the last several decades, researchers have conducted scores of "trait studies." Indeed, these studies indicated that attributes such as intelligence, enthusiasm, dominance, self-confidence, social participation, and equalitarianism often characterize leaders.[1] Other researchers found that physical traits were related to leadership ability. Leaders seemed to be larger, more active, energetic, and better looking . . . but not *too* good looking![2] Other researchers described leaders as possessing tact, cheerfulness, justice, discipline, versatility, and self-control. It is alleged that one leadership study conducted by a branch of the military determined that leaders are often characterized by a love of good, red meat, and an aggressive pursuit of desserts.

The **trait perspective** of leadership is one of those things that seemed like a good idea at the time but actually yielded very little useful information. While correlations between traits and leadership have generally been positive, they have occasionally been weak.[3] It seems that traits which are useful in one situation, say leading troops into battle, are not necessarily those required for other leadership positions, such as conducting a business meeting.

A further problem with the trait approach is that it does not identify which traits are important to become a leader and which are important to maintain the position. Nor do these studies adequately distinguish between leaders and followers who possessed the same traits. In addition, trait studies do not approach leadership in ways which are useful to the group participant wishing to *improve* his or her leadership skills. After all, it is difficult for us to make ourselves larger, more energetic, or more aggressive pursuers of desserts. Therefore we shall relegate the trait approach to the "historical perspective" category and proceed from there.

FUNCTIONAL PERSPECTIVE

The **functional perspective** to studying **leadership** has proven to be informative to students and practitioners of small group communication. Rather than focusing on the characteristics of individual leaders, the functional approach examines leadership as a set of behaviors which may be performed by *any* group member to maximize group effectiveness. Barnlund and Haiman identify leadership behaviors as those which guide, influence, direct, or control others in the group.[4] This is a much more fruitful approach for those of us who are interested in *improving* our leadership abilities. Whereas the trait approach might help us identify the sort of person we should *appoint* to a position of leadership, the functional approach helps us understand what specific communicative behaviors need to be performed in order for the group to function effectively. By understanding these behaviors we can more effectively participate in group discussions.

According to advocates of the functional approach, leadership behaviors fall into two categories. The major distinctions are between **task leadership** and **process leadership** (also called group building or maintenance). Task-oriented behaviors aim specifically at accomplishing the group goal. Process-oriented behaviors help maintain a satisfactory interpersonal climate (*see* Chapter Five) within the group. *Both* types of leadership are essential.

Task Leadership

When groups convene for the purpose of solving problems, making decisions, planning activities, or determining policy, they are frequently hampered by the randomness of group members' behavior. Even when we have "gotten down to business," group process seems to stray. Discussion becomes tangential; we lose track of where the group is going. Sometimes one person monopolizes the conversation while the others remain silent. Sometimes the group just can't seem to get started. At times like these, it is easy for us to blame the designated leader for the group's failure.

The group leader has a responsibility to keep the group moving. But research in group process has shown that behaviors which keep the group on track are behaviors which *anyone* can perform. The fact that a person has the title "leader" does not necessarily mean that that person is best equipped to do the job. If we view leadership as a set of functions which are often distributed, the group is still quite capable of getting its job done regardless of who is designated "leader." If you are a member of a group which is disorganized, *you* can provide the leadership the group needs even though you are not the "leader."

In Chapter Four we presented a listing of functional leadership roles. Let's look at a few *task-leadership behaviors* and consider ways that these behaviors help the group toward its goal.

Initiating. In every task-oriented group discussion, ideas need to be generated. Sometimes these ideas are related to procedural matters; at other times the group needs to generate ideas to solve problems. If, for example, you had just finished our chapter on problem solving (Chapter Nine) and could see that your group was failing to adequately define the problem before suggesting solutions, you might say: "Listen. I'm afraid that we're all proposing solutions before we've really agreed on the nature of the problem itself. Let's take a few minutes and talk some more about the problem so that we know we're all discussing the same thing."

By proposing a change in the course of the group's action you are *initiating* a procedural change, in this case one which will probably benefit the group. To "initiate" means to "begin." If you say: "Let's get this meeting under way," you have begun a change (assuming the group follows your suggestion). If, later in the meeting, you offer: "Let's consider an alternate plan," or "Let's generate some more ideas before evaluating what we have here," again you are communicating in ways which will probably alter the course of the group's action. You are *initiating*. Without someone who initiates discussion, the group has no direction. The ability to initiate is an important group behavior and one which *anyone* can contribute.

Coordinating. Earlier in the book we pointed to the complexity of small group communication. Different people bring different expectations, beliefs, attitudes, values, and experiences to the group meeting. The contributions of each group member are unique and yet all are directed toward a common group goal. Given the diversity in small groups, *coordinating* is often an important leadership function. Communicative behavior which helps the group explore the relationships between the contributions of all group members is valuable. If, for example, you see a tie between the ideas brought to the group by two of its members, you should point it out to help focus the group. Coordinating the efforts of the members can help the group see the "groupness" of its efforts, thereby reducing uncertainty about the group, the problem, and the solutions.

Summarizing. Groups can get long-winded. Often in the middle of a discussion it is difficult to tell just where the discussion began and where it is going. It doesn't take many tangential remarks to get the group "off track." Even when the group is "on track" it is sometimes useful to stop and assess the progress made. *Summarizing* is a leadership behavior which reduces group uncertainty by showing how far the discussion has progressed and what it still needs to accomplish. By developing a sensitivity to when the group needs a summary—and then providing it—we can help move the group toward its goal. Even if your summary is not accepted by the group, you will still reveal discrepancies between the perceptions of the members, thus opening the door to more clarification and less uncertainty.

Elaborating. Sometimes good ideas fall on deaf ears until they are elaborated enough to be visualized. Suppose you are at a meeting of your fraternity or sorority at which you are trying to determine ways of increasing next year's pledge class. Someone in the group suggests that redecorating the recreation room might help. At this point in the discussion several things might happen. Among them: (1) The group might begin to evaluate the idea, some being in favor and some not, (2) another idea might be suggested and recorded, or (3) you (or someone else) might *elaborate* on the idea by describing how the room might look with new carpeting, a pool table, soft lighting, and a new sofa in one corner. Whereas the idea of redecoration might have fallen flat by itself, your elaboration gives it a fighting chance. Good ideas are often left unexplored because people fail to elaborate on them.

We have touched on four types of communicative behaviors which serve a task-oriented leadership function in small groups: initiating, coordinating, summarizing and elaborating. While these are some of the more important types of contributions you can make, the list is by no means complete (*see* Chapters Four and Eleven). Task leadership is *any behavior or set of behaviors which influence the group process and are directed toward accomplishing the group's designated task.* Making suggestions, offering new ideas, giving information or opinions, asking for more information, and making procedural observations or recommendations are *all* task-oriented leadership behaviors which can contribute to the group effort. Viewing leadership from the functional approach, leadership skill is associated with your ability to analyze the group's process and to choose the appropriate behavior.

Process Leadership

It is fairly obvious that for a group to accomplish its task, group members must address themselves to that task. What is less obvious, but equally important, is that in order for the group to function effectively, the group needs to concern itself *with itself!* Groups are composed of people, and people have needs. (In fact, the family is a small group specifically adapted to meeting individual needs.) People don't leave their needs at home when they come to a meeting; they bring those needs along. Effective group communication must be addressed to the external task of the group *and* to the needs of its members. Effective groups not only solve problems and make decisions but also provide their members with individual satisfaction. Failing to maintain a satisfying group climate can lead to a breakdown in the group's task performance. In this respect, small groups resemble the automobile. Automobiles are great for getting you where you want to go, but they require regular tuning and maintenance in order to run reliably and efficiently. In fact, failure to provide basic maintenance eventually will result in a breakdown. So it is with groups—they too need "tuning" and "maintaining."

Leadership research has consistently indicated that groups have *both* task needs and process needs. The process dimension is often called "group building and maintenance." *Process-leadership behaviors* are leadership acts that maintain interpersonal relations in the group and facilitate a group climate which is both satisfying to group members and conducive to accomplishing the task.

In Chapter Five we discussed group climate from the pespective of individual and interpersonal needs. Now let's look at some specific process-leadership behaviors from the perspective of leadership and group needs.

Tension Release. Think of times you've studied for an exam. You cram more and more information into your head until you reach a point where it all seems futile. Everything runs together. Ideas blur. You know it's time for a break. After a cup of coffee and some relaxing conversation you return to the books with your energy renewed.

Sometimes the most effective leadership you can provide for a group is suggesting a coffee break! When the group is tired, when the task is difficult, when the hour is late, when tension is high, when there is internal or external stress, the group needs relief. A joke, a bit of humor, a break, or even a move for adjournment can often provide just what the group needs. *Tension release* punctuates the group process. An occasional break or a good laugh can renew the group's energy level and improve member satisfaction.

Some people seem to be naturally sensitive to a group's need for tension release. But *knowing* that tension release is a necessary leadership function can alert anyone—even the most task-oriented individual—to that need.

Gate Keeping. As we noted in Chapter One, an advantage of working in small groups is that "several heads are better than one." The very diversity that makes group communication so complex also gives it strength. The collective experience and intelligence of the group is stronger than that of the individual. But that experience and individual insight is only useful to the group if it is shared.

We all know that some people like to talk more than others. We have all been in groups in which two or three people monopolize the conversation while others remain relatively silent. While this is a fairly common occurrence, it poses a problem for the group on two levels: First of all, quiet members are just as likely to possess useful information and ideas as are more vocal group members—ideas which may never surface unless these quiet members say something. Second, it has been found that people who talk more tend to experience more satisfaction with the group. The fact that some people are reticent (they don't talk much) can have a negative effect on the group at both the task and process dimensions.

Gate keeping is a leadership behavior aimed at coordinating discussion so that members can air their views. This may take the form of eliciting input ("Harvey, you must have given this a lot of thought. What are your views of the problem?") or even of limiting the more verbal members of the group ("Can we perhaps limit our comments to two or three minutes so that we can get everyone's ideas before we have to adjourn?"). Gate keeping is an important leadership function because it insures more input along the task dimension and higher member satisfaction along the process dimension.

Encouraging. Everyone likes to receive praise. We feel good when someone recognizes us for our contributions. But in order for us to receive praise, someone has to give it. *Encouraging* is a leadership behavior aimed at increasing the esteem of group members and raising the hopes, confidence, and aspirations of the group. Improving the morale of the group can increase cohesiveness, member satisfaction, and productivity.

Mediating. As we noted in Chapter Seven, conflict is a normal, healthy part of group interaction. However, *mismanaged* conflict can lead to hurt feelings, physical or mental withdrawal from the group, reduced cohesiveness, and general disruption. *Mediating* is leadership behavior aimed at resolving conflict between group members and releasing any tension associated with the conflict. Whenever conflict becomes person-oriented rather than issue-oriented, it is a particularly appropriate time for some mediation.

> Wanda: I think that the plan I'm proposing has considerable merit and meets our needs.
>
> Harold: That's ridiculous. It'll never work.
>
> Wanda: Get off my case, Bozo! I don't see you proposing anything better.

We have a potentially volatile situation here which could easily create a lot of disruption while Harold and Wanda "slug it out." We often have to work in groups with people we don't especially like. Obviously, Harold and Wanda don't get along too well. But groups can function effectively in spite of personality clashes. The key is to *focus discussion on issues rather than on personalities.* Note that there may be times when interpersonal difficulties become so severe that they cannot be resolved by simply focusing on the group's task. Such difficulties can be a serious encumbrance to the group and need to be dealt with either within the group setting or outside of the group. If this is the case, ignoring the problem won't make it go away.

Once again, our list of behaviors which contribute to the process or maintenance needs of the group is not complete. Several researchers have offered more complete lists which appear in Chapters Four and Eleven. The behaviors we have described are some of the more essential task and process leadership behaviors. We have included them here to illustrate their importance and to help you examine your own leadership behavior in groups.

Both task and process leadership are essential to the success of an ongoing small group. If the group does not make progress on the task, the members will probably feel frustrated and their satisfaction will be minimal. In addi-

For a group to be effective, a leader must be available to guide and control the group. However, leadership responsibilities can be assumed by anyone in the group if the group becomes disorganized.

tion, if a comfortable environment is not maintained, the members tend to focus their attention and energy on their own dissatisfaction with the group rather than on their assigned task.

SITUATIONAL PERSPECTIVE

Thus far in the chapter we have discussed the trait and functional approaches to leadership study and have explored some task and process leadership roles. The **situational perspective** to group leadership accommodates all of these factors—leadership behaviors, task needs, and process needs—but also takes into account the variables of leadership style and situation. When you complete the task process leadership questionnaire at the end of this chapter, you may have some new insights about your own leadership behavior in groups. In interpreting the results of that questionnaire, you will find that the degrees of concern for task and for people are related to **leadership style.**

Leadership Style

We asserted that your beliefs and attitudes about leadership will affect your behavior in small groups. *Leadership style is a relatively consistent pattern of behavior reflecting the beliefs and attitudes of the leader.* While no two people exhibit precisely the same leadership behavior, we can observe three basic styles: authoritarian (or autocratic), democratic, and laissez-faire.

Authoritarian leaders assume a position of intellectual and behavioral superiority in the group. They make the decisions, give the orders, and generally control all of the group's activities. *Democratic leaders* have more faith in the group than authoritarian leaders and consequently try to involve the group in making decisions. *Laissez-faire leaders* see themselves as no better or no worse than the other group members. Implicit in this style of leadership (or nonleadership?) is an assumption that direction will emerge from the group itself. The laissez-faire leader avoids dominating the group. In one of the earliest studies of the effects of leadership style, researchers compared groups of school children led by graduate students who had been specifically trained in one of the three leadership styles. The researchers defined the styles as shown in Table 10–1.

Table 10–1   Leader Behavior in Three "Social Climates"[5]

Authoritarian	Democratic	Laissez-faire
1. All determination of policy made by leader.	1. All policies a matter of group discussion and decision, encouraged and assigned by leader.	1. Complete freedom for group or individual decision; minimum of leader participation.
2. Techniques and activity steps dictated by the authority, one at a time, so that future steps are always largely uncertain.	2. Activity perspective gained during discussion period; general steps to group goal sketched, and when technical advice needed, leader suggests alternative procedures.	2. Various materials supplied by leader, making it clear he would supply information when asked, but taking no other part in discussion.
3. Particular work task and work companion of each member usually dictated by leader.	3. Members free to work with anyone; division of tasks left up to the group.	3. Complete nonparticipation of leader.
4. Dominator tending to be "personal" in praise and criticism of work of each member; remaining aloof from active group participation except when demonstrating.	4. Leader "objective" or "fact-minded" in praise and criticism, trying to be regular group member in spirit without doing too much of the work.	4. Infrequent, spontaneous comments on member activities unless questioned; no attempt to appraise or regulate course of events.

Briefly, here are the results of the study:

1. Groups with democratic leaders generally were more satisfied and functioned in a more orderly and positive way.
2. Groups with authoritarian leaders showed the highest incidence of aggressiveness as well as the highest incidence of apathy (depending on the group).
3. Members of democratic groups were more satisfied than the members of laissez-faire groups; a majority of group members preferred democratic to authoritarian, although some members were more satisfied in authoritarian groups.
4. Authoritarian groups spent more time engaged in productive work, but only when the leader was present.

It is tempting to conclude that humanistic, participatory, democratic leadership will invariably lead to greater satisfaction and higher productivity. Unfortunately, such a generalization is unwarranted by the evidence we now possess. (Remember, we warned you in Chapter One that group communication is complex. Generalizations are hard to come by.) Several studies have shown that no leadership style is effective in *all* situations. What works at General Motors may not work at the local church. An effective student-body president may be disastrous as a camp counselor. The expectations in one group differ from the expectations in another group.

Recent research on the effectiveness of different leadership styles has suggested that leadership effectiveness is contingent on a variety of interrelated factors such as culture, time constraints, group compatibility, and the nature of the group's task. While the functional approach to leadership reveals the importance of fulfilling various leadership roles in the group, it does not tell us which roles are most appropriate in which situation. Clearly we need to consider the setting in which leadership behavior occurs.

Situational Factors in Leadership Behavior: A Case Study

The situational approach to leadership views leadership effectively as an interaction between style and various situational factors. Consider the following case study.

Having been offered some very attractive extra retirement benefits by top management, Arthur agreed to take early retirement at age sixty-two. Once an ambitious and young junior executive for the company, Arthur had, in recent years, taken a rather relaxed, "anything goes" attitude as director of his division. As a result, his group had been showing the lowest productivity record in the company. Because of low productivity, Arthur's subordinates were not receiving attractive salary increments and other rewards from top management. Morale was very low and the employees were discontent.

Hoping to rejuvenate the group, management replaced Arthur with an extremely bright, dynamic, and aggressive young manager named Marilyn. Marilyn's instructions were these: Get your group's productivity up by 20 percent over the next twelve months or we'll fire the whole group and start from scratch with a new manager and new employees.

Marilyn began by studying the records of the employees in her new group to determine the strengths and weaknesses of each. She then drew up a set of goals and objectives for each employee and made assignments accordingly. A rigid timetable was set for each employee and all employees were directly accountable to Marilyn herself.

The employee response was overwhelmingly positive. Out of chaos had come order. Now each person knew what was expected and had tangible goals to achieve. There was a sense of great unity behind their new leader as they all strove to achieve their objective of a one year, 20 percent increase in productivity.

At the end of the year, productivity was up not 20 percent but 35 percent! Management was thrilled and awarded Marilyn a large raise in salary and the company's certificate of achievement.

Feeling that she had a viable formula for success, Marilyn moved into the second year as she had into the first; setting goals for each employee, holding them accountable, and so forth. But the second year things went less smoothly. Employees who had been quick to respond to her every wish the first year were less responsive. While the work she assigned was usually completed on time, the quality of the work was declining. It soon became evident that there was a morale problem among employees. Those who had once looked up to Marilyn as "Boss" were now calling her, sarcastically, "Queen Bee" and reminiscing about "the good old days" when Arthur was their manager.

Marilyn's behavior as manager had not changed over time, yet her leadership was no longer effective. Something needed to be done, but what?

David Korten has proposed that under certain conditions there is pressure to have a centralized, authoritarian leadership but that as these conditions change, a more democratic, participative form of leadership is likely to arise. Korten's work may give us an answer to Marilyn's problem.

Korten says that in situations where there is high goal structure and high stress, there is a move toward authoritarian leadership. Our case study is an example of this situation. When Marilyn took over as manager, the group was given a very specific goal—to raise productivity by 20 percent. At the same time, there was a good deal of stress; if they failed, they would lose their jobs. In such situations, the authoritarian style is effective and, in fact, appreciated by the group. Think of times in your own groups when there has been a clear goal but much uncertainty about how to achieve it. Remember when there has been high stress because of an impending deadline or a group grade. At such times a group will gladly follow any leader who can give the group direction and show them the means to that goal. But when the situation changes, that is, when there is less uncertainty, less stress, and a lower goal structure, the need for authoritarian leadership diminishes and is replaced by a need for more participative democratic leadership. To clarify this point, let's return to the case study.

While Marilyn's style of leadership the first year was appropriate, the situation changed at the end of that year. The goal had been reached and replaced by a much more loosely structured goal—that of *continuing* what the group had been doing. Simultaneously, external stress was reduced. The group no longer operated under the "20 percent ultimatum." Having learned what they had to do *as a group* to succeed, the employees were now ready to attend more to their *individual* needs in the group. The need for a more democratic, people-oriented style of leadership had arisen.

Figure 10-1 gives a graphic representation of Korten's situational leadership model. The model is applicable even on an international scale. Consider the differences between leadership and goal structure in the Soviet Union and in the United States. The Russians have been seeking a new way of life as yet unattained, therefore their goals are structured, concrete, and operational (*high goal structure*). By contrast, Americans focus on maintaining a process rather than on achieving change (*low goal structure*). The relationship of these goals to leadership styles in the two countries is obvious.

Figure 10-1   Relation of Stress, Goal Structuring, and Leadership Patterns

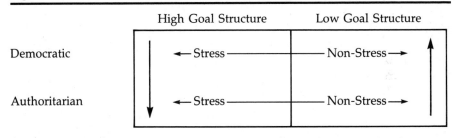

This figure drawn from "Situational Determinants of Leadership Structure" by David C. Korten is reprinted from *Journal of Conflict Resolution* Vol. 6, No. 3 (September 1962) pp. 222–235 by permission of the Publisher, Sage Publications, Inc.

Let's summarize this section and then return to the case study. Situational stress tends to lead to an increase in goal structuring. High goal structuring in the group arises from group (as opposed to individual) needs, task orientation, and a need for change. In such situations, authoritarian leadership patterns are likely to emerge. In the absence of stress, a group tends to maintain less structured goals. At such times there is an emphasis on the status quo and on individual (as opposed to group) needs. Democratic leadership is more appropriate here.

If Marilyn is to lead effectively, she has two basic options. She can either change her leadership style toward encouraging more participation from her employees (more process, less task), or she can continue in the authoritarian role by creating new stress or the illusion of stress. While the latter solution seems rather unethical, we mention it here because it is not an uncommon phenomenon.

A Contingency Model of Leadership Effectiveness

After fifteen years of examining over sixteen hundred small groups, Fred Fiedler developed a theory of leadership effectiveness which relates the effectiveness of a group to the situational variables which enable a leader to exert influence. His major finding—one which we shall explore further—was this: *Most people are effective leaders in some situations and ineffective in others.* Fiedler related two leadership styles ("task-oriented" and "relationship-oriented") to three situational variables (leader-member relations, task structure, and position power). Figure 10-2 graphically describes the ways in which *situational favorableness* may be related to the three situational variables.

Leader-member relations is assumed to be the most influential dimension of situational favorableness. The leader who is well-liked, respected, and trusted by other group members has little trouble exerting influence in that group.

Task structure ranks second in importance. Fiedler observed that most groups exist for the purpose of performing tasks required by an organization of which the group is a subunit. Since the organization has a rather large stake in the success or failure of the group, one way to assure compliance with the organization's task objectives is to give the group leader a standard set of operating instructions to follow, or a step-by-step way of tackling the problem. According to Fiedler:

> One important feature of the highly programmed or structured task is that the organization through the leader can maintain quality control over the process and over group behavior at every step. This also enables the organization to back up the leader whenever someone gets out of line. In effect, by structuring the task the organization is able to provide the leader with power, irrespective of the power of the position which he may occupy.[6]

Figure 10-2 Determinants of Situational Favorableness[7]

	1	2	3	4	5	6	7	8
Leader-Member Relations	GOOD				BAD			
Task Structure	HIGH		LOW		HIGH		LOW	
Leader Position Power	Strong	Weak	Strong	Weak	Strong	Weak	Strong	Weak

Position power is the least influential of the three determinants of situational favorableness identified by Fiedler. But Fiedler cautions us that this hierarchy must not be seen as "eternally fixed." Large differences in rank or status may outweigh task structure in some situations, but these situations are considered exceptions to the rule.

Returning to Figure 10-2 we can see that the model describes all possible combinations of conditions along these three dimensions. The eight cells of the model describe the eight possible combinations. Cell 1, indicating all dimensions high, represents the most favorable leadership situation. Cell 8, with all dimensions low, represents the least favorable leadership situation. The intervening cells, particularly Cell 4 and Cell 5, describe situations of *intermediate favorableness.*

The relationship of leadership style with situational favorableness was researched and described by Fiedler in terms of the leader's motivations. As we pointed out earlier in the chapter, most people are primarily motivated by either task concerns or maintenance concerns. Different group members usually perform these two functions. Fiedler identified those individuals who were primarily motivated by task concerns and those who were more motivated by human relations. Then he studied their effectiveness as leaders in situations of varying favorableness. Here is what Fiedler found:

> Leaders who are task motivated and task-controlling perform best under conditions that are very favorable or are relatively unfavorable for them. Considerate, relationship-motivated leaders perform best under conditions that are intermediate in favorableness.[8]

In other words, if you are highly task-oriented and lean toward the authoritarian style, you are likely to be most effective as a leader in groups where the situation is either very favorable or very unfavorable. Consider an unfavorable situation such as a fire in a theater. A leader who is considerate of the feelings and attitudes of the audience and who will not act before discussing decisions with the group is not going to gain a great deal of esteem from the panicking crowd. Rather, the people need decisive, authoritarian direction: "Let's get out of here! Follow me!" In a highly favorable situation where leader-member relations are strong, the task is clear-cut, and the leader has a position of authority, the task-motivated leader is operating under optimum conditions because the group is ready to work.

In the intermediate range of situational favorableness the process-oriented democratic leader is most effective. If position power is weak, the ability to influence must be based on the respect which group members hold for the leader. A democratic leader is more likely to gain this respect. When leader-member relations are bad or when there is confusion over the task, the group needs the confidence and cohesiveness which democratic leadership can foster. Again, when the situation is so bad that it appears hopeless, the call is for strong, authoritarian leadership to "bail out" the group.

Let's take another look at the contingency model from the leader's perspective. Fiedler suggests that while each of us is *primarily* motivated by task or process concerns, we are *secondarily* motivated by whichever concern was not our primary concern. If Harold is a real taskmaster as a leader and finds himself in a situation where the task is easily accomplished (as in high situational favorableness), Harold can then become more congenial toward his workers and thus satisfy both his primary and secondary needs. Harold will be satisfied *and* effective. If Wanda finds herself in a group where there are some relationship problems, she can satisfy her process motivational needs by helping resolve the conflict and then, secondarily, helping accomplish the group's task.

It is assumed, then, that *each of us is motivated toward both task and process concerns but that one of the two is a primary motivation.* Highly task-oriented individuals seem to function best in highly favorable or unfavorable situations, while the more process-oriented among us are more effective in situations of intermediate favorableness. Matching style to situation allows us to fulfill our motivation needs in order of their primacy.

The utility of Fiedler's theory and research is that if we can assess the situation in which we are working, we can determine the leadership style which will be most effective. Of course, changing our personalities is no easy task, but often we can bring about changes *in the situation* which will help us become more effective as leaders. In situations where we know we are not effective, we can lend our support to those in the group who *are* best equipped to deal with the situation. Furthermore, there may be times in your life when you must appoint a group leader. Fiedler's theory can help you select the most appropriate person for the job.

Some Observations on the Situational Approach to Leadership

The situational approach, at first glance, seems to cover all of the bases. It looks at style, task needs, process needs, and situational variables which influence the group. Unfortunately, most research utilizing this approach has focused on the behavior of leaders rather than on leadership as a total process of realizing group goals.[9] Thus, while the situational approach is useful, it is, perhaps, not as helpful to the student of small group communication as is the functional approach. The process of achieving a group goal involves *everyone* in the group, not just the leader. A continuing concern of students and scholars is the influence that group members' verbal and nonverbal statements have on the group goal.

EMERGENT LEADERSHIP IN SMALL GROUPS

A fascinating series of leadership studies conducted at the University of Minnesota (the "Minnesota Studies") sought the answer to the question: "Who is most likely to emerge as the perceived leader of a leaderless discussion group?" Led by Professor Ernest Bormann, the Minnesota Studies formed and observed "test-tube groups" which engaged in leaderless group discussions.

Most of us have an almost intuitive sense of the leader as someone who takes charge and organizes the discussion. Predictably, group members often perceive as leaders those who actively participate in the group and who direct their communication toward procedural matters. For example, a friend of ours has been called to jury duty on three occasions. Each time, when the jury has been dismissed to deliberate, our friend went to the head of the table, slapped his hands on it and said, "Well. I think our first order of business is to elect a foreman." He was, of course, elected to that position all three times.

While studies have shown a clear correlation between perceived leadership and talkativeness, it is not just those who talk the most who become leaders in a leaderless group. In fact, most groups do not select leaders at all. The Minnesota Studies showed that leaders *emerge* through a *method of residues* in which group members are rejected until only one remains. The first members to go, it seems, are the very quiet ones who do not actively participate in the early stages of the group's life. The next members eliminated are the talkative but overly aggressive or dogmatic members who are perceived as too inflexible for the leadership position.

After this initial phase of elimination, the group enters a second phase in which roughly half of the group members remain in contention for the leadership role. This phase of role emergence moves much more slowly than the first phase and it is a good deal more painful and frustrating. One by one, contenders are rejected until only one or two remain. Often, would-be leaders are rejected because their style is perceived as disturbing. In the classroom discussion groups of the Minnesota Studies, the authoritarian style was often rejected on the grounds that the person was "too bossy" or "dictatorial." Of course we must keep in mind that the authoritarian style, while perceived as inappropriate in a classroom discussion group, may be highly appropriate in other situations, especially those which involve extreme stress. In this second phase of role emergence the Minnesota Studies also found that, to some extent, the groups rejected female contenders, but only in groups with two or more men. In groups containing only one man, a female leader often would emerge and the man would be isolated—a pattern which may be changing.

Group members who were primarily task-motivated often rejected a contender who was perceived as too process-oriented, that is, too concerned about everyone's feelings and moods to be decisive. Likewise, members who were primarily process-oriented tended to reject those who they saw as overly concerned with the task.

According to Professor Bormann:

> In the final analysis groups accepted the contender who provided the optimum blend of task efficiency and personal consideration. The leader who emerged was the one that others thought would be of most value to the entire group and whose orders and directions they trusted and could follow.[10]

The Minnesota Studies give us some fascinating insight into the process through which group leaders emerge. While this information doesn't tell us specifically how to behave in order to rise to leadership positions, it does alert us to the process through which such things take place. These studies also remind us of the complexity of small groups and explain, to an extent, why a person who assumes a leadership role in one group may not in another and why a person who is perceived as a leader in two groups may not assume the same role in each.

LEADERSHIP TRAINING

One of the most consistently supported findings in small group research is that the productivity of a group will improve if training is provided for its members.[11] By **training** we mean instruction to develop skills. Whereas most of the instruction you receive in university classrooms primarily involves what and how you *think,* training shifts the emphasis to what you can *do.*

The simplest form of leadership training is providing group members with feedback on their performance.[12] There is evidence that when such feedback is provided, group members tend to work harder, particularly when they are being evaluated by an expert.[13] This technique of observation and feedback is the mainstay of most leadership training programs. Whether feedback is provided by other group members, an observer, or a video monitor, we need a more objective eye than our own to see what we are doing and how we can do it better. Beyond the basics, leadership training ranges from the simple (and inexpensive) to the elaborate (and expensive). Given the variable definitions of leadership we have outlined in this chapter, the training may justifiably encompass any or all of the principles and skills outlined in this book. Often, the training course will include a **simulation** exercise.

Simulations are structured exercises that create conditions that participants might confront outside of the training environment. The simulation provides a context in which participants can experiment with new behaviors without any risks. The "war games" that are a part of military training are one example of simulation; the conditions of war are re-created so that trainees can try out their new behaviors in a situation that is not life threatening. Likewise, many leadership and management training programs recreate the conditions of the work environment—through written reports, financial documents, and background information—in which trainees can experiment. Thus simulations are important to leadership training because they add a working context that approximates the actual circumstances for which participants are being trained.

While most training focuses more on behavior than it does on cognition, good training is multidimensional; that is, it incorporates more than one level of learning. Good training should provide us with a) an expanded set or repertoire of behaviors available to us, and b) the understanding and awareness to make judgments about why, how, and when to use those behaviors. To learn effectively, we need both principles and practice.

MANAGING MEETINGS EFFECTIVELY

Thus far in the chapter we have covered a great deal of material about leadership which, if applied properly, can help you become a better group leader or member. In this section of the chapter we're going to be more specific and prescriptive than usual. This section is about the "nuts and bolts" of managing meetings effectively as a designated leader. No matter how well informed and sensitive you are to leadership and group dynamics, there are some basics that we'd rather have you learn here than through trial and error.

Planning the Meeting

Many of the potential problems encountered by designated group leaders can be avoided by careful planning. Planning is one area of leadership that is often overlooked. There are a number of factors involved in planning a meeting. We have organized these factors under three rules that have been suggested by Professor Harry L. Ewbank, Jr.[14]

> Rule #1: Meet only when there is a specific purpose and when it is advantageous or desirable to solve problems and make decisions as a group.

One of the first decisions in planning meetings is whether or not to hold a meeting. Professor Ewbank reflects the sentiments of countless frustrated people when he says that "Any time is a good time *not* to hold a meeting."[15] Much time is wasted in meetings that are scheduled with no particular purpose in mind. Most people will be grateful to find fewer meetings on their calendars. Therefore, reflect carefully on the purpose of the meeting you are scheduling. Ask yourself whether the task to be done is the group's responsibility or if it might be accomplished more effectively through other channels.

> Rule #2: Meet with all (and only) those necessary to do the job.

If you have a choice about who is to attend the meeting you are calling, it is important to consider what resources the group will need to accomplish its task most effectively. Groups are often frustrated in their efforts when there are more or less individuals present than necessary. If there are certain types of information the group will need, be sure the people who have the information are present. On the other side, individuals who don't know why they are at the meeting usually prove to be disruptive.

Rule #3: Plan and distribute an agenda well in advance of the meeting time.

Be sure that all group members know the time and place of the meeting with enough advance notice to fit it into their schedules, or for you to reschedule the meeting if there are too many schedule conflicts. This type of planning is crucial, particularly when group members must travel to get to the meeting. In addition to the time and place of the meeting, the agenda should include all items to be discussed. This allows group members to prepare and gather whatever resources they need to contribute to the group's effort. The agenda should also include a time in which new business may be introduced by any group member, and a time at which the meeting is scheduled to conclude.

Plan your agendas carefully. A good agenda is realistic; it is an accurate reflection of what the group should be able to accomplish in the allotted time frame.

Directing the Meeting

Different groups accept (or tolerate) differing levels of direction from their designated leaders. One simple rule of thumb is this: When the designated leader is the natural, emergent leader of the group or, when he or she is the leader of a one-time-only *ad hoc* group, then the group will allow the leader to be much more directive. Beyond this simple rule, there are tasks that generally are expected of designated leaders. Two of the most important are getting the meeting started and keeping the group focused on its agenda.

To begin a group meeting with "Well, group, what shall we do tonight?" is an open invitation for personal agendas and leadership battles. Assuming that the group has an agenda, the discussion leader needs to 1) be sure that the group has enough (but not too much) time for orientation (see Chapter Eight), and 2) see that the group gets down to business. There are a variety of ways to initiate discussion. One of the most effective is to remind the group of its agenda and follow with an open-ended question (one that cannot be answered with a "yes" or "no").

As we have stressed throughout the book, it is important for group members to share a mutual understanding of the group's goals. When this is accomplished, the group's agenda for each meeting should provide a "road map" for moving toward those goals. It is often the responsibility of the designated leader to keep the group "on course." One of the most effective tools for doing this is *summarizing*. Periodically, take time to review your understanding of the group's progress and to check out that understanding with the other group members. Such summaries help the group take stock of what it has done and what it has yet to accomplish. Other leadership behaviors that help the group stay on the agenda are the functional roles we discussed earlier in the chapter (*see* also, Chapter Four) of "initiating," "clarifying," and "gatekeeping."

LEADERSHIP: PUTTING PRINCIPLE INTO PRACTICE

Leadership, whether we view it as a set of functions distributed throughout the group or as a behavior exhibited primarily by a designated leader, is an interplay among the needs of the group, the needs of the individuals within the group, and the ability of a person or persons to meet the needs and expectations of all.

In this chapter we have presented a variety of theories about and approaches to leadership. We stated at the outset and we reaffirm here that your attitudes toward leadership affect your behavior in small groups. For example, if you believe that a group leader should be the ultimate boss, you will probably be a bossy leader. This chapter is intended to provide you with more realistic and flexibile attitudes (and, therefore, behaviors) about group leadership. To review the chapter:

- There are three perspectives to the study of group leadership. The trait approach attempts to identify specific characteristics common to successful leaders. The functional approach views leadership as a set of behaviors which may be shared by all group members. The situational approach relates effective leadership to an interaction between leadership style and the group's situation.

- Three styles of leadership are authoritarian, democratic, and laissez-faire. Each of these styles has its benefits and drawbacks. The authoritarian style, for example, may be most efficient in many situations but often results in reduced member satisfaction over a longer period of time.

- Studies made at the University of Minnesota give us insight into the way leaders emerge in a leaderless group discussion. These studies suggest that those perceived by other group members as leaders are not chosen by the group *per se,* but are selected as leaders after a process of elimination or "method of residues."

- There is a considerable body of evidence suggesting that leadership training improves the productivity of small groups. At the core of most leadership training are the processes of observation, evaluation, and feedback.

All of the theory and research points to the conclusion that *the most effective leadership behavior is that which best meets the needs of the group.* Groups have both task and process needs which must be met. These and other situational variables determine the most appropriate type of leadership behavior. Here are some suggestions on how to apply what you've learned.

If you are the designated leader or chairperson of the group:

- The rest of the group will have certain expectations of you as leader. For example, they will probably expect you to be particularly influential on matters of procedure. Such expectations should be met.

- Prepare a realistic agenda well in advance and distribute it to all group members. At the meeting, help the group stick to its agenda.
- Analyze the group's situation—time constraints, goal structure, task structure, stress, leader-member relations, position power, and so on.
- Consider your own orientation toward group work. Are you motivated primarily by task concerns or by people concerns? Some situations call for decisive, authoritarian action. Is this what you're good at? If not, you may want to delegate authority to someone who is more task oriented, at least until the crisis has passed. Does your concern for task outweigh your concern for group-member relations? There may be times when you should follow the laissez-faire leadership style and let person-oriented members take over for a while. Adapt your style to the situation and use the resources of the group to everyone's advantage.
- In an ad hoc group that meets only once or twice, the style of leadership you choose is not nearly as important as it is in a committee that meets regularly over a long period of time. In most long-term situations, a democratic style of leadership is preferable. Provide procedural structure for the group, but encourage as much participation as possible. If you have the time, increased participation can breed a better quality decision or problem solution.
- Remember that groups have task *and* process needs. They need to get the job done, but they also need encouragement, praise, and thanks.

If you are *not* the designated leader or chairperson of the group:

- While you have less control in this situation because of the different set of expectations the group has of you, you are still influential. You can still demonstrate leadership behavior.
- Use your knowledge about small group communication—leadership, problem solving, growth, and development—to analyze what is going on in the group. Consider your own strengths as a group member. What roles do you fulfill best in the group? Use your strengths to provide what the group needs and support those who have other needed skills.
- Occasionally the designated leader does not seem up to the task and there is a leadership void in the group. This often occurs when leaders are appointed by an outside source or when the leader is elected at the first meeting, before group members have had an adequate opportunity to evaluate each other as potential leaders. In these cases, rely on the functional approach since *any* member of the group (including yourself) can provide leadership. Watch out for delicate egos. When people (including our designated leaders) don't live up to our expectations we tend to experience negative feelings toward them. In a small group this can result in an attempt to overthrow the designated leader or in a resentful and ineffectual group climate. The group's actual task is set aside while group

members hassle over the issue of "who's running the show." Almost invariably, the results are unsatisfactory, with bruised egos being the most common injury. For a more effective strategy, work around—don't overthrow—an ineffectual leader (to every rule, of course, there are exceptions). Leadership can come from *any* group member while the designated leader's self-esteem remains intact.

- Sometimes a small group contains a wealth of leadership talent. Leadership is not (or *should* not be) a contest for status and power. Individual goals must be placed behind group goals. Good leaders need good followers and supporters.

In every group the effectiveness of the leadership you provide depends upon the situation, your sensitivity to the needs of the group, and your ability to adapt your communicative behavior to meet those needs.

PRACTICE

Task Process Leadership Questionnaire[16]

The following items describe aspects of leadership behavior. Respond to each item according to the way you would most likely act if you were the leader of a work group. Circle whether you would most likely behave in the described way: always (A), frequently (F), occasionally (O), seldom (S), or never (N).

A F O S N   **1.** I would most likely act as the spokesman of the group.

A F O S N   **2.** I would encourage overtime work.

A F O S N   **3.** I would allow members complete freedom in their work.

A F O S N   **4.** I would encourage the use of uniform procedures.

A F O S N   **5.** I would permit the members to use their own judgment in solving problems.

A F O S N   **6.** I would stress being ahead of competing groups.

A F O S N   **7.** I would speak as a representative of the group.

A F O S N   **8.** I would needle members for greater effort.

A F O S N   **9.** I would try out my ideas in the group.

A F O S N   **10.** I would let the members do their work the way they think best.

A F O S N   **11.** I would be working hard for a promotion.

A F O S N   **12.** I would tolerate postponement and uncertainty.

A F O S N   **13.** I would speak for the group if there were visitors present.

A F O S N   **14.** I would keep the work moving at a rapid pace.

A F O S N   **15.** I would turn the members loose on a job and let them go to it.

A F O S N   **16.** I would settle conflicts when they occur in the group.

A F O S N   **17.** I would get swamped by details.

A F O S N   **18.** I would represent the group at outside meetings.

A F O S N   **19.** I would be reluctant to allow the members any freedom of action.

A F O S N   **20.** I would decide what should be done and how it should be done.

A F O S N   **21.** I would push for increased production.

A F O S N   **22.** I would let some members have authority which I could keep.

A F O S N   **23.** Things would usually turn out as I had predicted.

A F O S N   **24.** I would allow the group a high degree of initiative.

A F O S N   **25.** I would assign group members to particular tasks.

A F O S N   **26.** I would be willing to make changes.

A F O S N   **27.** I would ask the members to work harder.

A F O S N   **28.** I would trust the group members to exercise good judgment.

A F O S N   **29.** I would schedule the work to be done.

A F O S N   **30.** I would refuse to explain my actions.

A F O S N   **31.** I would persuade others that my ideas are to their advantage.

A F O S N   **32.** I would permit the group to set its own pace.

A F O S N   **33.** I would urge the group to beat its previous record.

A F O S N   **34.** I would act without consulting the group.

A F O S N   **35.** I would ask that group members follow standard rules and regulations.

Task Process Leadership-Style Profile Sheet[17]

To determine your style of leadership, mark your score on the *concern for task* dimension (T) on the left-hand arrow in the figure on page 237. Next, move to the right-hand arrow and mark your score on the *concern for people* dimension (P). Draw a straight line that intersects the P and T scores. The point at which that line crosses the *shared leadership* arrow indicates your score on that dimension.

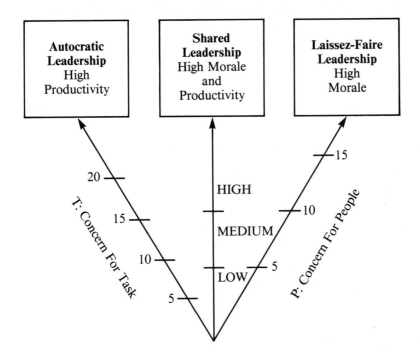

**Shared Leadership Results from
Balancing Concern for Task and Concern for People**

Leadership Exercises

1. Observe a working group and analyze the situation from the perspective
    of Fiedler's contingency model. What type of leadership is most appropri-
    ate for this situation? What type of leadership is actually taking place?

2. Consider the stages in problem solving described in Chapter Six. Identify
    which leadership functions might be most appropriate at each stage of
    development.

3. At some time you have probably been in a position of leadership. How
    does the style of leadership you choose relate to the way you feel about
    yourself as a person, a leader, or a discussant? How does it relate to the
    way you feel about groups? Other people? Do you want to assume leader-
    ship?

4. Consider the dialogue between Harold and Wanda presented early in this
    chapter. List five responses you might make which would help the group,
    and especially Harold and Wanda, resolve the conflict.

Notes

1. A. Paul Hare, *Handbook of Small Group Research,* 2nd ed. (New York: The Free Press, 1976).

2. Dane Archer, "The Face of Power: Physical Attractiveness as a Non-Verbal Predictor of Small-Group Stratification," *Proceedings of the 81st Annual Convention of the American Psychological Association* 8, Part 1: 177–78.

3. Hare, p. 278.

4. Dean Barnlund and Franklyn Haiman, *The Dynamics of Discussion* (Boston: Houghton Mifflin Company, 1960), pp. 275–79.

5. Ralph White and Ronald Lippitt, "Leader Behavior and Member Reaction in Three 'Social Climates' " in *Group Dynamics,* 3rd ed., Dorwin Cartwright and Alvin Zander, eds. (New York: Harper and Row, Publishers, Inc., 1968), p. 319.

6. Fred Fiedler, *A Theory of Leadership Effectiveness* (New York: McGraw-Hill Book Company, 1967), p. 144.

7. Adapted from Fred Fiedler, "Personality and Situational Determinants of Leadership Effectiveness" in *Group Dynamics,* Cartwright and Zander, eds.

8. Fiedler, "Personality and Situational Determinants of Leadership Effectiveness," p. 372.

9. Dennis Gouran, "Conceptual and Methodological Approaches to the Study of Leadership," *Central States Speech Journal* 21 (Winter 1970): 217–23.

10. Ernest Bormann, *Discussion and Group Methods,* 2nd ed. (New York: Harper and Row, Publishers, Inc. 1975), p. 256.

11. For a list of studies that support this assertion, see A. Paul Hare, *Handbook of Small Group Research,* 2nd. ed. (New York: The Free Press, 1976), p. 354.

12. Rita Spoelders-Claes, "The Effect of Varying Feedback on the Effectiveness of a Small Group on a Physical Task," *Psychologica Belgica* 13 (1): 61–68.

13. Murray Webster, Jr., "Source of Evaluations and Expectations for Performance," *Sociometry* 32 (3): 243–58.

14. Henry L. Ewbank, Jr., *Meeting Management* (Dubuque, IA: Wm. C. Brown Company Publishers, 1968).

15. Ibid., p. 8.

16. The T-P Leadership Questionnaire was adapted from Sergiovanni, Metzcus, and Burden's revision of the Leadership Behavior Description Questionnaire, *American Educational Research Journal* 6 (1969), pages 62–79.

17. Ibid., p. 12.

11 Observing and Evaluating Group Communication

After studying this chapter, you should be able to:

■ Explain the relationship between group communication theory and systematic observation of small group phenomena.

■ Describe three classes of observational systems and the circumstances under which each is appropriate.

■ Record group interaction with an interaction diagram, apply one or more category systems, and interpret the results.

■ Use at least two self-report instruments to measure role perceptions and group cohesiveness.

■ Explain why self-report measures can be helpful to a group.

■ Observe, record, and interpret group interaction using Bales' Interaction Process Analysis.

■ Observe and evaluate group leadership using one of the systems presented in this chapter.

■ Design and implement a post-meeting reaction sheet.

Observing and Evaluating Group Communication

By reading the first ten chapters of this book and by participating in classroom activities you have learned about a variety of factors which contribute to effective communication in the small group. You have learned *what* you need to observe in studying small group communication; now you will learn *how* to observe these variables in a systematic way. Having such knowledge can benefit both you and the small groups in which you participate. While few of you will become serious theorists and researchers of small group communication, all of you will find ample opportunity to apply your knowledge and skills. What you have learned so far should make you more sensitive to the dynamics which affect small group communication. The material presented in this chapter will provide you with a way to *validate* your observations, thereby giving you an additional tool with which to help your groups. For example, if you see a particular communication network or role distribution emerging in the group, making an interaction diagram and applying a category system can confirm your observations and offer you a means of recording changes in those patterns over time. If terms like "interaction diagram" and "category system" are new to you, read on.

THEORY AND OBSERVATION: A NATURAL RELATIONSHIP

As we pointed out in Chapter Two, building theories is a very basic human process which takes place whenever we try to make sense of the events and phenomena surrounding us. Theories are *explanations* which can lead us to more successful *predictions*. Theories reduce uncertainty. We have presented a lot of theoretical material in this book: theories about group formation, growth and development; theories about leadership effectiveness; theories about conflict and "groupthink," and so forth. These theories give us a way of breaking down group process into its constituent elements and some guidance in analyzing the relationships between them. Before you took this course you were, no doubt, aware of the frustrations of working in small groups but you did not have the tools to explain what was happening. Now you do. Theories serve as our tools to explain—they are observation systems unto themselves. Once we have a theoretical description of small groups we no longer look at group phenomena, we look *for* them. *Our theoretical understanding guides our practical observations.* In essence, then, this entire book has been devoted to enhancing your skills in observing and evaluating the communication in small groups. Each chapter has taken one or more components of group process and has theoretically described how these components combine to enhance or detract from the effectiveness of the group.

This chapter will provide you with some tools with which you can *validate* the observations you make. Some of these tools you can readily use during any small group meeting. Others require more preparation and structure. All of these tools will enable you to systematically describe many of the variables discussed in this book as they apply to working groups. We will begin with a simple but effective way of describing interaction patterns in the small group, then we will examine several systems for analyzing group interaction. These systems fall into three general areas of classification: *Interaction categories* give us various classes for "pigeonholing" the observed behavior of group members; *interaction ratings* involve the observer judging the communicative acts according to a set of criteria; *self-report measures* ask group members to describe their own situations.

OBSERVING COMMUNICATION NETWORKS: INTERACTION DIAGRAMS

In Chapter Five we suggested that communication networks—who talks to whom—have an effect on group cohesiveness, leadership patterns, and group productivity. A few minutes spent observing small group interaction can show you clearly that group members infrequently address the group as a whole; instead, they tend to address specific group members. An **interaction diagram** can reveal a lot about the interaction patterns in your group. It tells you who is talking to whom and how often. You can identify the most active and the more reticent members. You can pattern the relationships that form between group members. By combining an interaction diagram with a **category system** , you can recognize the nature of the contributions each group member makes to the group. Interaction diagrams are extremely useful tools. Here's how to make one:

1. Draw a circle for each member of the group, arranging your circles in the same relative positions as that in which group members are seated (Figure 11–1).
2. Refer to Figure 11–1. If Nancy were to open the meeting by asking Phil

Figure 11-1   Interaction Diagram

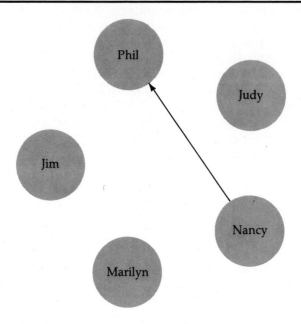

for the minutes from the last meeting, you would draw an arrow from Nancy's circle to Phil's, indicating the direction and destination of Nancy's communication. Each subsequent remark made by Nancy to Phil would then be indicated by a short crossmark at the base of the arrow.

3. Repeat this process each time someone in the group addresses someone else. If Phil were to address the minutes to Nancy, you would put an arrowhead at the other end of the line that connects the two.

4. Indicate communication addressed to the group as a whole with a line pointing away from the center of the group. Again, note subsequent remarks with crossmarks.

5. Figure 11-2 is an example of what a completed interaction diagram might look like.

If you take a few moments to examine Figure 11-2 you will see some patterns beginning to emerge. For example, Phil seems to be the most vocal in the group. Furthermore, most members address their remarks to Phil which suggests that Phil is perceived as the group's leader. Additional support for this observation is found in the frequency with which Phil addresses the group as a whole. The amount of communication shared between Phil and Jim indicates a strong relationship there, perhaps that of a leader and his "lieutenant."

Figure 11-2   Completed Interaction Diagram

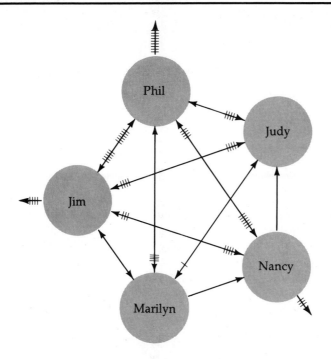

The interaction diagram is an easy way to describe *graphically* the interaction patterns in the group. Also, this method of observation can be used without seriously disrupting the regular workings of the group. By updating the interaction diagram during several meetings, you can observe changes in group interaction and, as we shall soon see, the addition of a category system to the interaction diagram renders this a most powerful descriptive tool.

OBSERVING GROUP CLIMATE

We learned in Chapter Five that groups tend to be more cohesive when all group members participate actively. The interaction diagram is clearly a way to measure this dynamic and a good deal more. If we apply **a category system** to our interaction diagram we can make some observations about the *content* of the communication in addition to measuring its *amount* and *direction*.

As we noted earlier, *interaction categories* are classifications of behavior into which our various communicative attempts may fall. In Chapter Five we introduced you to two such systems: Gibb's categories of defensive and supportive communication and Sieburg's categories of confirming and disconfirming responses. Let's consider Sieburg's categories and see how they might be used in conjunction with an interaction diagram.

Confirming and Disconfirming Responses

As you may recall, Sieburg described the types of responses which cause people either to value themselves more or to value themselves less. Clearly an understanding of these "confirming" and "disconfirming" typologies can assist us in improving the group climate. After all, when people treat us in ways that devalue us, it doesn't exactly enhance a sense of warmth and a bond of friendship. If a group has little cohesiveness, if interpersonal trust is low, and if the group is going nowhere, the ways in which group members are responding to one another may be to blame. We can use Sieburg's system for charting interpersonal responses in the group to find out.

If we wanted to analyze this phenomenon in detail, we would videotape the group in action and carefully analyze each interpersonal response according to Sieburg's system. More informally, we can note types of responses on an interaction diagram as they occur.

The first step in this endeavor is to become thoroughly familiar with the different kinds of responses so that you can recognize them. Secondly, as you draw the interaction diagram, take note of types of responses and keep a list of these responses next to the circle representing the person who *elicited* the response. For example:

Mike: Well gang, I stayed up all night working on the problem and I think I've finally figured out a way to rig the boat to get that extra wind power we need to win the race this weekend.

Betsy: Peggy, did you get around to pricing those new winches we need for the foredeck?

Figure 11-3   Interaction Diagram

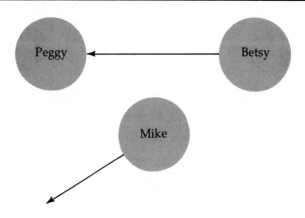

In Figure 11–4, note that Betsy's "impervious response" is recorded next to Mike's name. This may seem a bit illogical at first but there's good reason for it. Sieburg's theory describes the effects of Betsy's "impervious response" on Mike. If we are going to examine the group's cohesiveness or morale, we need to look at particular communicative behaviors in terms of their *effects* on the *receivers* of those acts.

There's another good reason for recording confirming and disconfirming responses in this way. Imagine that you are attending a group meeting at which another member is busily taking notes and drawing interaction diagrams. Toward the end of the meeting, he reports that he would like to provide the group with a little feedback. He presents his interaction diagram, then turns to you and says, "I don't suppose that you were aware that you gave three tangential responses, one impervious response, two irrelevant responses, and interrupted others eleven times?" How would you feel? A bit defensive, eh?

By focusing attention on the *receivers* of disconfirming responses, you can identify behaviors which may be detrimental to the group climate without attacking the *senders.* If we openly criticize others, we are likely to increase defensiveness in the group. Many of us inadvertently disconfirm other group members' responses. We interrupt and often fail to acknowledge what others have said before we throw in our "two cents." The effects of these behaviors need to come to our attention, but we do not need to be openly criticized for that which we did not intend. Note, however, that there may be times when, *with the group's consent,* we might gain considerable benefit from identifying confirming or disconfirming behaviors with those who *emit* them.

Many category systems may be used effectively with an interaction diagram. We have mentioned Sieburg's and Gibb's systems as ways of measuring some of the dynamics which affect group climate. Diagrams and category

Figure 11–4   Interaction Diagram With Categories

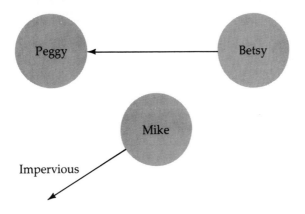

systems can be very helpful to the group. If you suspect a problem in your group, such a system strengthens your observations. It provides tangible evidence for the group and it detaches you from your observations—important considerations if you don't want your group to respond defensively to you in your role as evaluator. Be careful, though, not to cast yourself as an outsider. If you are a part of the group you are observing, use observational systems only with the group's consent. Then, with the information you provide, the group can achieve greater insight into its process and, ideally, more effective communication.

OBSERVING ROLES AND ROLE PERCEPTIONS

In Chapter Four (Relating to Others in Small Groups) and Chapter Ten (Leadership) we discussed the importance of role formation, role perceptions, role expectations, role enactment, and role behaviors as leadership functions. In this section we will describe some methodologies for clarifying role behavior in small groups: Group Role Inventory and Benne and Sheats' categories of Functional Roles.

Group Role Inventory

When there is a difference between the way we see ourselves and the way others see us, when there is a difference between role perception and role enactment, and when our expectations of people cloud our perceptions of them, there is a potential source of uncertainty, confusion, frustration, and conflict. The Group Role Inventory was designed to help members become more aware of the roles they play and of how others perceive those roles. It is time consuming—at least forty-five minutes are needed—but often worth the time and effort it takes, particularly when the group is having trouble establishing norms. The Group Role Inventory can also be an effective means for dealing with one or two "problem members" by bringing everyone's role expectations into the discussion rather than by "ganging up" on the troublesome members.

Group Role Inventory

Objectives:	To become aware of the roles we play in our group and of how others perceive our roles
Materials:	Group Role Inventory Sheet (attached)
Time:	Forty-five minutes
Partici-pants:	On-going groups
Procedures:	1) Fill out Group Role Inventory Sheet.

2) Go over the list and check the role you would like
   to have performed but did not perform.
3) Go over the list again and star (*) the role you
   performed but would rather not have performed.
4) Discuss results with your group.

Applica-   The exercise should make members aware of how roles are
tion: used in their groups.

Group Role Inventory Sheet

Who in your group, including yourself, is most likely to:

1. Take initiative, propose ideas, get things started?
2. Sit back and wait passively for others to lead?
3. Express feelings most freely, frankly, openly?
4. Keep feelings hidden, reserved, unexpressed?
5. Show understanding of other members' feelings?
6. Be wrapped up in personal concerns and not very responsive to others?
7. Interrupt others when they are speaking?
8. Daydream, be lost in private thoughts during group sessions, be "far away"?
9. Give you a feeling of encouragement, warmth, friendly interest, support?
10. Converse privately with someone else while another member is speaking to the group?
11. Talk of trivial things, superficial chitchat?
12. Criticize you, put you on your guard?
13. Feel superior to other members?
14. Be listened to by everyone while speaking?
15. Feel inferior to other members?
16. Contribute good ideas?
17. Contradict, disagree, argue, raise objections?
18. Sulk or withdraw when the group is displeasing?
19. Be the one you would like to have on your side if a conflict arose in the group?
20. Agree or conform with whatever is said?
21. Be missed, if absent, more than any other member?

Functional Roles

If we view leadership as sets of behaviors which are distributed throughout the group (*see* Chapter Ten), we should be able to observe group interaction and identify leadership roles. Such observations can help us pinpoint which leadership roles are being filled and which are being omitted, thus showing us how leadership roles function in relation to the group's purpose or task.

Kenneth D. Benne and Paul Sheats designed a category system which we discussed in Chapters Four and Ten. Their system includes *group task roles, group building and maintenance roles, and individual roles.*[1] Used alone or in conjunction with an interaction diagram, these categories of functional roles are powerful observational tools.

Table 11-1 Seashore Index of Group Cohesiveness[2]

Check one response for each question.

1. Do you feel that you are really a part of your work group?
   _____ Really a part of my work group
   _____ Included in most ways
   _____ Included in some ways, but not in others
   _____ Don't feel I really belong
   _____ Don't work with any one group of people
   _____ Not ascertained

2. If you had a chance to do the same kind of work for the same pay in another work group, how would you feel about moving?
   _____ Would want very much to move
   _____ Would rather move than stay where I am
   _____ Would make no difference to me
   _____ Would want very much to stay where I am
   _____ Not ascertained

3. How does your work group compare with other similar groups on each of the following points?

	Better than most	About the same as most	Not as good as most	Not ascertained
a. The way the members get along together	_____	_____	_____	_____
b. The way the members stick together	_____	_____	_____	_____
c. The way the members help each other on the job	_____	_____	_____	_____

OBSERVING GROUP COHESIVENESS

Self-Report Measure: A Cohesiveness Index

Cohesiveness, as we stated in Chapter Five, is often described as the attraction which a group holds for its members. You can measure this variable by asking individual group members to describe their feelings toward the group. *Self-report measures* are easy to design and can provide a great deal of useful information. Seashore's Index of Group Cohesiveness (*see* p. 248) exemplifies the self-report methodology.

OBSERVING GROUP INTERACTION

A widely-used and time-tested scheme for observing group interaction is the *Interaction Process Analysis* (IPA), designed by Robert Bales in 1950. While the IPA was originally intended for formal, empirical research application, it can be adapted readily for more informal group observation. Bales' category scheme consists of twelve classes of statements which fall into four general types: *positive reactions, attempted answers, questions,* and *negative reactions.* Use the Interaction Process Analysis by observing group interaction, counting the number of statements which fall into each category, and analyzing the data as it applies to that group's phase of development in the problem-solving process. As with the use of interaction diagrams and category systems, Bales' Interaction Process Analysis can reveal a great deal about the structure of small group communication.

Interaction Process Analysis

Table 11–2 lists Bales' categories of interaction. While these categories are only part of a complete Interaction Process Analysis, they are sufficient for most informal uses.

As we mentioned earlier, Bales' categories can be used informally to record and analyze interaction patterns in groups. Goldberg and Larson describe a simple but effective way of doing so:

> For simple class-related activities, you can develop a form sheet to record your observations. List the twelve basic categories down the left-hand margin of a sheet. Draw vertical lines down the sheet so that a series of columns is present. Number the columns consecutively at the top of the sheet. When completed, the sheet will consist of a large matrix, the rows defined by the twelve categories and the columns numbered across the top. Each column may be used to record a single interaction unit. When the scoring is completed, the sequence of the interaction units will be recorded and numbered in keeping with the columns. Usually, members are identified by code numbers, from one to N. Who speaks to whom can be recorded simply by a series of coupled numbers. Remarks addressed by members to the group as a whole are indicated by a zero. Thus, 2–0 would refer to group member number 2 addressing the group as a whole.

Table 11-2 Bales' Interaction Categories[3]

Positive Reactions	1. Shows solidarity, raises others' status, gives help, rewards
	2. Shows tension release, jokes, laughs, shows satisfaction
	3. Shows agreement, shows passive acceptance, understands, concurs, complies
Attempted Answers	4. Gives suggestion, direction, implying autonomy for others
	5. Gives opinion, evaluation, analysis, expresses feeling, wish
	6. Gives information, orientation, repeats, clarifies, confirms
Questions	7. Asks for information, orientation, repetition, confirmation
	8. Asks for opinion, evaluation, analysis, expression of feeling
	9. Asks for suggestion, direction, possible ways of action
Negative Reactions	10. Disagrees, shows passive rejection, formality, withholds help
	11. Shows tension, asks for help, withdraws out of field
	12. Shows antagonism, deflates others' status, defends or asserts self

Whether a group progresses through certain phases in problem solving, whether task and social-emotional behaviors are balanced or disproportionate, whether certain members disproportionately engage in specific forms of behavior, whether specific member's behavior vary with respect to the problem phase (orientation, evaluation, control, etc.) through which the group is progressing, whether certain members talk disproportionately to certain other members, whether group interaction assumes a particular form or pattern following decision proposals, and many other questions may be explored tentatively on the basis of your analysis and observation of member behaviors conforming to these twelve basic categories.[4]

Clearly, the use of Bales' Interaction Process Analysis can yield a great deal of information about a group's processes—information which can help you understand small group communication and attempt to make it better.

OBSERVING GROUP LEADERSHIP

The ability to lead a small group is, to a large extent, the ability to communicate effectively, to send and receive messages clearly and without disruption, to channel, focus, and interpret the communication of others so that the meanings of messages are shared by all, and to help the group avoid "anything that needlessly inflates the time and energy required to exchange meanings."[5] When we observe and evaluate leadership, then, we are analyzing the *quality of communication* in the small group. In this section we present two *rating scales*. Rating scales are particularly valuable for measuring leadership in that they go beyond the descriptive properties of category systems by including an *evaluative* component which is essential if we are to measure the *quality of communication*.

Leadership Rating Scale

Table 11–3 Barnlund-Haiman Leadership Rating Scale[6]

Instructions: This rating scale may be used to evaluate leadership in groups with or without official leaders. In the latter case (the leaderless group) use part A of each item only. When evaluating the actions of an official leader use parts A and B of each item on the scale.

INFLUENCE IN PROCEDURE

Initiating Discussion

A.	3	2	1	0	1	2	3
	Group needed more help in getting started			Group got right amount of help			Group needed less help in getting started

B. The quality of the introductory remarks was:

Excellent	Good	Adequate	Fair	Poor

Organizing Group Thinking

A.	3	2	1	0	1	2	3
	Group needed more direction in thinking			Group got right amount of help			Group needed less direction in thinking

B. If and when attempts were made to organize group thinking they were:

Excellent	Good	Adequate	Fair	Poor

Clarifying Communication

A.	3	2	1	0	1	2	3
	Group needed more help in clarifying communication			Group got right amount of help			Group needed less help in clarifying communication

B.   If and when attempts were made to clarify communication they were:

Excellent	Good	Adequate	Fair	Poor

Summarizing and Verbalizing Agreements

A.   3   2   1   0   1   2   3

Group needed more help in summarizing and verbalizing agreements		Group got right amount of help		Group needed less help in summarizing and verbalizing agreements	

B.   If and when attempts were made to summarize and verbalize agreements they were:

Excellent	Good	Adequate	Fair	Poor

Resolving Conflict

A.   3   2   1   0   1   2   3

Group needed more help in resolving conflict		Group got right amount of help		Group needed less help in resolving conflict	

B.   If and when attempts were made to resolve conflict they were:

Excellent	Good	Adequate	Fair	Poor

INFLUENCE IN CREATIVE AND CRITICAL THINKING

Stimulating Critical Thinking

A.   3   2   1   0   1   2   3

Group needed more stimulation in creative thinking		Group got right amount of help		Group needed less stimulation in creative thinking	

B.   If and when attempts were made to stimulate ideas they were:

Excellent	Good	Adequate	Fair	Poor

Encouraging Criticism

A.   3   2   1   0   1   2   3

Group needed more encouragement to be critical		Group got right amount of help		Group needed less encouragement to be critical	

B.   If and when attempts were made to encourage criticism they were:

Excellent	Good	Adequate	Fair	Poor

Balancing Abstract and Concrete Thought

A.   3   2   1   0   1   2   3

Group needed to be more concrete	Group achieved proper balance	Group needed to be more abstract

B.   If and when attempts were made to balance abstract and concrete thought they were:

Excellent	Good	Adequate	Fair	Poor

INFLUENCE IN INTERPERSONAL RELATIONS

Climate-Making

A.   3   2   1   0   1   2   3

Group needed more help in securing a permissive atmosphere	Group got right amount of help	Group needed less help in securing a permissive atmosphere

B.   If and when attempts were made to establish a permissive atmosphere they were:

Excellent	Good	Adequate	Fair	Poor

Regulating Participation

A.   3   2   1   0   1   2   3

Group needed more regulation of participation	Group got right amount of help	Group needed less regulation of participation

B.   If and when attempts were made to regulate participation they were:

Excellent	Good	Adequate	Fair	Poor

Over-all Leadership

A.   3   2   1   0   1   2   3

Group needed more control	Group got right amount of control	Group needed less control

B.   If and when attempts were made to control the group they were:

Excellent	Good	Adequate	Fair	Poor

Feedback Rating Instrument

A somewhat more complex scale to measure the quality of communication has been designed by Dale Leathers. This scale, or *instrument,* examines *feedback* to determine whether "one's messages seem to produce confusion or tension or inflexibility or all three," based on the assumption that, "effectiveness and efficient communication in discussion demand that the sender of a message receive feedback of maximum 'self-correcting' potential if the sender is to possess the flexibility of response so necessary in small group communication."[7] The basic unit to be observed is the "feedback event," usually a complete utterance by an individual group member that is immediately preceded and followed by statements from another group member.

> Georgette: I've been trying to figure out what the company's policy is on this issue so I went and spoke with the first vice-president.
>
> Roger (facetiously):   I'll bet *that* was an enlightening experience.
>
> Georgette: C'mon, Roger, you're not being fair to him.

The statements above constitute feedback. Roger's facetious remark is feedback to Georgette. When we look at Georgette's first statement, Roger's feedback, and Georgette's second statement, we can see a disruptive effect: Whatever it was that Georgette was going to say to the group was thwarted. Examining feedback events allows us to see their *immediate effects* on the small group communication process.

Leathers' Feedback Rating Instrument is based on findings which suggest that every feedback response has nine dimensions: (1) Deliberateness, (2) Relevancy, (3) Atomization, (4) Fidelity, (5) Tension, (6) Ideation, (7) Flexibility, (8) Digression, and (9) Involvement. Definitions of each of these are provided on the scales in Table 11–4.

Table 11–4   Leathers' Feedback Rating Instrument[8]

	Symbol			Deliberateness			Signal
Scale	3	2	1	0	1	2	3
#1							

Symbol response represents a deliberate, carefully reasoned, logical response; signal response represents an immediate, unthinking, largely automatic, visceral response of Y to X.

	Relevant			Relevancy			Irrelevant
Scale	3	2	1	0	1	2	3
#2							

Relevancy—extent to which Y seeks to establish the connection between X's comment and the comment that immediately preceded X's comment.

	Unified			Atomization			Atomized
Scale	3	2	1	0	1	2	3
#3							

Degree to which Y's contribution involves incomplete, fragmented, or disjointed thought; includes running a number of ideas together, a number of people talking at the same time.

	Clear			Fidelity			Confused
Scale	3	2	1	0	1	2	3
#4							

Extent to which Y's response to X exhibits confusion as to the meaning and/or intent of X's original message; characterized by the necessity of Y's seeking clarification, definition, expansion, etc., from X.

	Relaxed			Tension			Tense
Scale	3	2	1	0	1	2	3
#5							

Degree to which nonverbal gestures like laughter, sighs, groans, etc., indicate Y's relative state of tension or relaxation.

	Ideational			Ideation			Personal
Scale	3	2	1	0	1	2	3
#6							

Ideational responses involve an appraisal or evaluation of X's ideas; personal responses represent the degree to which Y's comments involve direct or implied criticism of X, as a person.

	Flexible			Flexibility			Inflexible
Scale #7	3	2	1	0	1	2	3

Inflexible response indicates Y's unwillingness to modify his position in response to X's contribution; may include a counterassertion.

	Concise			Digression			Digressive
Scale #8	3	2	1	0	1	2	3

Degree to which Y inhibits X's immediate response, primarily by means of lengthy and discursive utterances.

	Involved			Involvement			Withdrawn
Scale #9	3	2	1	0	1	2	3

Degree to which Y seeks to avoid comment on X's contribution by attempting to withdraw from the discussion of X's contribution.

In order to make an evaluation using the nine scales it is necessary to approach the discussion with a strategy for selecting feedback responses to evaluate. In an ongoing group one strategy might be to rate the feedback responses of individual members over time. In a "one shot" observation, you might select every Nth feedback response to evaluate.

EVALUATING GROUP MEETINGS

An extremely useful tool for providing feedback to a group about its perform-ance and progress is a post-meeting reaction sheet. These can be designed in any way that provides the most useful information for the group or group leader. They take only a few minutes to fill in, and can provide information that can dramatically improve how the group functions. An example follows.

Post-Meeting Reaction Sheet

Date:

Meeting #:

Was the purpose of this meeting understood clearly by all group members? Were all aware of the agenda?

How would you characterize the social climate of this meeting?

Was there relatively equal participation by all group members or did one or two monopolize the discussion?

Was there conflict during this meeting? If so, how well did the group manage it?

Did the group work through its agenda successfully?

Make three suggestions for improving the next meeting.

Any additional comments?

OBSERVING AND EVALUATING GROUP COMMUNICATION: PUTTING PRINCIPLE INTO PRACTICE

This chapter has presented a number of ways in which you can observe, measure, and evaluate small group communication processes. While most of the measures described were developed for the purpose of small group research, they can be extremely helpful in reducing uncertainty about the dynamics of *any* group. The theories, descriptions, and examples throughout this book, and the tools presented in this chapter provide you with knowledge which will help your groups become more effective.

Take a moment before you close the book and return to the model of small group communication presented in Chapter Two. To be understood fully, all of the components of that model—goals, leadership, outcomes, norms, roles, cohesiveness, and speech communication—need to be seen as interconnected and as mutually influential. By necessity we have treated these components one at a time, but in reality these phenomena occur in unison—either in harmony or in dissonance. They operate all the time: in senate committees, in business offices, in families, over matters of state, over matters of business, and over matters of love.

Use your knowledge well.

PRACTICE

1. Use one of the scales presented in this chapter to observe and evaluate a group discussion (either in or out of class). Compare notes with classmates. What do your findings imply? How do you interpret the results? What recommendations would you make to this group based on your observations?

2. As a group, develop a set of criteria for selecting a measurement instrument to observe and evaluate small group communication. Under what circumstances would you use what method(s)?

3. Observe a live or videotaped group meeting. Then design a post-meeting reaction sheet that you feel would be helpful to the group or the group leader. Be able to explain the observations that led you to your choices of questions.

Notes

1. Kenneth Benne and Paul Sheats, "Functional Roles of Group Members," *Journal of Social Issues* 4 (Spring 1948): 41–49.

2. Stanley Seashore, *Group Cohesiveness in the Industrial Work Group* (Ann Arbor, Michigan: University of Michigan Institute for Social Research, 1954).

3. Robert Bales, *Interaction Process Analysis: A Method for the Study of Small Groups* (Reading, Massachusetts: Addison-Wesley Publishing Company, Inc., 1950), p. 59.

4. Alvin A. Goldberg and Carl E. Larson, *Group Communication: Discussion Processes and Applications* (Englewood Cliffs, New Jersey: Prentice-Hall, Inc. 1975), pp. 99–100.

5. Halbert E. Gulley and Dale G. Leathers, *Communication and Group Process: Techniques for Improving the Quality of Small-Group Communication,* 3rd ed. (New York: Holt, Rinehart & Winston, 1977), p. 128.

6. Dean C. Barnlund and Franklyn S. Haiman, *The Dynamics of Discussion,* (Boston: Houghton Mifflin Company, 1960), pp. 401–4.

7. Gulley and Leathers, pp. 41–42.

8. Dale Leathers, "The Feedback Rating Instrument: A New Means of Evaluating Discussion," *Central States Speech Journal* 22 (Spring 1971): 32–42.

Glossary

A

activity track. The primary function of a group's activity at a given point in the group's discussion. The activity can be either task process, relational, or topical.

adaptors. Nonverbal behaviors that help us respond to our immediate environment.

affect displays. Nonverval behaviors that communicate emotion.

affection. The human need to express and receive warmth and closeness.

B

brainstorming. A creative problem-solving technique to help a group generate and eventually analyze and evaluate possible solutions to a problem.

breakpoint. A point in a group's discussion when the group members shift to a different activity.

buzz group. A small group formed from a larger group to respond to a question or problem and, after a short period of deliberation, to summarize their responses to the larger group.

bypassing. A communication barrier that occurs when two people assign different meanings to the same word.

C

category system.   Any list of terms for related behaviors used to determine the frequency of those behaviors. May be used alone or with other observational methods such as the interaction diagram.

closed-ended question.   A question which asks a respondent to choose among several responses supplied by the person asking the question.

cohesiveness.   The degree of attraction group members feel toward one another and the group.

committee.   A small group that is given a specific task by a larger group or organization.

communication network.   Pattern of interaction within the group; who talks to whom.

complementarity.   Refers to the tendency to feel attracted to others who possess knowledge, skills, or other attributes that we do not possess but that we admire or believe would be useful to us.

confirming responses.   A communication response that causes a person to value himself/herself more.

conflict.   Disagreement over available options, resulting from having seemingly incompatible goals and perceiving interference from each other in achieving those goals.

conflict phase.   The second phase of Fisher's phases of group interaction in which disagreement and individuals' differences usually surface.

consensus.   Occurs when all members of a group agree with and are committed to the group decision.

control.   The human need for status and power; varies from person to person in terms of the need to control others and the need to be controlled by others.

criteria.   Standards or goals for an acceptable solution to a problem.

D

decision making.   Making a choice among several alternatives.

defensive communication.   Communicative behavior that arouses a perceived need to protect the self-concept.

descriptive problem-solving approach.   An approach which seeks to help people understand how a group solves a problem.

disconfirming responses.   Those that cause the other person to value himself less.

E

ego-conflict.   Occurs when individuals become defensive because they feel they are being personally attacked.

emblems.   Nonverbal cues which have a specific verbal counterpart. Emblems take the place of spoken words, letters, or numbers.

emergence phase.   The third phase of Fisher's phases of group interaction in which the group begins to manage conflict and disagreement.

explanatory function.   The power of theories to explain.

F

forum presentation.   A discussion format which encourages audience members to respond to an issue or idea. Forum presentations frequently follow a panel discussion or a symposium presentation.

functional perspective.   Views leadership as behaviors that may be initiated by any or all group members.

G

group climate.   The emotional context of group interaction; affects and is affected by group communication.

group cohesiveness.   The degree of attraction group members feel toward one another and the group.

group maintenance roles.   Behaviors that help the group maintain the social dimension of the group.

group task roles.   Behaviors that help the group accomplish its purpose or reason for meeting.

groupthink.   Occurs when a group strives to minimize conflict and reach a consensus at the expense of critically testing, analyzing, and evaluating ideas.

I

ideal solution format.   A problem-solving format that helps a group define the problem, speculate as to what the ideal solution to the problem is, and identify the obstacles which prohibit the ideal solution from being implemented.

illustrators.   Nonverbal behaviors that accompany and embellish verbal communication.

immediacy.   A dimension of nonverbal communication which refers to our liking or disliking others.

inclusion.   The basic human need for affiliation with others.

individual roles.   Behaviors that call attention to individual contributions of group members.

interaction diagram.   A means of identifying and recording communication networks in groups, as well as the frequency and direction of communication.

interdependence.   A quality of relationship among components of a system wherein a change in any part effects a change in all of the other parts.

interpersonal needs.   Basic human needs that can be fulfilled by other individuals or groups.

J

Johari window.   A model which illustrates relationships between self-disclosure, self-perception, and perception of others.

L

leadership.   Behavior that influences, guides, directs, or controls the group.

leadership style.   A relatively consistent pattern of behavior reflecting the beliefs and attitudes of the leader; may be classified as authoritarian, democratic, or laissez-faire.

listening.   An active, complex process of selecting, attending, understanding, and remembering.

M

metacommunication.   One aspect of the communication message (e.g., nonverbal cues) providing information about how the total message should be interpreted; communication about communication.

metadiscussion.   A statement about the discussion process rather than the topic of discussion; discussion about the discussion process.

mutuality of concern.   The degree to which group members share the same level of commitment to the group or its goals.

N

nominal group technique. A group problem-solving method in which group members work individually on a specific idea or question and then report their ideas to the group for discussion. Suggested solutions are ranked individually by group members and then presented for summary rank ordering.

nonverbal communication. Communication behavior that does not rely upon a written or spoken linguistic code, but that creates meaning intrapersonally, or between two or more individuals.

norms. Rules or standards that distinguish appropriate from inappropriate behavior.

O

open-ended question. A question which permits a respondent to answer freely without providing choices or constraints.

orientation phase. The first phase of Fisher's small group interaction in which group members seek to understand the nature of each other and the task confronting the group.

P

panel discussion. A group discussion which takes place before an audience to inform the audience about issues of interest, to solve a problem, or to encourage the audience to evaluate the issues of a controversial question.

paralanguage. Vocal cues such as pitch, rate, volume, and quality, which provide information to others.

potency. A dimension of nonverbal communication which communicates status and power.

power. The sum of the resources an individual possesses and uses to exert control over others.

predictive function. The precision with which theories allow us to predict events.

prescriptive problem-solving approach. An approach that suggests specific agendas or techniques of improving group problem solving.

primary group. A group whose main purpose is to fulfill our basic need to associate with others.

primary tension. Feelings of anxiety and uneasiness that occur when a group first gets together.

problem solving.   A multi-step process which attempts to overcome or manage an obstacle to achieve a goal.

process leadership.   Communication directed toward maintaining interpersonal relations and facilitating a positive group climate; also called group building and maintenance.

pseudo-conflict.   Occurs when individuals perceive disagreement which is the result of inaccurate communication.

public communication format.   An organized group discussion which is presented to an audience.

Q

quality control circles.   A small group of people who participate in corporate decision making by meeting on a regular basis for the purpose of improving productivity, morale, and work quality, using brainstorming and other group problem-solving methods.

question of fact.   A question that asks whether something is true or false.

question of policy.   A question that considers whether a change in procedure or behavior should be made.

question of value.   A question that considers the worth or desirability of something.

R

reflective thinking.   A multi-step problem-solving format developed by John Dewey which includes the following steps: (1) identify and define the problem, (2) analyze the problem, (3) suggest possible solutions, (4) suggest the best solution(s), and (5) test and implement the solution.

regulators.   Nonverbal behaviors which help control the flow of communication.

reinforcement phase.   An expression of positive feelings toward the group and the group's final decision; the fourth phase of Fisher's phases of group interaction.

relational activity.   An activity which deals with those behaviors which sustain or damage the quality of interpersonal relationships among group members.

responsiveness.   A dimension of nonverbal communication that communicates activity, energy, and interest.

risk technique.   A group discussion technique that is designed to assess how individuals may respond to and manage a change in policy or procedure.

role. A consistent behavior pattern as a result of expectations an individual has about himself, an individual's actual behavior, and the expectations others have toward the individual.

S

secondary tension. The development of conflict over group norms, roles, and differences of group members' opinions.

self-concept. A composite of the characteristics or attributes an individual uses to describe himself.

self-disclosure. The deliberate communication of information about yourself to others.

similarity. Refers to the tendency for individuals who share similar experiences, beliefs, attitudes, and values to be attracted to one another.

simple conflict. Occurs when two individuals each know what the other person wants, but neither can achieve his goal without also keeping the other from achieving his goal.

simulation. A structured exercise that creates for participants conditions that they might confront outside of the training environment.

single-question format. A problem-solving agenda which helps the group identify the key issues and subissues of a problem.

situational perspective. Views leadership as the interrelationships among group needs and goals, leadership style, and situation.

small group communication. Face-to-face communication among a small group of people who share a common purpose or goal, feel a sense of belonging to the group, and exert influence upon one another.

small group ecology. The use of space by group members as illustrated by seating arrangement and physical closeness to others.

small group. At least three people who are interacting with one another.

speech communication. 1. The human symbolic process through which we make sense of the world and share that sense with others. 2. What we say and how we say it.

status. An individual's position of importance.

study group. A group whose primary purpose is to gather information and learn new ideas and concepts.

survey research. A method of sampling several individuals' attitudes, beliefs, values, behavior, or knowledge.

symposium presentation. A series of short speeches unified by a central theme or issue.

system. An organic whole composed of interdependent elements that adjust to one another continually in order to maintain the system.

T

task leadership. Communication directed toward accomplishing the group's task or goal.

task-oriented small group. A group with a specific objective to achieve, problem to solve, or decision to make.

task process activity. An activity the group enacts to manage its task or its reason for convening.

territoriality. Use of space to claim or defend a given area.

theory. A symbolic representation of a phenomenon that seeks to explain and predict events within the phenomenon.

therapy group. A group led by a trained professional whose primary purpose is to provide treatment to help individuals with personal problems.

topic focus. A group activity which deals with the general themes, major issues, or arguments of concern to the group at a given point in the discussion.

training. A course of instruction emphasizing skill development.

trait perspective. A view of leadership ability as personal attributes or qualities possessed by leaders.

Index